The 104th (New Brunswick) Regiment of Foot in the War of 1812

New Brunswick Military Heritage Series, Volume 21

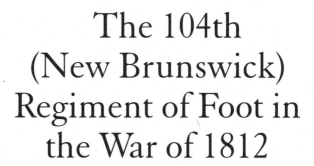

The 104th (New Brunswick) Regiment of Foot in the War of 1812

John R. Grodzinski

GOOSE LANE EDITIONS and
THE NEW BRUNSWICK MILITARY HERITAGE PROJECT

Major Tom Hambley   *Dec 2015*

Edited by Brent Wilson and Barry Norris.
Cover design by Julie Scriver
Page design by Chris Tompkins.
Cover illustrations: (front) *The Battle of Lundy's Lane* (detail), a canvas giclee print based on an engraving from *Harper's Weekly*, June 16, 1866; (back) *A View of Fort George, Upper Canada, from Old Fort Niagara* (detail) by Edward Walsh (LAC C-000026)
Printed in Canada.
10 9 8 7 6 5 4 3 2 1

Library and Archives Canada Cataloguing in Publication

Grodzinski, John R. (John Richard), 1960-, author
    The 104th (New Brunswick) Regiment of Foot in the War of 1812 / John R. Grodzinski.

(New Brunswick military heritage series ; 21)
Includes bibliographical references and index.
Issued in print and electronic formats.
Co-published by: New Brunswick Military Heritage Project.
ISBN 978-0-86492-447-6 (pbk.).—ISBN 978-0-86492-794-1 (epub)

1. Great Britain. Army. Regiment of Foot, 104th (New Brunswick).
2. Canada—History—War of 1812—Regimental histories. 3. Canada—
History—War of 1812—Regimental histories—Sources. 4. New Brunswick—
History, Military—19th century. 5. Great Britain—History, Military—
19th century. I. Title. II. Series: New Brunswick military heritage series ; 21

FC442.G76 2014   971.03'4   C2014-900115-0
                                             C2014-900116-9

Goose Lane Editions acknowledges the generous support of the Canada Council for the Arts, the Government of Canada through the Canada Book Fund (CBF), and the Government of New Brunswick through the Department of Tourism, Heritage and Culture.

Goose Lane Editions
Suite 330, 500 Beaverbrook Court
Fredericton, New Brunswick
CANADA E3B 5X4
www.gooselane.com

New Brunswick Military Heritage Project
The Brigadier Milton F. Gregg, VC,
Centre for the Study of War and Society
University of New Brunswick
PO Box 4400
Fredericton, New Brunswick
CANADA E3B 5A3
www.unb.ca/nbmhp

RECYCLED
Paper made from
recycled material
FSC
www.fsc.org   FSC® C103567

To the memory of the officers, NCOs, men, and boys of the 104th Regiment of Foot, and the women who marched with them, whose service and sacrifice helped to preserve the independence of British North America in the War of 1812.

Contents

9   **Foreword**

13   **Introduction**

17   **Chapter One**
Garrison Duty in New Brunswick,
the War of 1812, and the March to
Kingston

57   **Chapter Two**
Kingston, Sackets Harbor, and the
Niagara Peninsula, April-June 1813

87   **Chapter Three**
The Blockade and Reconnaissance of
Fort George and Return to Kingston,
July-December 1813

101 **Chapter Four**
Kingston, the Upper St. Lawrence River,
and the Flank Companies on Detached
Service in the Niagara Peninsula,
January-December 1814

137 **Chapter Five**
The End of the War of 1812 and the
Disbandment of the 104th Foot

149 **Appendix**

163 **Acknowledgements**

165 **Endnotes**

193 **Selected Bibliography**

201 **Photo Credits**

203 **Index**

219 **About the Author**

Foreword

The Canadian militia in the War of 1812 has received much attention but what is often forgotten is that regular Canadian soldiers also fought in the conflict—and fought well. The five fencible corps and the various units raised by the provincial governments constituted an important component of the defence of British North America. There was, however, only one Canadian regiment "of the line," meaning a unit of the British Army liable for service anywhere in the globe. That unit was the 104th (New Brunswick) Regiment of Foot, and in this book John Grodzinski tells its story.

Although the author concentrates on the record of the 104th Foot during the war years of 1812-1815, he provides a proper context for the unit's history, discussing its early days up to the outbreak of hostilities. He also admirably dissects the complexities of the British Army's arcane system of organization, recruiting, and promotion.

The author rightfully spends time on the seven-hundred-mile epic march from Fredericton to Kingston made by six companies of the 104th in the late winter of 1812-1813. This notable feat of arms—almost certainly the longest winter march made by a British regiment up to that time—is covered in detail, particularly its logistical arrangements, because marching troops in the winter is one thing, but feeding them along the way is quite another. It is only fitting that, two centuries later, volunteers and personnel

A private of the light
company, or "Light
Bobs," of the 104th
Foot. Watercolour by Don Troiani

from militia units along its course restaged this journey to commemorate
the wartime original. As John Grodzinski reminds us, however, perhaps
too much attention can be paid to this aspect of the history of the 104th
Foot because it also saw considerable active service.

The unit's first combat occurred when it participated in the raid on
Sackets Harbor, New York, in late May 1813. The 104th performed well
but suffered heavy casualties. Following this incident, it deployed to the

Niagara Peninsula, where it spent a frustrating and sickly summer as part of the British force blockading the American-held Fort George near present-day Niagara-on-the-Lake.

In the autumn of 1813, it was brought back to Kingston when American forces threatened the St. Lawrence lifeline, and remained there over the winter. In the following summer, the two flank, or elite, companies of the 104th were again sent to the Niagara, where they fought in some of the bloodiest actions of the war, including the vicious nighttime battle of Lundy's Lane, the bloody assault on Fort Erie, and the action at Cook's Mills. With the coming of peace, most of the regiment was concentrated in Lower Canada, where it remained until disbanded in 1817.

Although John Grodzinski stresses the bright high points of the history of the 104th Foot, he does not neglect the darker areas, and discusses problems of leadership, desertion, and illness. The result is a complete but compact history of a Canadian military unit that has long been overlooked.

It is only fitting that the bicentenary of the War of 1812 has resulted in the full restoration of the wartime Colours of the 104th Foot. Even more welcome is the decision of the federal government to allow units of the modern Canadian Army to perpetuate units of that earlier conflict and to receive the Battle Honours gained by them during the War of 1812. Thus, the modern Royal New Brunswick Regiment is officially linked with the 104th (New Brunswick) Regiment of Foot and has received the two Battle Honours, "Defence of Canada, 1812-1815" and "Niagara, 1814," earned by its predecessor.

Donald E. Graves
"Maple Cottage"
Valley of the Mississippi
Upper Canada

Introduction

Throughout the course of its history, the British Army has been expanded and reduced in size based on the needs of the government. Until 1862, regiments were generally identified by numbers, and, in some cases, by a territorial association as well. The numerical title determined the seniority of the unit, and when peace came and reductions followed, the more junior, higher-numbered regiments were usually the first to go.

This routine expansion and contraction has resulted in a regiment having borne the number "104th" on five previous occasions. The first came in 1761, during the Seven Years' War, when the 104th (King's Volunteers) Regiment of Foot was raised; it was disbanded in 1763. The number was resurrected as the 104th between 1780 and 1783, during the American Revolutionary War, and again in 1794-1795 as the 104th (Royal Manchester Volunteers), during the war with revolutionary France. In 1810, the New Brunswick Fencible Infantry was redesignated the 104th Regiment of Foot and, after serving in Upper and Lower Canada during the War of 1812, was disbanded in 1817. The final iteration of the 104th came in 1861, with the redesignation of the 2nd Bengal Fusiliers as the 104th Bengal Fusiliers. In 1881, the regiment was amalgamated with the 101st (Royal Bengal Fusiliers) Regiment of Foot to become The Royal Munster Fusiliers, which was disbanded in 1922. None of these regiments shares any lineage with the others that have borne the number or with any modern British regiments.[1]

The story of the unit that is the subject of this book owes its origin, as noted above, to a fencible regiment from New Brunswick. Between 1791 and 1816, the defence of the province was augmented by the formation of one provincial regiment and two regiments of fencible infantry. The first regiment of fencibles, The King's New Brunswick Regiment, existed between 1791 and 1802; in 1803, it was followed by The New Brunswick Fencible Infantry, which was later taken into the line as the 104th Foot. Finally, in the autumn of 1812, a new regiment, the New Brunswick Regiment of Fencible Infantry, was raised; it was disbanded in 1816. Like their regular counterparts, fencible regiments were subject to orders from the British Army, not the New Brunswick militia.

This book briefly examines the history of the 104th Regiment of Foot, which was formed in New Brunswick during the Napoleonic Wars and fought in the War of 1812. The 104th Foot is distinct in that it was the only regular infantry regiment raised in British North America between 1803 and 1815. Thereafter, however, its employment in the Canadas mirrored that of other British regiments that served in the conflict: sent piecemeal, often as companies, to the most threatened regions, then redeployed to a central location, such as Kingston, once the situation stabilized.

This war of companies that the 104th Foot experienced in no way diminishes its record. In 1812, the 104th contributed to the defence of New Brunswick, Prince Edward Island, and Cape Breton. When it was ordered to Upper Canada in 1813, the regiment arrived in Kingston at a time when the scale of the war had increased dramatically from that of the previous year. The arrival of British reinforcements, the embodiment of the Upper Canadian militia, the transformation of the war on the Great Lakes by the arrival of the Royal Navy, and the rejuvenation of the US Army are but a few of the changes that had taken place.

The arrival of the 104th Foot in Kingston allowed the British to consider indirect means of attacking their enemy, and the regiment promptly provided the majority of the troops committed to the raid on the American naval base at Sackets Harbor, New York. Several companies were then sent to the Niagara Peninsula, where they were involved in a number of actions before returning to Kingston at the end of the year. In 1814, as the line companies garrisoned posts between Kingston and Prescott on the important line of communication between Montreal and Kingston, the grenadier and light companies joined the Right Division of the Army of Upper Canada in the Niagara Peninsula, where, over a four-month period they were nearly wiped out. The end of the war saw the 104th in Montreal, where it was disbanded in 1817.

Although the unit is often styled the 104th (New Brunswick) Regiment of Foot, readers will soon discover that the regiment included a diverse group of men not only from New Brunswick, but also from Nova Scotia, Newfoundland, Lower and Upper Canada, England, Scotland, Ireland, and elsewhere. From the contemporary Canadian perspective, the 104th Foot can be considered as a national endeavour whereby men from a group of loosely associated British colonies, known as British North America, and Britons served side-by-side in defending those colonies from foreign aggression. Not only did they succeed in doing so, but many remained in the colonies and helped to build what eventually would become the Dominion of Canada.

Today, aside from some commemorative plaques, a bridge named in the regiment's honour, and a few artefacts, there is little to remind us of the exploits of the 104th Foot. Perhaps, however, the award of War of 1812 Battle Honours to units of the Canadian Army, and the numerous projects surrounding the bicentenary of the War of 1812 will allow Canadians to appreciate the story of the soldiers of the War of 1812, including the history of the only regular regiment of the British Army to be raised and employed on this continent during the Napoleonic Wars and the War of 1812.

A Note to the Reader

The proper designation of British numbered infantry units in the Napoleonic Wars was as "regiments of foot." Many regiments also acquired territorial affiliations, including British counties, North American provinces, or cultural associations such as "Highland." Not all of these designations received official sanction, and did not appear in the Army List. Thus, although the regiment that is the subject of this book is often identified as the "104th (New Brunswick) Regiment of Foot," it appeared only as the "104th Foot" in the Army List. So, for purposes of brevity, I identify it hereafter by that shorter name or simply as the 104th.

Military records are notoriously inaccurate, especially when it comes to strength returns, routine reports that showed personnel by rank, whether they were present and fit for duty, and other details that staff officers thought important. A close reading of the text will reveal discrepancies between the figures presented here, depending on whether they were drawn from town or district orders, provincial or theatre returns, and medical reports. In some cases, such as when the flank companies of the 104th were in the Niagara Peninsula in 1814, the pace of military operations and the continual shifting of units between locations meant these reports were never completed, or were compiled in haste. Greater precision is normally found in returns involving the payment of funds, but these, too, are subject to error and, on occasion, deliberate fabrication due to graft on the part of the reporting staff officer, non-commissioned officer (NCO), or clerk. Although I have tried to reconcile these differences and omissions, it proved impossible to resolve the conflicting data completely; I thus present "ballpark" figures and inconsistent data, and leave the reader to contemplate the possible conclusions.

Chapter One

Garrison Duty in New Brunswick, the War of 1812, and the March to Kingston

In all respects fit for any service.

— Inspection Report, 104th Foot, June 1812

The King's New Brunswick Regiment, The New Brunswick Fencible Infantry, and the Formation of the 104th Foot

During the eighteenth century, a series of conflicts shaped the early political boundaries of North America. By 1783, three major political groupings had emerged: Britain held colonies in the northeast; to the south were the United States of America; and to the west, the colonial holdings of Spain. A commercial company, the Hudson's Bay Company, controlled a vast tract of land in the northwest. The First Nations peoples inhabiting these territories did not always recognize these boundaries, which remained ill-defined for nearly a century. Ongoing competition between the respective governments for additional territory and fears for their own security soon combined with wider political differences in Europe to ensure another war in the early nineteenth century.

Even with the loss of thirteen of its North American colonies in 1783, Britain's colonial possessions in the New World remained vast, with the largest group of colonies becoming known collectively as British North America: the provinces of Quebec and Nova Scotia, the Island of Cape Breton, the Island of St. John (later, Prince Edward Island), and Bermuda; the Colony of Newfoundland was not included in this structure. The displacement of a large number of refugees from the United States, popularly known as Loyalists but also including a significant number of First Nations peoples, to the remaining British colonies and to Britain transformed the boundaries of British North America. In 1784, the province of Nova Scotia was partitioned and the province of New Brunswick created, while in 1791, the province of Quebec was divided into the largely English-speaking province of Upper Canada and the predominantly French-speaking Catholic province of Lower Canada.

In general terms, peaceful relations dominated the years immediately following the American Revolutionary War. The most serious threat occurred on the west coast, where, in 1789, the establishment of a Spanish outpost at Nootka, on Vancouver Island, nearly led to war between Spain and Britain. The peaceful conclusion of this crisis by treaty in 1790 was followed four years later by a reduction in tensions with the United States. The Treaty of Amity, Commerce and Navigation, more popularly known as Jay's Treaty — after the senior American negotiator, John Jay — resolved many of the boundary disputes between the United States and the British colonies to the north. Despite the rapprochement, however, mutual suspicion remained, and the ongoing war between the United States and First Nations groups in Ohio and the Michigan and Illinois Territories had the potential to spill over into Upper Canada.[1]

These events, however, were minor against the backdrop of a wider global war that erupted in 1793, when Britain joined a coalition of several European countries to oppose revolutionary France. As France defeated its opponents on the continent, Britain's command of the sea allowed it to secure several important victories in the Mediterranean and the West Indies.[2]

The perceived threat to the Atlantic provinces from both France and Spain fuelled public support and saw a swelling of willing recruits for military service. In July 1793, a French naval squadron with 2,400 troops arrived off New York, where they began recruiting Americans and seeking the support of the United States for an attack on the British Atlantic colonies. The threat posed by the French using Saint-Pierre and Miquelon as naval bases to strike at the Atlantic provinces was removed in May 1794 when a contingent of four hundred British soldiers and members of the Nova Scotia Regiment took the islands. The appearance of a combined Franco-Spanish squadron of twenty vessels carrying 1,500 troops off Newfoundland intensified the completion of defensive works, while a landing by the enemy at Bay Bulls resulted in little more than looting by French soldiers.[3]

Although the British relied upon regular troops to defend their North American provinces, the active theatres in Europe and the West Indies left few such troops available for service elsewhere. The colonial militia forces, raised from among all able-bodied men ages sixteen to sixty and controlled by each province, were inadequately trained, and lacked much of the necessary arms and equipment to be useful in the field. The fortifications protecting key points, such as cities and harbours, were in a poor state or lacked ordnance.[4]

The military situation in New Brunswick was acute. Since 1790, Governor Thomas Carleton had warned of the exposed state of the communities along the Bay of Fundy, the ruinous state of the fortifications, and the lack of arms. The impending withdrawal of the last British regulars from the province would leave the militia responsible for repelling any attack. Unfortunately, little had been done to prepare the force created by the 1787 militia act. Many companies and regiments lacked a full complement of men, and many of the officers owed their appointments to political patronage, rather than to martial skill. Musters were dominated by administrative activity and social events, and the lack of weaponry provided few opportunities for effective drill instruction. Fortunately, by 1791, British officials had presented a solution for improving the state of the garrisons throughout British North America with the creation of fencible and provincial regiments.[5]

Although they had ancient precedents, fencible regiments originated during the Seven Years' War when Britain established several such regiments to defend itself from invasion. Equipped, trained, disciplined, and paid as regulars, fencible infantry and cavalry regiments were raised with the understanding that their deployment would be restricted to within national boundaries or other specified geographic areas, such as a county, and that their service could be extended abroad only by their volunteering for this service. When the war with France began in 1793, Britain accordingly expanded its regular Army for employment overseas, while fencible units augmented the militia in England, Scotland, and Ireland. This system was extended to North America, where the formation of a number of regiments of fencible infantry would release the regular regiments garrisoned there for employment elsewhere.[6]

Beginning in 1791, fencible regiments were raised in several provinces of British North America. Among the units were the Queen's Rangers in Upper Canada, the Royal Nova Scotia Regiment, the Island of St. John's Volunteers (from 1800, the Prince Edward Island Fencibles), and the Royal Newfoundland Regiment. In 1794, the two-battalion Royal Canadian Volunteers was divided between Upper Canada and Lower Canada.

Provincial regiments presented another means of augmenting local forces. Normally raised for the duration of a conflict, they were officered by professional officers, dressed, equipped, and trained like regulars, and employed in a specified geographic area, although they often ventured outside their boundaries. The appeal of this type of unit was that it provided a solution to a local problem by bolstering the defences vacated by regular troops, at less cost than a regular regiment. The specifics regarding officers' commissions, the pay and benefits to officers and the rank and file, employment of the regiment, and command and control varied with the orders provided for the raising of each provincial unit.

In February 1793, given the state of New Brunswick's defences, the Secretary of State for War, Henry Dundas, instructed Governor Carleton to raise a six-hundred-strong unit to be known as The King's New Brunswick Regiment. The regiment was to be headquartered in Fredericton, and the posting of six of its companies to Fredericton, Saint John, and St. Andrews would allow the withdrawal of the 6th Foot, the last regular regiment in the province, for employment in the West Indies. Carleton, who welcomed this decision and became colonel of the regiment, controlled the officer appointments. All officers above the rank of ensign were selected from a list of half-pay officers or were veterans of the American Revolutionary War. As the regiment was "merely provincial and for the service of New Brunswick only,"[7] the officers' commissions provided them with local rank, as they were not granted regular Army commissions. Despite its provincial status, which normally meant it fell under the provincial militia structure, The King's New Brunswick Regiment was subject "to the Control and Orders of the Commander in Chief of His Majesty's Forces in North America or to such other orders as in His Majesty's wisdom he may think proper to give."[8] Lieutenant-Colonel Beverly Robinson, who was born in the colony of New York and served, along with his father, in the Loyal American Regiment during the American Revolutionary War before relocating to British North America, was appointed commanding officer.[9]

Not everyone shared Carleton's enthusiasm for the formation of this regiment, and one member of the provincial assembly questioned whether the removal of "one fifth of the population capable of bearing arms and at least one-third of the more active young men"[10] would benefit the province. There might have been some truth in this, as recruiting in Fredericton and Saint John, the settlements bordering the St. John River, and at St. Andrews, on the frontier of the province, progressed slowly. By July 1794, only three hundred of the four hundred and fifty men on the roll were considered effective, and the number was well below the establishment of six hundred.[11] Despite these difficulties, the regiment was immediately put to work improving defensive works and roads. This activity was interrupted by occasional alarms, caused by reports or, more often, rumours of the presence of French naval forces or landings on the Fundy shore, none of which amounted to anything. By the end of the decade, the threat of invasion had subsided, and interest in defence matters in the province declined.

By 1802, as French successes on the European continent left Britain without allies and facing a strong threat from Napoleon's forces, the two countries entered into a peace agreement known as the Treaty of Amiens. Peace was welcomed, and through the summer and autumn of 1802, all the fencible and provincial regiments in North America were disbanded. Confronted more by scares than by actual threats, these units nevertheless had created a firm basis for the defence of the colonies, and demonstrated that British North Americans could serve alongside British regulars effectively. The detachments of The King's New Brunswick Regiment serving outside Fredericton were recalled, and in August 1802 the regiment was disbanded. In consideration of their service, the officers were placed on half-pay and the men received grants of land.[12]

The peace was short lived, however, and within fourteen months war was renewed, requiring the resumption of improvements to the defences of British North America. As the regular garrison would not be returned to its previous strength, the British government ordered the raising of four fencible regiments of infantry: The Canadian Fencibles in Lower Canada, the Royal Newfoundland Fencibles, the Nova Scotia Fencibles, and The New Brunswick Fencible Infantry. For now, no regiment was to be formed in Upper Canada.[13]

In June 1803, Brigadier-General Martin Hunter (the following year he was promoted to major-general) was appointed colonel of The New Brunswick Fencibles, the titular head of the regiment who oversaw its institutional well-being, which included advising the commanding officer on regimental matters, including officer appointments. On paper, the organization of The New Brunswick Fencibles[14] was similar to that of a British line regiment according to the "new" establishment that had been introduced in 1804: with 1,123 officers, NCOs, and rank and file distributed among a twelve-man headquarters, eight "centre" or "line" companies of 111 officers, NCOs, and men each, and two "flank" companies, one of grenadiers with 112 all ranks, and the other, a 110-man strong "light" company. Each line company consisted of a captain commanding, two lieutenants, one ensign, five sergeants, five corporals, two drummers, and ninety-five privates. The flank companies had a similar structure, although an additional lieutenant was provided in lieu of an ensign, and the grenadier company had fifers instead of drummers. (More will be said of the differences between the line and flank companies later.) There was no allowance for a paymaster or pay sergeants.

Instead of a commissioned assistant surgeon, at first two senior non-commissioned surgeon's mates saw to the unit's medical needs.[15] In 1807, however, William Dyer Thomas, an experienced surgeon who had commenced his career in 1800 with the 1st Dragoon Guards, was appointed to The New Brunswick Fencibles. The surgeon's duties included the administration of the regimental hospital, the care of the sick, and the

Lieutenant-General Sir Martin Hunter was instrumental in raising The New Brunswick Fencible Infantry and its subsequent transfer to the line in 1810 as the 104th Foot. He also served as the colonel of both regiments.Courtesy of Martin Bates and NBM X15765(2)

treatment of battlefield casualties. In contrast to physicians, who held high academic qualifications, surgeons had a more modest education, although they generally possessed a university degree (or at least proof of attending medical lectures and experience in a practice), a licence from the College of Surgeons, and had successfully completed an examination by the Medical Board. Assistant surgeons had some education, and were required to pass an exam set by the surgeon. Surgeons were ranked as, but not equivalent to, captains and their assistants as lieutenants.[16] Requirements concerning medical appointments varied during the Napoleonic Wars, but by the time William Thomas became surgeon, controls had become stricter and, aside from the recommendation of his commanding officer, his appointment required approval by the Medical Board. Thomas later served with the 104th Foot until he went on half-pay in 1816.

One of the two assistant surgeons was Thomas Emerson. His military service began during the American Revolutionary War, when he joined the Royal Fencible Americans, after which he was granted land in Nova Scotia. In 1793, he became surgeon's mate (the title was changed to assistant surgeon in 1796) in The King's New Brunswick Regiment. Then, in August 1804, he signed up as assistant surgeon with The New Brunswick

Fencibles. Another assistant surgeon was Charles Earle, who served until January 1812, when he went on half-pay. Earle was replaced by William Woodford until May 1814, when Woodford transferred to the newly formed New Brunswick Regiment of Fencible Infantry, although he remained with the 104th until the summer of 1814.[17]

The unit establishment made no mention of pioneers — soldiers who were given special equipment and some training to build or clear minor obstacles, clear routes, and do other heavy work. According to the Army Regulations, however, "no regiment is considered fit for service unless the Pioneers are completely equipped."[18] The Regulations specified that one corporal and ten privates (one per company) were to be appointed as pioneers, and the colonel of a regiment was responsible for their having "Tools and Appointments [equipment]…in a complete and serviceable state."[19] Special equipment included one apron per man and their tools included bill-hooks, spades, picks, felling and broad axes, saws, and mattocks.

Many pioneers were black.[20] The British services increased the available source of manpower through the recruitment of blacks in Africa, the West Indies, and North America. These men served in line regiments, colonial corps, specially recruited regiments from the West Indies, a regular corps of pioneers and artificers, and in the Royal Navy and the Royal Marines. In 1814, the Corps of Colonial Marines was formed in the West Indies from runaway American slaves. The "Company of Coloured Men" was raised in Upper Canada at the outset of the War of 1812, and in October 1812, it fought at the Battle of Queenston Heights. A number of blacks also joined the Glengarry Light Infantry Fencibles, although their number is difficult to establish as the records make no distinction by race. Sixteen blacks are said to have joined The New Brunswick Fencible Infantry as pioneers, many of whom later served in the 104th Foot. One man, Henry Grant, who joined The New Brunswick Fencibles in 1808, eventually became a bass drummer in the regimental band.[21]

The eighteen drummers and two fife players in the battalion should not be confused with musicians or the "band of music."[22] The drummers and fifers played an integral role in the internal regulation of the companies, for which they received extra pay and allowances. The drummers' uniforms were more lavish than those of the fifers and, later, buglers, who were dressed like the rest of the men in the regiment. General Regulations also permitted the colonel to form a band, consisting of one private per company plus a sergeant as bandmaster. All of these men "were to be Effective to the Service as Soldiers, are to be perfectly drilled, and liable to serve in the Ranks on any emergency."[23] Although a band was not authorized upon The Fencibles' establishment, one appears to have been formed shortly afterward, and included the company drummers and fifers and a number of musicians who played other instruments. An 1810 inspection report indicates that bugles had replaced the drums in each company, although by 1813, when the 104th Foot was preparing to march to Canada, it was reported to have both drummers and buglers.[24]

As was the practice with the other fencible regiments raised in British North America, The New Brunswick Fencibles were allowed to recruit in "any part of the British colonies in America."[25] Recruiting parties accordingly ventured throughout New Brunswick and into Lower Canada, and Nova Scotia, and enjoyed some success in attracting colonists to the colours. The story was different in Newfoundland, where Governor Vice-Admiral Sir Erasmus Gower ordered the recruiting parties, for reasons unknown, to leave the colony. Authority was also granted to recruit in Scotland, and the recruiting parties there extended their reach into Ireland. Experienced NCOs and men also came from other regular regiments, such as the 37th and 60th Regiments of Foot.[26]

The standards for recruitment specified that enlistment was to be voluntary and open to all "stout and well made"[27] males over five feet five inches in height and, ideally, between seventeen and thirty years of age. As an inducement to join The New Brunswick Fencible Infantry, each recruit would receive a bounty of six guineas, a sizable sum, which would be paid in increments following examination by a surgeon, attestation, and inspection by a senior officer.[28] They would also receive up to five hundred acres of land when the regiment was reduced. The Fencibles were also allowed to recruit boys and lads who were "perfectly well limbed, open chested, and what is commonly called long in the fork [long legged],"[29] not less than five feet tall and aged between ten to fifteen years of age. The recruitment of boys was always strictly controlled, as they were an extraordinary source of manpower and could be employed only on general duties or as drummers, until they became seventeen, when they could carry arms and be employed in the infantry as privates. Many learned to read and write in regimental schools, which groomed them for future appointments as NCOs. Many of the boys were related to soldiers serving in the regiment.[30]

To find additional men, Hunter sent Major John White "out to Canada on the Recruiting Service."[31] White was given additional authority to recommend six suitable gentlemen for appointment to the rank of captain, lieutenant, and ensign. Operating from Montreal and Quebec, White succeeded in recruiting a number of men, whom he dressed in uniforms found in Montreal for the 60th Foot, which was currently stationed in England and not expected to return to Canada. White died in March 1804, and Captain Thomas Christian was appointed commander of the recruiting effort in the Canadas, while Captain Dugald Campbell took command of the recruits at Quebec, assisted by Captain A. Sutherland. Earlier in the year, to get to Quebec, Campbell had completed an arduous journey from New Brunswick overland on snowshoes. Additional recruiting parties commanded by Lieutenants René-Léonard Besserer and David Miller were sent further inland to Kingston and York (later Toronto), respectively.[32]

By April 1805, 121 recruits had been collected at York, Kingston, Montreal, and Quebec, although difficulties then arose in approving their enlistment. A proposal put forward by Captain Christian to have Lieutenant-General Peter Hunter, the lieutenant governor of Upper Canada, inspect the men, which would confirm them as being suitable recruits before they were sent to New Brunswick, was refused, as Hunter claimed he lacked the authority to do so. At Fredericton, Major-General Martin Hunter then petitioned London for approval, which was granted later that year, albeit after the recruits in the Canadas had marched overland from Quebec to New Brunswick. Recruiting continued in the Canadas until the spring of 1808, when it was ordered halted by Sir James Craig, the commander-in-chief and governor of British North America.[33]

An officer's coatee from The New Brunswick Fencible Infantry. The coatee is scarlet with light buff colour cuffs, lapels, and turnbacks, with silver buttons.

Courtesy of the Fredericton Region Museum 1969.2547.1

Unlike the broad conditions permitted for the recruitment of the rank and file, the Horse Guards, the headquarters of the British Army in London, closely regulated the appointment of officers. Thus, unlike The King's New Brunswick Regiment, the officers assigned to The New Brunswick Fencible Infantry received permanent rank in the Army, and would be eligible for half-pay once the regiment was reduced. Over three quarters of the officers appointed to the regiment already held regular commissions, including the commanding officer, both majors, and all of the captains. Many of the subalterns — the ensigns and lieutenants — also came from regular regiments and a number were newly appointed, including a few who were recruited locally.[34]

Major George Johnston of the 29th Foot was promoted to lieutenant-colonel and placed in command of The New Brunswick Fencibles. Since they were currently in Scotland, Johnston and several of the recently appointed officers decided to remain there and see to recruiting soldiers. Other officers came from the 46th Foot, the 11th West India Regiment, and the Cape Regiment; most of them were on active service, while a few were on half-pay. As was the custom at the time, two important officer appointments were made from NCOs. Sergeant Major Edward Holland of the 40th Foot was appointed an ensign and made adjutant; in 1812, he was promoted captain and given command of a company. Sergeant James Hinckes of the 43rd Foot became the quartermaster, in charge of regimental equipment, forage (for the horses), and rations.[35]

When, in January 1806, Lieutenant-Colonel Isaac Tinling, the deputy quartermaster general at Halifax, inspected The New Brunswick Fencibles at Fredericton, he found the regiment in good order and discipline, and rejected as unsuitable for service only a few of the 692 officers, NCOs, and men on parade. This figure was an important milestone, since a minimum of five hundred rank and file had to pass inspection—meaning they had to receive a senior officer's final approval that they were fit for service—before the regiment could be placed on the Army's official establishment. The King responded favourably to Tinling's report, and ordered The New Brunswick Fencible Infantry to be placed "on the regular establishment of the army as of 25th June 1805."[36]

Not long afterward, the regiment commenced its duties, although recruiting efforts continued in order to bring the regiment to its authorized strength of a thousand men. From its base in Fredericton, the regiment was distributed among garrison outposts on the Fundy Shore. In September 1807, a company was posted to Saint John and another divided between Saint John and St. Andrews, and in early 1808, four companies were sent to Saint John. In June, No. 1 Company was sent to Sydney, Nova Scotia, and No. 4 Company to Charlottetown, Prince Edward Island. Both would remain in those locations for the next two years.[37]

On January 1, 1806, at a ceremony held in Fredericton, Major-General Hunter presented The New Brunswick Fencible Infantry with a set of Colours. The stand of Regimental Colours included two flags, the King's Colour and the Regimental Colour. Both were made of silk and measured six feet six inches in the fly and six inches on the pike. Each was carried on a pike nine feet six inches long, including a four-inch spearhead. Atop of each pike were two three-foot-long silk cords and tassels. The King's Colour was the Union Flag, while the field of the Regimental Colour was the same as the unit's facing Colour, with the cross of St. George and a small Union Flag in the canton. The regimental name appeared in the centre of each Colour, surrounded by a wreath of roses, thistles, and shamrocks. Unfortunately, the true appearance of the stand of Colours belonging to The Fencibles will never be known, as they have disappeared, although there is speculation that they were modified when the regiment became the 104th Foot; these later Colours are displayed at the New Brunswick Museum in Saint John.[38]

In June 1807, Anglo-American relations underwent a serious reverse following the *Chesapeake-Leopard* incident, in which the British frigate HMS *Leopard* intercepted, fired on, and then boarded an American warship off the coast of Virginia. As Britain and the United States appeared to be on the point of war, in late 1807 British authorities decided, in response to the poor state of Nova Scotia's defences, to combine under a single person the head of the civil government and commander of the forces in that province. This was part of a wider trend that saw the colonial administration in British North America becoming increasingly military in character. In August 1807, Lieutenant-General Sir James Craig was appointed captain-general and governor-in-chief of British North America. Subsequently, in January 1808, Major-General Sir George Prevost succeeded the aging Sir John Wentworth as governor and commander of the forces in the Maritime provinces with the local rank of lieutenant-general.

Garrison duty, in light of growing tensions with the United States, did little to satisfy the desire of the officers and many of the men of The New Brunswick Fencibles to see action. In 1808, an opportunity presented itself when it was learned that Prevost was to command a division preparing to take the French-held island of Martinique in the West Indies. A brigade of regulars would accompany Prevost as a show of strength against the Americans.[39] In November, after discovering a contingent was being readied to embark from Halifax, The Fencibles' officers requested Major-General Hunter to forward their petition to join the Prevost expedition. The offer was forwarded to Governor Craig at Quebec, but no reply had been received when Prevost sailed with the brigade of regulars on December 6, 1808, bound for Jamaica.

When he arrived in Nova Scotia with three battalions of infantry in 1808, Prevost had distributed the regulars and fencibles among New Brunswick, Nova Scotia, Cape Breton, and Prince Edward Island to counter the potential threat from the Americans. Over the next two years, however, as the crisis with the Americans appeared to diffuse, four of the regular battalions were transferred elsewhere. The reductions commenced in July 1809, when the 101st Foot, which had arrived in Halifax in 1807, departed for Jamaica. In June 1810, the 1/7th Foot left Nova Scotia for Portugal, followed by the 1/23rd in October. In August 1811, Prevost departed Halifax to take up the post of captain-general and governor-in-chief of British North America, and Lieutenant-General Sir John Sherbrooke replaced him as governor of Nova Scotia and commander of the forces in the Maritime provinces.[40]

In the meantime, trade continued to dominate the political differences between Britain and the United States. In May 1810, the US Congress had replaced the Non-Intercourse Act of 1809, which forbade American trade with Britain and France and their colonies and which proved impossible to enforce, with Macon's Bill No. 2 — named after the chairman of a congressional committee — and restored trade between the United States and Britain. Then, in August 1810, France promised to withdraw its trade restrictions on the United States if that country re-imposed non-intercourse with Britain. In November, the United States announced it would comply with Napoleon's terms and issue a revised Non-Intercourse Act in the new year, although the French then reneged on their promise. The British responded by declaring that the re-imposition of non-intercourse was unjustified, and threatened to embargo American trade through Orders-in-Council unless US President James Madison provided proof that the French decrees had been lifted. This demand placed Madison in a difficult situation, as any response would have amounted to an admission that he had been tricked by Napoleon. Furthermore, it became clear to Madison that, until Napoleon was defeated, the Orders-in-Council would remain in force, which was an unacceptable condition. In July 1811, Madison chose instead to call the Congress into an early session in November, which "amounted to no less than a decision to prepare the United States for war with Great Britain."[41]

British military leaders in the Maritime provinces faced a difficult situation. The success of the show of force by the arrival of a brigade of regulars had been illusory. The backbone of the local defences provided by the regular garrison had been weakened with the departure of four regular battalions, and although the shortfall was partially overcome with improvements to the militia forces of each province, more regular troops were required. Undaunted by their failure to accompany the expedition to Martinique, the officers of The New Brunswick Fencibles made a second offer to Governor Craig to extend the regiment's sphere of service and become a regiment of the line, but that offer, too, was refused. The regiment tried again the following year, this time under the leadership of Major Charles McCarthy, acting since December 1809 in place of Lieutenant-Colonel Johnston, who was on a leave of absence in England. Again, The Fencibles' officers sent their request to Major-General Hunter, but this time Hunter chose not to communicate with Craig, perhaps since he was aware that the governor was ill. Instead, he forwarded the application, with his endorsement, to the adjutant general at the Horse Guards in London, where it was to be laid "before the Commander in Chief for his favourable Consideration."[42] This time, the application was successful, and within weeks a Royal Warrant was issued for The "New Brunswick Fencibles being made a Regiment of Line and numbered the 104th Foot."[43]

Into the Line: The 104th Regiment of Foot, 1810-1813

British policy prior to the beginning of the war with France in 1793 had been to augment the Army by raising new regiments, rather than by expanding existing ones. During the war, the number of regiments rose to 135, the majority of which were disbanded following the peace of 1802. In reforming the system, the Duke of York, the commander-in-chief of the Army, chose to abandon the practice of creating new regiments and instead increased the Army's establishment by adding additional battalions to the existing 96 infantry regiments. The added flexibility of this new system allowed manpower to be used where it was needed. The mass of men serving in militia, volunteer, and fencible units was done away with, and newly raised battalions could be used for home defence duties or employed as a "disposable force" anywhere in the world.[44]

Accordingly, between 1807 and 1815, only three new regiments were added to the establishment of the Army. This was achieved by drafting two unnumbered colonial regiments and a reserve battalion into the line, rather than drafting them into other regiments. The 102nd was raised from the New South Wales Corps, the 103rd was created from the 9th Garrison Battalion, and The New Brunswick Fencible Infantry became the 104th Regiment of Foot.[45]

The establishment, or personnel strength, of a regiment included a number of fixed and variable elements that set the number of the rank and file at between eight hundred and twelve hundred men. Factors influencing which establishment a unit received included whether it had more than one battalion, and if it was to be garrisoned at home — meaning Britain or Ireland — or overseas, or deployed on field operations. Regular battalions normally consisted of a headquarters, eight line companies, each of the same strength, and two flank companies with minor differences in strength. When a single-battalion regiment or all of the battalions of a regiment went overseas, a recruiting company for each battalion was authorized to remain behind.[46]

Once taken into the line, the 104th Foot was placed on an establishment of eight hundred men, which was increased in November 1812 to one thousand rank and file. Its eight line companies were each commanded by a captain, assisted by one lieutenant, an ensign, four sergeants, and four corporals. In each company, eighty men filled out the ranks for a total, including two drummers, of 89 men. More specialized roles went to the grenadier and light companies, each with a similar number of officers, NCOs, and men as the line companies. The tallest and most experienced men went to the grenadier company, which the commanding officer employed as a shock or assault force. The light company — or "Light

A plate of the 104th Foot as worn by an enlisted man on the 1812 pattern shako.
New Brunswick Museum R2009.1

Bobs," as they were nicknamed—acted as skirmishers, deploying around the regiment in extended order as an advance, flank, or rear guard, to cover the main body as it manoeuvred. The flank companies enjoyed greater independence from the line companies and, on campaign, it was common for them to be detached and employed separately. Finally, the regimental headquarters included a colonel—an honorary appointment almost always bestowed upon a general officer who never served with the regiment—a lieutenant-colonel as the commanding officer, two majors who commanded larger detachments or wings of the regiment in the field, a paymaster, an adjutant, a quartermaster, a surgeon and his two mates, the regimental sergeant major, a paymaster sergeant, a quartermaster sergeant, and an armourer sergeant.[47]

Those officers of The New Brunswick Fencible Infantry who held temporary commissions and were selected for the 104th now received regular Army commissions. Thus, the commission for Charles Rankin, who held temporary rank as a lieutenant, had seniority in the Army from November 1, 1811. Currently serving officers, such as Ensign Henry Moorsom, of the 24th Foot, or young gentlemen such as John Le Couteur, who held an approved application for a commission, also joined the 104th. Another notable officer, William Drummond, a Scot and a veteran with fourteen years' service in the West Indies, had transferred in 1809 from the 60th Foot to The New Brunswick Fencibles. Whatever plans Drummond might have had for retirement at the time ended in 1810 when, following the departure of Major McCarthy to join the Royal African Corps, he accepted appointment as senior major of the 104th.[48]

Appointed as the first commanding officer of the 104th was Lieutenant-Colonel Alexander Halkett. He had joined the 23rd Foot as an ensign in 1790 and in 1800, following a period in the West Indies and England, obtained a lieutenant-colonelcy in the 93rd Foot, which, in a situation similar to the 104th Foot, had been taken into the line from the Sutherland Fencibles. The regiment remained in Britain and Ireland until 1805, when it embarked for the Cape of Good Hope, where it remained in a state of inactivity until 1814, when it was transferred to the Gulf Coast of the United States.[49] Halkett seems to have made little impression during his command of the 93rd, and his appointment as commanding officer of the 104th might have resulted from his previous experience in taking a fencible regiment into the line. Halkett was well known for his enjoyment of a drink; one member of New Brunswick society described him in 1811 as "very much given to drink and appears to want common understanding, but is of a good family."[50] Halkett also appeared to have encouraged "the natural taste for drinking in others."[51] A harsher view was offered by Captain Jacques Viger of the Voltigeurs Canadiens, who in 1813 described Halkett as an "indolent man, mellowed by wine."[52]

Although the role the commanding officer played in establishing the efficiency, or effectiveness, of an infantry battalion was critical, much of the success or failure of a unit was pinned on the conduct of the senior major and the adjutant. Whereas the modern adjutant functions as the primary administrator to the commanding officer, exercising authority over personnel administration, regimental correspondence, and the dress, deportment, and conduct of the officers, in the Napoleonic era supervisory duties over the officers were performed by the senior major, who was to "superintend the drill of all officers on their first joining" the regiment, and to provide the junior officers with "the best advice and instruction."[53] Circumstances might also place the senior major in temporary command due to the prolonged absence of the commanding officer caused by employment on the staff (those working in a commander's headquarters) or his becoming a casualty.

As Army Regulations provided for generous leaves of absence in peacetime for up to a third of captains who commanded companies and wartime absences due to employment on the staff, sickness, or casualties often left junior subalterns in control of companies, the "drilling of recruits" and their performance of the manual and platoon exercise — the tactical drill of the period — was the principal duty of the adjutant. As the adjutant "instructed" and "checked" the sergeant major and sergeants in the training of the men, he was often selected from among the sergeants. The adjutant was answerable to the commanding officer or, more often, to the senior major for the "progress and improvement"[54] of the men. When the regiment was on the march, the adjutant and his sergeants oversaw the formation and dressing of the troops. The adjutant also had disciplinary duties, including carrying out punishments imposed by regimental courts martial, and administrative responsibilities, including compiling the monthly returns and regimental books.[55]

Between 1810 and 1817, Charles McCarthy, William Drummond, Robert Moodie, and Thomas Hunter held the post of senior major of the 104th Foot. Lieutenant Edward Holland, a former sergeant major, was adjutant of the 104th Foot from its formation until June 1812, when he was promoted and given company command. Determination of the officers who followed Holland is complicated by contradictory records, but they appear to have included Lieutenant John Jenkins, who replaced Holland, but left the 104th when he was offered a captaincy in the Glengarry Light Infantry Fencibles; Lieutenant George Jobling, who was adjutant until July 1813, when Ensign William McDonald, who had been sergeant major until he was commissioned as quartermaster in 1812, replaced him; and Lieutenant Fowke (Frederic) Moore, who followed McDonald in April 1814.[56]

William Gilpin was appointed regimental agent to the 104th Foot to assist the officers with the management and purchase of their commissions and exchanges between regiments and to manage the complexities of funds for recruiting, maintaining the regimental accounts, arranging contracts with clothiers and other contractors on behalf of the commanding officer, and acting as a bank on behalf of the Horse Guards and the Pay Office. Located on the Strand in London, Gilpin's agency was one of twenty such offices that represented the financial interests of line infantry and cavalry regiments. The 49th Foot, then stationed in Canada, was the only other regular regiment Gilpin represented, but he also provided services to the militia in England. Gilpin had also served as agent for The New Brunswick Fencible Infantry, whereas the large firm of Greenwood, Cox and Company represented the Newfoundland, Nova Scotia, and Canadian fencible regiments.[57]

Many residents of New Brunswick welcomed the transfer of The Fencibles to the line, but it posed a number of difficulties for British officials, the most significant being the unit's manning. The remarkable growth of the Army during the Napoleonic Wars was being offset by the loss of 23,000 men per year, which exceeded the number of available replacements. With the need to employ a force for home duties, garrison the Empire — including a host of recently obtained colonies — and support an offensive strategy in Europe, finding men to fill the ranks of over a hundred regiments, many with more than one battalion, was becoming difficult. Recruitment, rather than controlled centrally, rested with the individual regiments, which either kept a battalion at home to serve as a depot for new recruits or, if it became necessary to send all its battalions overseas, maintained a regimental cadre in Britain or Ireland to continue with recruitment. This was not the case, however, with the 104th.[58]

To bring the unit up to strength, recruiting parties, normally consisting of an officer, a few NCOs, privates, and, when possible, a drummer, fanned out across New Brunswick and Nova Scotia. Their efforts, while enjoying success, were frowned upon, however, by Lieutenant-General Prevost, who interpreted them as being in violation of the general rules for recruitment, which did not permit foreigners to serve in regiments of the line.

The main source of manpower for the regular establishment of the British Army was voluntary enlistment or transfers from the militia in

Britain and Ireland. Extraordinary sources of manpower adopted during the Napoleonic Wars included convicts, foreigners, foreign deserters, prisoners of war, and British boys. Convicts, prisoners, and deserters gained an unenviable reputation, however, and were generally useful only in penal corps. The recruitment of boys, who had to be at least sixteen years of age and at least five feet tall, was strictly controlled by the Duke of York, and they were never considered part of a unit's operational strength.[59] Foreigners—who included anyone not born in England, Scotland, or Ireland, or whose service did not make a demand on British manpower—provided a valuable source of manpower, and by 1813 they constituted just over 20 percent of the strength of the British Army. Before the Napoleonic Wars, the Army had often hired foreign troops, but after 1793 the French occupation of many European countries cut off the supply of men. Thereafter, dedicated foreign units, including the King's German Legion, were created. Although concerns over the loyalty of foreigners serving in line regiments meant they "met with disapproval,"[60] a number did make their way into the rank and file—including a number from British North America—but their total never amounted to more than 3.4 percent of the Army. Included in the roll of foreign units were the fencible units raised in British North America for local defence, releasing regular troops for service elsewhere.[61]

As it was raised outside of Britain, the 104th Foot faced unique challenges regarding its recruitment, which was exacerbated by unclear communication between the Horse Guards and the senior commanders in British North America. Raised abroad and without the advantages of a second battalion in Britain, the 104th was unable to recruit from "Home," a complication that also rendered it unable to pay recruits a bounty, as did other regiments of the line. Indeed, in New Brunswick, Major-General Hunter's proposal to Colonel Henry Torrens, the military secretary to the commander-in-chief of the Army, to raise a second battalion in Canada was rejected, as it would have exacerbated the manpower problem. Prevost's opposition to the 104th's efforts to recruit in the Canadas continued when he moved to Quebec, and in early 1812, knowing that a new fencible regiment was to be raised in Upper Canada, Colonel Edward Baynes, the adjutant general of the forces in British North America, instructed Hunter that recruiting in Canada was to cease that spring.[62]

In 1812, the matter was resolved when Gilpin, the 104th's regimental agent, asked Baynes to clarify the "misconception of the Instructions and Regulations intended exclusively for Regiments which recruit at home" and "prevent the Recruiting Parties of that Corps [the 104th] being sent away from the Canadas."[63] The Horse Guards responded promptly, and in April advised Prevost that "it was never in contemplation to prohibit" the 104th "from receiving Recruits . . . from the several Provinces in British North America," and that "it has always been the expectation, that from this source alone, this Regiment could be constantly kept Effective to its Establishment." Torrens concluded with instructions that it was "His Royal Highness' desire that every facility may be given on your part, towards the furtherance of this object."[64]

With authority to recruit throughout British North America now clarified, the recruiting parties were permitted to proceed and, as was customary with single-battalion regiments serving overseas, an eleventh, or recruiting, company was formed for that purpose.[65] Nonetheless, as had been anticipated, competition for the limited manpower grew between the recruiting parties from the 104th and those of other regiments, including the newly formed Glengarry Light Infantry Fencibles, which was authorized for service in Upper Canada and also permitted to recruit throughout British North America, and a new provincial regiment, the Voltigeurs Canadiens, which was formed in Lower Canada. In the Maritime provinces the Nova Scotia Fencibles needed to be sustained, and in October 1812 a new fencible regiment in New Brunswick was formed, all of which added to the growing demand for men.[66]

Nonetheless, the 104th Foot found recruits, although this success was partially offset by routine losses to the regiment's strength. Whether in peace or war, units routinely lost personnel for various reasons. For example, between September 1811 and June 1812, ninety-six "excellent" recruits joined the 104th and seven deserters decided to return to the colours, but their numbers were reduced by fourteen deaths, seventeen desertions, and the need to provide drafts to other regular regiments, including the 49th and 101st. The net effect was to reduce the 104th's gain of 103 personnel to sixty-four.[67] Indeed, whether in combat or not, the 104th Foot would continue to lose men to illness and desertion—a difficulty that would plague the regiment during its time in the Canadas.[68]

An inspection report for the 104th compiled in June 1812 provides excellent insight into the composition and character of the regiment. The return reported there were 54 sergeants, 50 corporals, 22 drummers, and 864 privates, for a total of 990 men. Of these, 391 identified themselves as English, Scottish, Irish, or foreign; 599, or 60 percent of the total, were described as "British Americans." Unfortunately, the return does not identify the province of origin of these men, but many undoubtedly came from New Brunswick and Nova Scotia. One man listed his birthplace as the United States.[69]

Because of their prior affiliation with The New Brunswick Fencible Infantry, many of the men had some previous military service. Most of the privates had between one and seven years of continuous military service, but ninety-nine had served for less than a year. Nearly half the sergeants had served for ten or more years, and one was reported as having been in uniform for thirty-three years. A similar level of experience was reported among the corporals. The 104th was also a youthful regiment, with half the men being between eighteen and twenty-five years of age; in contrast, two corporals were over age fifty-five.[70]

The regiment's establishment consisted of forty-four officers: one colonel, one lieutenant-colonel as commanding officer, two majors, ten captains, twenty-two lieutenants, and eight ensigns. As was the case with the 104th's predecessor, the majority held a regular commission in the Army. Most of the officers were present for duty, but two captains and ten lieutenants and ensigns were absent without leave; as well, five captains were on detached service, recruiting in the Canadas or holding staff appointments. Only three of the officers were identified as British Americans; the remainder were English, Scottish, or Irish. One, Captain George von Gerau, or Gerau de Hautefeuile, was foreign. Altogether, 114 men held commissions in both The New Brunswick Fencibles and the 104th, and of these sixty served with the 104th Foot during the War of 1812.[71]

As The Fencibles had been allowed to recruit in Scotland, many Britons accepted commissions in that regiment and continued their service with the 104th Foot. Such was the route taken by Coun Douly Rankin, a Scot who also helped to recruit thirty-four men from the Scottish Highlands whom he then brought to Fredericton. In 1810, the opportunity to gain a regular commission prompted him to seek a lieutenancy in the 104th. After the 104th departed for Canada, Rankin remained behind in New Brunswick and, in July 1816, following a dispute over his recruiting expenses, he was exchanged into the 8th Foot.

The 104th found its officers from other sources as well. In 1796, Andrew George Armstrong became an ensign in the 38th Foot, and in 1803 transferred to The New Brunswick Fencibles from the 6th West India Regiment. Three sons of James Rainsford, a Loyalist who settled in Fredericton following the American Revolutionary War, found appointments to the 104th, one of them later obtaining a commission in the New Brunswick Regiment of Fencible Infantry when it was formed in October 1812.[72]

From an operational perspective, the regiment was assessed as fit for service, and the majority of the men were fit and available for duty. Only forty-nine personnel were in hospital. The two field officers (majors) and the officers commanding companies (captains) were "effective and totally acquainted with their respective duties." The NCOs were "attentive and tolerably instructed." The privates were "strong, "hearty," and "a good body of serviceable men, healthy and clean, but not well drilled." The interior economy of the regiment was reported as "tolerable." The regimental clothing was "according to regulation," but lacking in certain pieces due to the distance they had to be brought. The 104th was equipped with 1,000 stands of arms that were also "serviceable, clean" and "in good order."[73]

Major-General George Smyth, the officer who carried out the inspection and who had replaced Hunter earlier in the year as the president of the council and commander-in-chief in New Brunswick, was able to visit only eight of the companies, as the other two were on detached service. Six companies were in Fredericton, two in Saint John, and one each in Prince Edward Island and Cape Breton. Events would soon change this disposition and see the regiment move to the Canadas.[74]

The War of 1812: June 1812 to February 1813

In May 1812 US President Madison became convinced that further negotiations with Britain were useless. At the beginning of June, he therefore presented Congress with four charges against Britain — the impressment of American seamen, the violation of neutral rights and territorial waters, the blockade of American commerce, and the trade restrictions imposed by the Orders-in-Council — as sufficient grounds for a declaration of war. Congressional support was not unanimous, but following a close vote, both houses of Congress gave their approval. On June 18, a proclamation was issued declaring that "war exists between the Kingdom of Great Britain and Ireland and the dependencies thereof, and the United States of America and their territories."[75]

In New Brunswick, news of the American declaration of war arrived at Saint John after midnight on June 27. Major-General Smyth pleaded restraint in light of a declaration of neutrality by the District of Maine. In Halifax, Smyth's superior, Lieutenant-General John Sherbrooke, repeated this call for restraint.[76] Nonetheless, defensive preparations continued, and improvements were made to the defences around Saint John's harbour. On Carleton Heights, five companies of the 104th under Major Drummond erected a blockhouse that became known as Fort Drummond (or the Drummond Blockhouse) and a battery armed with two guns to cover the western approaches to the town. As there were too few gunners to work all the ordnance, forty men commenced daily artillery practice under the direction of the Royal Artillery's Lieutenant John Straton, who was also aide-de-camp to Major-General Smyth.[77]

Little work had been done prior to the war to improve the important communication route between Saint John and Quebec known as the Grand Communications Route. In autumn 1811, anticipating the need to transfer troops from the Maritime provinces to Quebec, Prevost ordered two officers to test a canoe-and-portage route across the line of the Maine-New Brunswick boundary to Rivière-du-Loup on the St. Lawrence River. Communications between New Brunswick and Nova Scotia were also improved, and in the early weeks of the war, Smyth sent one of his aides-de-camp, Captain Thomas Hunter of the 104th, to determine a route from the St. John River to Fort Cumberland on the Bay of Fundy. Hunter was to proceed by bateau from Lake Washademoak and then locate portages and a suitable location on the Petitcodiac River, where a bateau drawing six inches of water could continue to Fort Cumberland. Finally, control of the St. John River and the route to Quebec City was to be maintained by posting a detachment from the 104th at the fork of the Oromocto River, where it was also to help construct a blockhouse.[78]

The Royal Navy's presence ensured that Nova Scotia and New Brunswick were protected from any direct military threat from the United States. It was a different story on the high seas, however, as the US Navy and American privateers commenced a vigorous campaign against British merchant shipping. In July 1812, the privateer *Madison* succeeded in taking a British government transport of 295 tons that was en route from London to Saint John. The prize included bales of superfine cloths for officers' uniforms, ten wine casks, one hundred quarter-casks of powder, drums, trumpets, camp equipage, and "830 suits uniforms for the 104th Regiment British infantry."[79]

This would not be the last time the 104th would lose uniforms to the enemy. In March 1814, Callender Irvine, commissary general of purchases for the US Army, reported purchasing "eleven hundred Coats captured by a Salem Privateer which coats were intended for the 104th Regiment." At four dollars each, Irvine considered them a "fortunate purchase," as "there is no scarlet cloth in market."[80] Inefficiencies in the American supply system had created shortages of uniforms and caused delays in their distribution to units. A persistent shortage of blue wool cloth, the official US uniform colour, was partly overcome by the distribution of captured uniforms, including the coats intended for the 104th. Irvine described the clothing as "red Coats, white or buff collar, cuffs & tips handsomely ornamented,"[81] and of "very superior quality."[82] Many of these uniforms were distributed to American soldiers, including enough for a "full band of musick"[83] issued to the band of the US Regiment of Riflemen.[84]

In January 1813, as he prepared for the opening of the campaign season, Prevost learned that, in addition to a naval contingent, he would receive

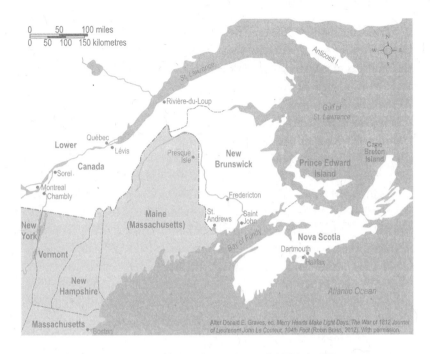

Northeastern British North America and the United States.
The 104th Foot was stationed in New Brunswick, Prince Edward Island,
and Cape Breton. MB

reinforcements from other British garrisons. Experience had taught Prevost that the movement of troop convoys was subject to many disruptions that could delay their arrival at Quebec until the late spring or summer. In addition, transatlantic voyages in crowded troopships often left soldiers sick and weakened, requiring them to undergo a period of rest and recuperation before they could be employed. Unwilling to gamble on the timely arrival of the troopships and faced with evidence of American preparations for an offensive against Upper Canada early in the year, Prevost looked within the North American colonies for additional manpower. As part of this redistribution of troops, six companies of the 104th Foot based at Fredericton and a detachment of artillery were ordered to march overland to Quebec.[85]

Typically, the troops were not informed of what was being planned, but as training was stepped up to include marching on snowshoes, everyone knew something was afoot. Then, in early February 1813, the 104th learned it was to march to Quebec City and thence to Upper Canada. At the time, the regiment occupied the following garrison posts in New Brunswick, Cape Breton, and Prince Edward Island (including company commanders):

Fredericton:
Regimental Headquarters, Lieutenant-Colonel Alexander Halkett
No. 2 (Light) Company, Captain George Shore
No. 5 Company, Captain Edward Holland
No. 7 Company, commander unconfirmed
No. 8 Company, Captain Thomas Hunter
No. 9 (Grenadier) Company, Captain Richard Leonard

Saint John:
No. 3 Company, Captain William Bradley
No. 6 Company, Captain Andrew George Armstrong
No. 10 Company (Half), commander unconfirmed

St. Andrews:
No. 10 Company (Half)

Sydney:
No. 1 Company, Captain George Gerau

Charlottetown:
No. 4 Company, Captain William Proctor

The orders for the march were issued on February 5, 1813. For now, four companies, Nos. 1, 4, 7, and 10, and the boys were to remain where they were. The remaining six companies were concentrated at Fredericton, where the regimental headquarters would oversee the final preparations.

The regimental headquarters and several companies of the 104th Foot
were stationed in Fredericton until early 1813, when the headquarters
and six companies left for Upper Canada.

Painting by W.S. Wolfe, LAC C-122463

Local militia were called up to replace the vacated posts at Saint John
until the 2nd Battalion of the 8th Foot could arrive from Halifax to replace
them.[86]

The twenty-two officers, one paymaster clerk, the drum major, thirty-one
sergeants, thirty-three corporals, fourteen drummers and buglers, and 452
privates were divided into six divisions, each based on a company that was
to depart over five consecutive days. The regimental headquarters under
Lieutenant-Colonel Halkett and the Grenadier Company commanded by
Captain Leonard, forming the first division, left Fredericton on February
16, accompanied by four First Nations guides. Following them were Nos.
3, 6, and 8 Companies (the order by which these three companies marched
cannot be confirmed), under Captains Bradley, Armstrong, and Hunter.

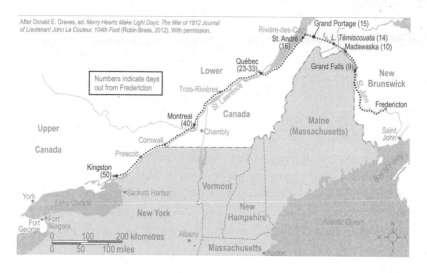

The Overland March of the 104th Foot in 1813. MB

On February 20, No. 5 Company under Captain Holland left, followed the next day by the Light Company commanded by Captain Shore. One soldier who was especially pleased to be leaving New Brunswick was Private Henry Grant. During a brawl in Saint John, Grant had killed a man, for which he was sentenced to two years in prison. With the 104th facing the potential of combat operations and requiring every man to be with his company, the officers arranged a pardon for Grant to accompany the regiment.[87]

As was customary, the departure of the regimental headquarters and individual companies was witnessed by the local populace, and the bugles "struck up the merry air"[88] "The Girl I Left Behind Me," an Irish tune with obscure origins, the words of which reflected a soldier's sorrow over his parting from his beloved girl.

One important piece of regimental property that was carried on the march was the stand of Regimental Colours. When The New Brunswick Fencibles became the 104th Foot, the centre of the Regimental Colour was altered to include a badge with the numeral "104" in arabic lettering on a red circle, enclosed by a blue girdle with narrow white edging that stated "**NEW BRUNSWICK REGIMENT**" in gold letters, surmounted by a crown. A rose, thistle, and shamrock wreath surrounded the badge. Few references to the Colours appear, however, in period documents. One source is a recollection recorded nearly half a century after the march by Lieutenant Andrew Playfair, who remembered the fires lit during halts that sometimes consumed the brush and wood huts the soldiers constructed. On one occasion, during a fire in the officers' camp, "the colours of the regiment" had "a very narrow escape."[89] Another reference to the Colours appears in April 1813, when Lieutenant-Colonel Halkett, accompanied by Captain Holland, his adjutant, took the Colours with them when they departed Quebec for Montreal. The location of the Colours thereafter remains unclear, but they might have been deposited at Montreal or in Kingston. Either way, given the piecemeal employment of the regiment in Upper Canada, it is improbable that the Colours of the 104th Foot were ever taken into the field or were present with the regiment in battle.[90]

The journey from Fredericton to Kingston was no small feat. The 104th was to cover a distance of some seven hundred miles, not by a well-defined road, but by a path that twisted and turned to avoid rapids, patches of bad ice, and difficult terrain along the St. John and Madawaska Rivers. The weather was abnormally cold, with greatly above average snowfall. The temperature dipped as low as −27 °C, and the troops endured at least one blizzard. These brutal conditions are even more striking given the clothing worn by the average soldier. The men had a black felt shako, red woollen coatee, white breeches — or, more likely, heavier grey trousers — and long black or grey gaiters. The red coatee was lined in light buff, which was also the regiment's "facing colour," a dress distinction that appeared on the collar, cuffs, lace (woven braid on the front of the coatee), shoulder straps, and turnbacks (the turning back of the coattails allowed freedom of movement, and exposed the inside colour of the coatee), and aided identification of the regiment. The double-breasted grey great coat provided some warmth and protection, and other items of winter dress, including wool and fur caps, mitts, scarves, and plume covers for the shakos, might have been issued. Footwear consisted of low-heeled shoes that were often poorly made or moccasins. The men also received a blanket to serve as bedding, and snowshoes were also provided on occasion.[91] One participant

By modern standards, the winter dress worn by the 104th Foot for the march from Fredericton to Kingston was insufficient. Aside from their uniforms, a double-breasted grey greatcoat provided some warmth and protection; other items of dress included wool and fur caps, mitts, and scarves. Footwear consisted of low-heeled shoes or moccasins.

Illustration by Drew Kennickell, courtesy of the St. John River Society

described the clothing "as poor and scanty, their snow-shoes and moccasins miserably made; even their mitts were of poor, thin yarn."[92]

Each soldier's accoutrements included sixty rounds of ammunition, carried in a cartridge box worn over the left shoulder, a haversack made of coarse linen or light canvas to carry rations, worn over the right shoulder, a bayonet and belt, and a wooden water canteen. On his back was a knapsack, also made of canvas or linen, which carried other clothing, such as shirts, a pair of shoes, stockings and socks, and toiletries, and when full weighed about forty pounds. Finally, there was the musket and sling. Altogether, the weapons and accoutrements weighed sixty pounds.[93]

Most of the soldiers were armed with the British Short Land Musket, India Pattern, more popularly known as the "Brown Bess." Weighing nine pounds, eleven ounces, and measuring fifty-five inches in length, with a barrel length of thirty-nine inches, the Brown Bess could fire a .71-calibre

The "Brown Bess," the primary weapon issued to
the soldiers of the 104th Foot. Courtesy of the Fredericton Region Museum

lead ball (the barrel had a .75-calibre bore) to a theoretical range of 250 yards. Due to imperfections in the powder, shot, and weapon, and the windage created by the smooth-bore barrel, the ideal range was between 100 and 150 yards. It took eleven drill movements to load, present, and fire the weapon, and despite claims that a rate of up to four or five rounds a minute was possible, a well-drilled soldier generally fired three to four rounds per minute in battle. Impurities in the powder, the build-up of residue in the firing mechanism, and damp weather could also result in a misfire rate of between 20 and 40 percent. As well, smoke from the weapon often impeded the target's visibility. These limitations necessitated the tactic of employing tightly packed formations of men, dressed shoulder to shoulder in ranks, whose volley fire would inflict maximum casualties on their opponents. A seventeen-inch-long socket bayonet could also be fitted to the Brown Bess, but it was normally used as a psychological weapon against the enemy — although, on active service, there would be many occasions for close-quarter fighting.[94]

When it was formed in 1810, the 104th inherited the remnants of the one thousand muskets and bayonets that had been issued to The New Brunswick Fencibles in March 1805. In October 1812, the 104th received six hundred light muskets and thirty sergeants' fusils — a lighter and shorter-barrelled version of the India Pattern musket that was often issued to boy recruits — and weapons that had become unserviceable were replaced during the march to Kingston and later during the course of wartime service in Upper Canada.[95]

A depiction of travel on the St. John River on the way to Quebec in early 1815 by Royal Navy purser and artist E.E. Vidal. New Brunswick Museum W6798

Instead of a musket, the officers carried edged weapons, which served as both status symbols and weapons. Most were equipped with the 1796 pattern straight-bladed infantry sword or the 1803 curved-bladed sword. The latter pattern was a particular favourite of the officers serving in the flank companies, especially among those in the light company. Sergeants also carried swords, but their sign of office was a seven-foot-long wooden staff surmounted by a thirteen-inch-long metal spearhead known as a spontoon or halberd. These staffs served a number of functions, including providing a useful tool for dressing the ranks, closing blank files caused by casualties, and as a rallying point during battle. Although swords and pikes fulfilled important requirements, they had limited tactical use and deprived the regiment of firepower.[96]

Except for those few occasions when sleighs were provided, the 104th marched on foot, with or without snowshoes. Each company was divided into a number of squads, with each pair of men using a small toboggan to carry their knapsacks and weapons; the officers carried their own knapsacks. The toboggans were made of hickory or ash, and were about six feet long and one foot wide. The men marched "Indian style," or in single file, so that each company formed a line about half a mile long.[97] According to Playfair, "[t]he train of the 104th (one company) consisted of upwards of 50 toboggans, containing each two firelocks and accoutrements, two knapsacks, two blankets..., and two pairs of snowshoes... each toboggan being drawn by one man in front and pushed or held back, as necessity required, by one man in the rear by a stick made fast to the stern of the toboggan, Indian fashion."[98]

Before leaving Fredericton, every man received fourteen days' rations. Each ration included one pound of pork and ten ounces of biscuits, tea, and coffee. The officers also provided supplements such as chocolate. At various points along the route, the commissariat issued additional rations, while the few civilians who were encountered offered wine, beer, and food. The physical exertions created by the difficult conditions and the cold caused the men to consume their rations faster than anticipated, leaving them without food on several occasions. Playfair recalled one instance when he "experienced a fast of 30 hours," after having consumed a "half pound cake of chocolate" for his breakfast, and there was "[n]o dinner that day, no supper that night, no breakfast the following morning." It was only when his column reached Rivière-du-Loup that he "found two men, with bags of biscuits and two tubs of spirits and water, handing each" man "a biscuit and about half a pint of grog."[99]

Accommodation, when it could be provided, varied from barracks, as when the regiment halted at Presqu'Ile, Grand Falls, Quebec, and Montreal, to houses, barns, and makeshift huts built by the men in the woods. Making the huts generally involved clearing an area of snow, "felling young pine trees [about fifteen feet in length] to form the rafters of the hut," then placing the trimmed trees "in a conical or lengthened form

When shelter was not available along the route of their march through
New Brunswick, the officers and men of the 104th Foot constructed huts,
as depicted here. The men used their snowshoes to dig into the snow, and
roofed over the huts using logs and tree branches.

Illustration by Drew Kennickell, courtesy of the St. John River Society

with ties at the top." The branches were then covered with a thatch of pine
boughs. Snow was thrown around the outer ring, forming a thick wall.
Inside, a floor was fabricated from small pine branches, and "a blazing
fire was then lit in the centre of the hut."[100] Pine branches were stacked
inside to make beds.

The route of the march through New Brunswick paralleled the St. John
River, and it took about twelve days to slog from Fredericton to the frontier
of Lower Canada. From there, the journey continued to the south bank
of the St. Lawrence River at Rivière-des-Caps, which the leading division
reached on March 8. The divisions then continued on foot along the south
shore of the river, averaging between eighteen and twenty miles a day, to
Point-Lévis, where they crossed to Quebec City. The first division arrived
there on March 13, having completed a journey of three hundred and fifty
miles in about twenty-four days. The last division entered the city three or
four days later. The men were quartered in the Jesuit barracks, and were
immediately placed on garrison duties.[101]

After such an arduous march, the troops must have found garrison duty an annoyance. Each day, the garrison contributed personnel to the guard that protected the city. Between them, they provided four duty officers (one field officer, and three captains and lieutenants, one to act as adjutant) and nearly three hundred NCOs and men to protect vital points, occupy pickets, conduct patrols, and provide escorts for prisoners and other personnel. On March 27, 1813, the guard was drawn from the Royal Artillery, and four infantry regiments, with the 104th providing thirty-six men for guard duty and another thirty-three to man the pickets. This routine continued until March 29. Until they left for Upper Canada, the commanding officer and other officers also made themselves available for other duties, including membership on boards of inquiry and courts martial, while Surgeon William Thomas temporarily gained responsibility for the sick of the 1st Foot, as its surgeon had been assigned elsewhere.[102]

Instructions also directed that, if Quebec were attacked, an alarm would be sounded by three guns firing in quick succession. All the gates to the city would be closed, and units in the garrison would occupy specific positions in the city. If the alarm sounded, the 104th was to occupy posts along the eastern edge of the Upper Town. Two companies were to hold a line between the governor's residence at the Palace of St. Lewis and the nearby Hope Gate; another company would be detached to Grand Battery, overlooking the river basin; while a fourth company was to take post between the Palace of St. Lewis and the Carronade Battery. The flank companies were to remain under arms at the Jesuit Barracks square, near the city centre, ready to react to any orders. Fortunately, no threat appeared to cause these plans to be implemented.[103]

In mid-March 1813, Prevost inspected the 104th Foot. On parade were 28 officers, the sergeant major, 32 sergeants, 31 corporals, 11 buglers, 469 privates, and a boy. Paying them the "highest compliments," Prevost "thought" them to be "really good wind."[104] In his report to the Horse Guards, he noted that the condition of the 104th was better "than was expected, from the severity of the season for which it has been performed."[105] Despite its recent ordeal, the sickness rate in the 104th was no worse than in most other units in the city's garrison. In the month from February 25 to March 24, 1813, twenty-five men of the 104th entered hospital, sixteen of whom were released. The diseases of those remaining in medical care included dysentery and ulcers to the body.[106]

After nearly a fortnight, the companies were ordered to continue on to Montreal and then to Kingston. The flank companies, commanded by Major Drummond, left immediately, while the remaining four companies would "march to Montreal and from thence to Kingston in two Divisions."[107] The first division, commanded by Major Robert Moodie left on March 29, and the second, under Lieutenant-Colonel Halkett, left the following day.[108]

Each soldier received six days' rations and a blanket, and the quartermaster general also provided sleighs to carry equipment and provisions. Shortfalls in weaponry were made up by the issuing of twenty-five muskets and twenty-four bayonets to the regiment. As the campaign season was about to open, speed was essential, and "no superfluous stores or heavy baggage was to be carried." Once the divisions arrived at Prescott, in Upper Canada, a detachment was to hasten to Kingston to give "notice of their arrival"[109] there. The first division left Quebec on March 25 and was in Montreal on April 1. The stop at Montreal would be brief, as the march was to continue the following day.[110] The flank companies under Major Drummond arrived at Kingston on April 12, followed by Moodie's division about four days later. Halkett and the last two companies went into barracks at Coteau-du-Lac, about fifty miles west of Montreal, until the beginning of May, when they proceeded to Kingston, arriving there on May 10.

The 104th had suffered a number of casualties during the march from Fredericton to Kingston. In March, Private William Lammy, from Captain Holland's company, had died near Woodstock. Private Stephen Wadine had frozen to death, and another five soldiers also might have died. Frostbite had afflicted an unknown number of men, including Private Reuben Rogers, who was left near the beginning of the Grand Portage Route; he later rejoined the regiment, only to perish under unknown circumstances in May 1814. One man had deserted. The survivors, in their worn and tattered uniforms, covered in mud and dirt from the final stages of the march, and sickly from their exertions, must not have appeared inspiring either to the officers and men of the Kingston garrison. To give an idea of the pace, the grenadier and light companies of the 104th had taken fifty-three and fifty-seven days, respectively, to march from Fredericton to Kingston, at an average rate of seventeen miles per day. Despite those lost and sick, however, the officers and men of the 104th Foot had achieved the goal they were given, and the six companies now undertook preparations for the coming campaign season.[111]

The final part of this story rests with the two line companies and boys that had remained behind in New Brunswick, and the soldiers' wives and children. Regulations and custom allowed regular regiments on overseas duty to embark with six "lawful wives" and their children to every "One Hundred Men."[112] As not all the families could accompany their men, the women would cast lots before the unit embarked. This rule did not apply to fencible units in North America, but when The New Brunswick Fencibles were redesignated the 104th Foot, the regulations would have allowed sixty wives to be with the regiment. Instead, the June 1812 inspection reported 157 wives and 280 children, only 16 of whom were age ten or older. To help meet the educational requirements of these children, in December 1811 Corporal Thomas Welsh was appointed schoolmaster sergeant, a new post recently approved for all regiments of the Army.[113]

In mid-March 1813, four companies of the 104th Foot were still in the Maritime provinces: No. 7 and No. 10 in New Brunswick, No. 1 in Prince Edward Island, and No. 4 in Cape Breton. Orders then went out that "all persons belonging to" the two New Brunswick-based companies were "to be assembled at St. John by the 11th of April for the purpose of embarking to Canada."[114] Prevost, who was keen to have the entire regiment concentrated at Kingston, also authorized, once the ice melted and St. Lawrence was reopened to navigation, the transportation of the "women and children of the 104th Regt. that have been left in New Brunswick"[115] to Quebec. Provision was made for each woman to receive half the daily ration given to the men, while each child received one-third of a ration. Joining them was Schoolmaster Sergeant Welsh, and together the soldiers, wives, and children sailed to Halifax in early May, where they were joined by a battery of artillery. There they waited for the St. Lawrence to reopen. Wives and children who, for sickness or other reasons, could not travel remained in New Brunswick. No longer eligible for rations, many of them faced hardship until the spring of 1814, when the lieutenant governor of the province authorized that rations be given to some of the dependents left behind, while others were allowed to make the journey to Canada by sea.[116]

The convoy and its escort, the frigate HMS *Minerva,* left Halifax carrying 215 sergeants, corporals, and privates, 35 boys, 113 women, 240 children, and the regiment's heavy baggage. Once they reached Quebec, one of the two line companies was sent immediately to Kingston, while the other stayed at Quebec with the families, where, due to the enemy threat and a shortage of rations in Upper Canada, it would remain for the rest of the war. In time, the company at Quebec would act as a depot for the regiment, holding the sick, wounded, invalids, and boys. In December 1813, the company moved to Three Rivers, although the invalids remained at Quebec.[117]

During the summer, Lieutenant-General Sherbrooke also hoped that the transfer of a detachment of the 10th Royal Veteran Battalion from Quebec to Halifax would allow him to relieve the last two companies of the 104th left in his command, stationed in Cape Breton and Prince Edward Island, and send them to the Canadas; the transfer proved impossible at that time, however, and it had to wait until the following year.[118]

Chapter Two

Kingston, Sackets Harbor, and the Niagara Peninsula, April-June 1813

Our young troops went into action admirably.
— Lieutenant John Le Couteur, May 29, 1813

At the outset of the War of 1812, Kingston was the largest community in Upper Canada, with a population of one thousand. Situated on the west side of Kingston Harbour, Kingston, or Cataraqui, as it was first known, was established in 1673, and eventually included a fort that served as a depot and transit point for French communication with the interior of the continent. In August 1758, a British force took the fort, leaving it in ruins and the area largely unsettled, until the end of the American Revolutionary War revived the strategic importance of the location. Beginning in 1783, the community was re-established, while across the harbour a naval base for the Provincial Marine, the naval force operating on the Great Lakes, was established at Point Frederick. In November 1812, a recently established US naval squadron on Lake Ontario chased the flagship of the Provincial Marine into Kingston's harbour, giving the Americans control of the lake.

By the spring of 1813, Lieutenant-Colonel Alexander Halkett had taken command of the garrison of Kingston from Lieutenant-Colonel Thomas Pearson, and assumed responsibility for the defence of the town, the Provincial Marine base at Point Frederick, and the recently established fortified camp atop Point Frederick, on whose slopes a tented campground accommodated a portion of the garrison and those units transiting to points farther west. Halkett was also responsible for ensuring the garrison's

The northern theatre of the War of 1812, depicting areas
where the 104th Foot campaigned. MB

logistical requirements. In May 1813, approximately 584 regulars were
stationed at Kingston, along with a varying number of sedentary militia.
Fourteen pieces of ordnance of differing calibres had been positioned in
blockhouses protecting the western approaches to the town and at Point
Frederick and Point Henry.[1]

During the course of the war, the naval and military presence grew
to dominate Kingston. The large number of officers, soldiers, and sailors
created crowded conditions, as the existing barracks space proved inadequate. Hired storehouses were converted to barracks to hold anywhere
from a few to 250 officers and men; a large tented camp was also erected at
Point Henry. By 1815, these newly acquired facilities could accommodate
between 1,700 and 2,800 men. The conditions during the spring of 1813,
however, made it impossible to concentrate the 104th Foot in one location, and the companies were dispersed between Point Henry — where
the light company was encamped in tents until the completion of proper

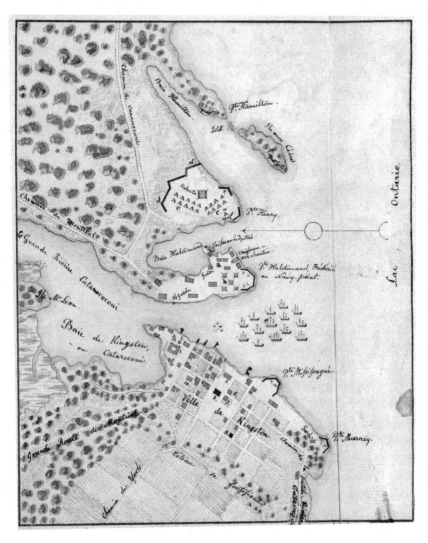

Map from 1839, based on an original drawn in the spring of 1813 by Captain Jacques Viger of the Voltigeurs Canadiens around the time the 104th completed its march to Upper Canada. During its stay in Kingston, the 104th Foot was garrisoned in the town and at Points Henry and Frederick. Courtesy of the Musée de la civilisation, Quebec City

During the winter of 1813-1814, Lieutenant John Le Couteur secured lodgings at this house belonging to Elizabeth Robison, the daughter of a prominent local merchant, politician, and militia officer, at the corner of Gore and King Streets in Kingston. Photograph by author

barracks — and Kingston, where sleeping quarters were provided in buildings, blockhouses (which could accommodate 120 men each), and other defensive works. Many of the officers, including Captain George Shore and Lieutenant John Le Couteur, found rooms in private dwellings, hotels, and other buildings set aside for this purpose.[2]

In April 1813, the Americans opened the campaign season by exploiting their control of Lake Ontario. Their plans called for a joint attack force of five thousand regulars and militia, who would assemble at Sackets Harbor to attack Kingston, York (Toronto), and Fort George on the Niagara front. As American intelligence indicated the defences at Kingston were formidable, it was decided to attack York and hold it until a British relief force could be detached from Fort George to reclaim the town. The Americans then would make a lightning move across Lake Ontario, reduce Fort George, and, aided by an army that would cross the Niagara River, secure the Canadian side. Afterwards, Kingston was to be blockaded to contain the British naval squadron. Commodore Isaac Chauncey would then proceed to Lake Erie to destroy British naval power, and thereafter "attack and take Malden and Detroit, & proceed into Lake Huron and attack & carry Machilimackinac [Mackinac]."[3] The American plan was complex in design and offered many challenges in execution.

The enemy's objective at York was to destroy naval stores and weaken British naval strength by capturing two 18-gun brigs under construction at the dockyard and two Provincial Marine schooners, which, according to Chauncey's sources, were wintering at the provincial capital. At York, Major-General Robert Sheaffe could muster only 413 regulars, 477 militiamen, 50 First Nations warriors, and about 100 miscellaneous personnel consisting of the staff, town volunteers, and members of the Provincial Marine. The town's main defences were a fort, four battery positions, and several unarmed works. Sheaffe actually anticipated that a determined attack on York would likely succeed, and he hoped to finish *Sir Isaac Brock,* the sole vessel being built at the dockyard, before the Americans could sail; he had already sent *Prince Regent* to Kingston as soon as the ice cleared. Completion of *Brock* was delayed by supply problems, however, and by difficulties between the shipbuilder and government officials.[4]

During the morning of April 27, 1813, the Americans began landing a large body of troops to the west of the town. Superior numbers and fire support by Chauncey's squadron overwhelmed the defenders, who began to withdraw to York. By the time he reached Fort York, Sheaffe realized the battle was lost, and ordered *Brock* and the naval supplies burned. He then prepared to withdraw to Kingston, leaving the militia, which had arrived too late to influence the outcome, to surrender the town.

One witness to the debacle was Captain Robert Roberts Lorimer. Born in England in 1789, Lorimer had joined the 49th Foot as an ensign in 1804, and two years later arrived at Quebec with his regiment. His commanding officer, Lieutenant-Colonel Roger Sheaffe, noted Lorimer's talent for staff work and appointed him adjutant. Another future wartime commander of Upper Canada, Gordon Drummond, also found Lorimer to be a talented officer; Drummond appointed Lorimer to his staff while he was at Quebec between 1808 and 1811 working for Sir James Craig, the governor-in-chief of British North America. In 1811, Lorimer accompanied Drummond back to Britain and, upon learning of the opening of hostilities with the United States, returned to North America, where he obtained a captaincy in the 104th Foot. In October, Sheaffe, now a major-general and commander of Upper Canada, brought Lorimer back to his staff as aide-de-camp.[5]

Lorimer was present when Sheaffe gave the order to evacuate York. They separated as Lorimer rode to Sheaffe's official residence, located near the grand magazine at Fort York, to retrieve what important documents and money he could find. A cataclysmic eruption took place when three hundred barrels of black powder in the grand magazine exploded, throwing tons of stone, earth, wood, and metal, as well as men, into the air. The falling debris killed Lorimer's horse, but despite sustaining a serious wound to his right arm, Lorimer got to his feet and continued eastwards on foot, and eventually reached Kingston.

The Americans, meanwhile, found their attack had been only partially successful.[6] The detonation of the grand magazine occurred just as the Americans approached the fort, and the debris, falling as far as five hundred yards away, caused two hundred and fifty casualties among the enemy, including Brigadier-General Zebulon Pike, commander of the troops ashore. Then, contrary winds and poor weather forced the Americans to remain at York for several days. By the time they could leave, fatigue and sickness had weakened their men so much that Major-General Henry Dearborn, commander of the northern theatre, cancelled plans for a direct assault on Fort George, and the American troops and naval squadron returned to Sackets Harbor to rest and refit.[7]

The state of the American forces was unknown to the British, however, and given the uncertainty of enemy intentions following the raid on York, the British troops at Kingston remained at high readiness to repel

Following the British evacuation of York in April 1813, elements of the 104th Foot deployed to the west of Kingston, where they were to guide the withdrawing troops into friendly lines and thwart any threat from pursuing American troops. Here, British troops destroy a bridge over the Don River as they begin their march to Kingston. LAC C6147

any attack. At the end of April, a report reached Halkett that York had been surrendered to the Americans and that the surviving British troops, including Sheaffe, were withdrawing to Kingston, pursued by American troops. Halkett immediately appointed Major Drummond to proceed with the grenadier company of the 104th and a group of First Nations warriors to the Bay of Quinte, about forty miles to the west, from where he was to support Sheaffe's column on the final leg of its march to Kingston. In compliance with a request from Sheaffe to send "up boats and Provisions for the troops,"[8] Halkett had bateaux loaded with enough food to feed a thousand men for three days. To protect the approaches to Kingston, Halkett established guards on the three bridges spanning the Cataraqui River, about three miles west of the town. Thirty Voltigeurs Canadiens, commanded by Captain Jacques Viger, and ten men from the 104th under Lieutenant Le Couteur were assigned the centre bridge, where Sheaffe and the remnants of the garrison from York were expected to cross.[9]

"Expecting that an engagement was at hand,"[10] Viger prepared the bridge for demolition, established sentry positions, and sent warriors ahead to scout for the enemy and to provide warning of the approach of Sheaffe's column. Conditions worsened, as it began to rain heavily, turning the roads into a muddy morass. The only contact came from "wayfarers, cattle drovers and countrymen," and militia sent to reinforce Viger's men. When it became apparent that the enemy was not approaching, all three detachments returned to Kingston. Sheaffe eventually arrived at Kingston on June 2, followed by the main body of the column from York three days later.[11]

The fallout from the surrender of York and logistical concerns were the least of the problems facing the 104th's commanding officer. Earlier, when Halkett had departed Montreal for Kingston, Major-General Sir Francis de Rottenburg, the commander of the district between those two points, had ordered him to halt at Coteau-du-Lac. Believing the order applied to the two companies he was travelling with and not him, Halkett continued to Kingston. When de Rottenburg complained to Lieutenant-General Prevost of this apparent disregard of his orders, the commander-in-chief issued a General Order chastising Halkett for his "direct disobedience to" de Rottenburg's "express orders" and ordering him "instantly"[12] to return to Coteau-du-Lac, where he was to explain his reasons for not following de Rottenburg's instructions. Disappointed by this turn of events, and slighted by this public rebuke that was so "injurious to" his "feelings,"[13] Halkett concluded that his "services" were "by no means properly appreciated" and requested a leave of absence to "return to Europe."[14]

In his defence, Halkett claimed that, since four companies of his regiment were already in Kingston, he considered it necessary to establish his headquarters there. Halkett did not help matters, however, when he wrote that, while he was in Quebec, the adjutant general for Canada, Colonel Edward Baynes, had informed him that "there was no necessity" for his "proceeding with the Regiment"[15] to Kingston, as his brevet promotion to colonel was expected and he should remain behind to await a new assignment, a detail that de Rottenburg likely knew. In May, the matter worsened following the arrival of Prevost at Kingston, accompanied by the new naval commander on the Great Lakes, Commodore Sir James Lucas Yeo. Prevost inspected the 104th "at their respective posts."[16] In contrast to his first inspection of the regiment in Quebec in March, where the regiment was found to be "in good health,"[17] Prevost now found the clothing, shoes, and other equipment to be worn out and the men "sickly ... not appearing in their usual good order and looks."[18] On the following day, the results of the inspection appeared in a general order, and Halkett became "fully convinced" that he had "no prospect of getting a Command."[19] Following approval of his leave of absence, Halkett left Kingston in May, just as the 104th was preparing for its first action, his request to accompany the troops having been unanswered. Dejected, Halkett returned to his home in Scotland, where, in June, he was promoted to major-general. Halkett was later knighted, but he never held another command.[20]

In June, following Halkett's departure, newly promoted Lieutenant-Colonel William Drummond "assumed command of the troops" on Point Frederick, and Robert Moodie, now also a lieutenant-colonel, replaced Drummond in "command of the troops at Point Henry."[21] Any hopes Drummond, the more senior of the two officers, had of taking command of the 104th ended in June, when the talented and experienced officer was appointed acting deputy quartermaster general, leaving Moodie in command. Captain Richard Leonard was appointed brigade major of the Kingston garrison, and became responsible for the readiness and employment of all the units stationed there, including the preparation and issuing of orders and instructions related to their duties.[22]

In the meantime, on May 27, 1813, the enemy struck again when, following a two-day bombardment of Fort George, an American army landed on the Niagara Peninsula. Its objective was to encircle and capture British forces in the area of Fort George. Brigadier-General John Vincent, commanding in the Niagara region, had anticipated that the enemy might be too strong for his own forces, and implemented a contingency plan, withdrawing his command to the safety of Burlington Heights. The following day, two American brigades, totalling three thousand soldiers, set out in pursuit. Heavily outnumbered, and with Chauncey commanding Lake Ontario, the British found themselves in a difficult situation.[23]

On May 26, Prevost was still at Kingston where, after studying reports that Fort George was under tremendous bombardment, he concluded that this was a prelude to an enemy assault on the fort, and proposed a bold plan to relieve pressure in the Niagara region and divert American attention by attacking the enemy naval base at Sackets Harbor. Prevost first conceived this idea on May 22, when an American spy confirmed that Chauncey's squadron was at the western end of Lake Ontario. A reconnaissance conducted on May 26 confirmed that Chauncey's squadron was indeed absent and the American garrison appeared weak. Once he knew that Fort George was under heavy bombardment and that Chauncey was supporting the assault on the fort, Prevost appointed Colonel Baynes to command the raid and began planning in earnest. Prevost was "[d]etermined in attempting a diversion in Colonel Vincent's favour by embarking the principal part of this small garrison of this place and proceeding with them to Sackett's Harbour [sic]."[24] Chauncey's departure for the Niagara Peninsula also made the naval stores and the *General Pike,* an American ship under construction, a tempting target. On May 27, units were mustered and the squadron readied for departure.[25]

The Raid on Sackets Harbor, May 27-29, 1813

In addition to the warships of Yeo's Lake Ontario squadron, the assault force included some nine hundred men of the Kingston garrison. The attack force was drawn from the light companies of eight different regiments and included two field artillery pieces and forty First Nations warriors. Fewer than one-third of the regular troops had seen any action. Whatever concerns Prevost had expressed about the 104th Foot following his inspection of the regiment were forgotten as Major Drummond was placed in command of a four-company detachment totalling nearly a third of the entire assault force. Which battalion companies were selected is not altogether clear from the returns and reports, but it is likely that the contingent included No.

3 Company commanded by Captain William Bradley, No. 6 Company under Captain Andrew George Armstrong, and both flank companies, No. 2 (Light) Company commanded by Captain George Shore, and Captain Richard Leonard's No. 9 (Grenadier) Company. Major Moodie and Captains Edward Holland and Thomas Hunter also accompanied the expedition.[26]

With the company bugles "sounding and Drums rolling" at Point Frederick and in Kingston, the detachments of the 104th manning the defences were quickly marched back to Kingston. At Point Frederick, a soldier from the light company informed Lieutenant Le Couteur that "there is some great move." Together, the two men rushed to find a means of crossing the harbour to Kingston. Unable to find a boat, the soldier, a native of New Brunswick and "thorough Canoeman," suggested they try one of the abandoned, unserviceable canoes. They clambered into one end, forcing its broken bow into the air, and crossed the harbour.[27]

One of the men rushing to the rendezvous was a volunteer serving in the ranks. On the eve of the War of 1812, John Winslow, who was from the same family that had disapproved of Colonel Halkett's enjoyment of alcohol, was a lieutenant in the 41st Foot at Fort George. A disagreement in the mess with another officer had resulted in a brawl, and when Major-General Isaac Brock learned of the incident, he demanded that both officers submit their resignations. Unable to salvage his career or Brock's opinion of him, Winslow decided to become a volunteer, and fought in the Battle of Queenston Heights. Impressed by this act, Brock's replacement, Major-General Sheaffe attempted to reinstate Winslow, but his appeal found little support; Winslow's commission was finally revoked in May 1813. By this time, Winslow was in Kingston, and in an effort to regain his name, he enlisted in the 104th Foot as a gentleman volunteer, meaning he would serve as a soldier until a commission became available.[28]

On May 27, Winslow embarked in one of the boats for Sackets Harbor, and later that year, when the 104th was sent to the Niagara Peninsula, he was attached to the light company. In 1814, he returned to the Niagara and fought at Lundy's Lane. Despite his commanding officer's frequent offers of an ensigncy, Winslow insisted that his name be cleared before he would accept a commission. In late 1816, Lieutenant-Colonel Moodie, who described Winslow's conduct as "conspicuously gallant" and his behaviour always "that of a gentleman,"[29] made one final appeal to Lieutenant-General Sir Gordon Drummond, who had replaced Prevost as captain general and governor-in-chief of British North America, to clear Winslow's name. The result was that, in October 1817, Winslow regained his commission, but as the Army was being reduced, he was placed on half-pay without any hope of active service.[30]

As the companies formed up in Kingston and the officers and NCOs checked to ensure the men carried their haversacks and sixty rounds of ball cartridge, word quickly spread that their destination was the American naval base at Sackets Harbor. Soldiers from Nos. 5 and 8 Companies, commanded by Holland and Hunter, were used to bring those companies selected for the expedition up to strength. Around midday, the men began filing onto the boats that had been assembled in Navy Harbour, between Point Frederick and Point Henry.[31]

Commodore Yeo's squadron included eight hundred sailors distributed among five ships armed with a total armament of eighty-two guns, a merchantman, thirty-three bateaux, three gunboats, and several canoes. With only a single civilian transport to carry part of the infantry and the two field guns, most of the soldiers were crowded onto the open decks of the warships, leaving little room for the ships' companies to do their work. Moreover, the extra load the vessels had to carry affected their handling. An unfortunate few men were also carried in the bateaux that were towed behind the ships for the thirty-six-mile journey. Just before sailing, a canoe delivered Prevost and his staff to Yeo's flagship, *Wolfe*.[32]

On the night of May 27, the squadron got under way and made good progress until early the next morning, when the wind died. During the night, an American schooner spotted the squadron and fired a shot to warn the garrison at the harbour before returning to base. By 4:30 a.m. on May 28, the British squadron was within sight of its objective, now about ten miles away. At dawn, Captain Andrew Gray, serving on the staff of the quartermaster general's department, made another reconnaissance while the troops prepared to land: Upon his return at 9:00 a.m., Gray offered the

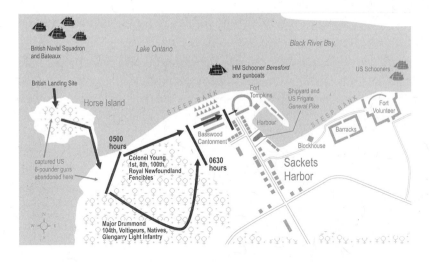

The Battle of Sackets Harbor, May 29, 1813. MB

welcome news that the American base appeared weakly defended. Elated by this intelligence, Major Drummond ordered his troops into the bateaux "to practice pulling,"[33] and then had them turn toward the landing site, only to be called back by one of Prevost's aides.

An hour later, the naval squadron and flotilla of bateaux were still seven miles from their objective when the wind faltered. Yeo then decided to make a personal reconnaissance; when he returned at 3:00 p.m., he and Baynes agreed to call off the attack and the squadron turned back to Kingston. Shortly thereafter, the wind shifted against the British once more. Then, a detachment of thirty-seven warriors and a number of regulars who had been sent out from the squadron in three canoes and a gunboat captured 115 American reinforcements en route to Sackets Harbor. Elated, Baynes and the other senior officers now decided that the ease with which fifteen boats from the American convoy had been captured—most of the 130 survivors in the remaining boats had landed at Stoney Point and scattered into the woods, and only a single boat arrived safely at Sackets Harbor—indicated that the troops at Sackets Harbor were of poor quality.

As a result, they recommended the attack go forward, and Prevost gave his consent.[34]

As the decision to proceed with the raid came late in the day and the squadron was still some distance from the proposed landing site, the British were forced to remain off the harbour that night. Several participants later claimed this delay allowed the Americans time to muster the militia and occupy their defensive positions, which might have been avoided had Yeo's recommendation for an immediate assault been acted upon. In fact, had the landings been conducted in the late evening or night of May 28, the attackers would have found the defenders already in position and with the coming darkness in their favour. As well, the weather to this point had been fine, but as night fell, a heavy rain soaked the men, who, in their haste to board the ships, had not taken their greatcoats.[35]

The defences at Sackets Harbor were considerable. Colonel Alexander Macomb, the officer who commanded the garrison in early 1813, had anticipated correctly that the British would avoid a direct descent on the base as the approaches were well covered by the guns of two forts. Instead, he expected they would establish a foothold on Horse Island, about a mile west, cross a narrow channel to the mainland, and then advance toward the village. Even if the British overwhelmed the troops defending Horse Island, they would still have to negotiate a massive obstacle constructed from hundreds of felled trees — known as an abattis — that encircled the town and dockyard. The main American defences centred on three log barracks, where a regiment of dismounted dragoons and elements of three regular infantry regiments, equivalent in number to the entire British assault force, were expected to defeat any attack. Behind them was Fort Tompkins, surrounded by a stockade and armed with a powerful 32-pounder gun. Farther beyond that, in the low ground, was Navy Point, covered by six guns ranging from 12- to 32-pounders manned by experienced sailors. Overlooking the harbour from the high ground to the east was Fort Volunteer, armed with six or seven guns. Altogether, the strength of the defenders amounted to 1,500 men, which outnumbered the attacker's ground force, and sixteen or seventeen pieces of ordnance, which gave them an eight-to-one advantage in artillery. To reach the naval base, the British would have to sweep aside the militia protecting the beachhead, get through the abattis, then overwhelm the regulars in the main defensive area. Even this was no guarantee of success, for the Americans were prepared to destroy the naval warehouses and their ship rather than let them to fall to the British.[36]

Around 4:00 a.m. on May 29, the tired, wet, and shivering troops moved into the bateaux, formed into line, and headed for the American shore. During the final run in, several of the officers induced Drummond to make his appearance less conspicuous by removing the epaulettes from his uniform, and he agreed, tucking them into his overalls. Any belief the landing would be unopposed was shattered when the New York State militia opened fire as the boats got within a hundred yards of the beach.[37]

As the men poured out of the boats onto the northern shore of Horse Island, the gunboats pulled ahead, firing into the trees and bushes with canister. The 32-pounder gun in Fort Tompkins then opened fire, and one round struck a boatload of grenadiers from the 104th, "killing and wounding a couple of men, cut the boat nearly in two, and down she went."[38] As morning dawned, troops from the companies pushed across the island to a causeway linking it to the mainland. The fire from the American 6-pounder gun and the militia increased, adding to the casualties. As the attack moved forward, Captain Leonard fell severely wounded, while Lieutenant Andrew Rainsford received a shot in the abdomen that knocked his sword from his hand, and Lieutenant James DeLancey was hit in the arm. Around them, other men fell killed or wounded.[39]

Nonetheless, the British secured the island, and the companies from the 100th, 1st, 8th, and 104th Foot, in that order, prepared to charge across the causeway to the mainland, while the gunboats positioned themselves to provide fire support. With their bayonets fixed, the 100th moved quickly onto the causeway, causing a stampede among the undisciplined defenders. The 104th followed, and as the men rushed across, they became engulfed in a dense cloud of grey smoke created by weapons firing. Suddenly, as they continued toward the shore, they came under volley fire that erupted from their rear. Understanding what had happened, Major Drummond ran back, waving his arms at the grey-clad soldiers firing from the island and yelling that they were firing at friends. It turned out that,

The main battlefield at Sackets Harbor. The American defences were among the three barracks buildings located in the wooded area at the centre of the photo. Despite repeated assaults, the British and Canadian attackers were unable to break through the defences and reach their objective, the naval dockyard beyond. Photograph by author

moments earlier, as Drummond's men began crossing the causeway, the Voltigeurs Canadiens, the last unit to land, had moved to the southern end of Horse Island and established a firing line. Thinking that the troops moving through the smoke to their front were Americans, the Voltigeurs had opened fire, but instead of finding the enemy, their rounds had struck the backs of the 104th. Drummond's intervention came quickly, but not before eight of his men had fallen.[40]

Meanwhile, the forward companies had cleared the enemy from the far shore. During the action, Drummond, with sword in hand, had charged toward the Americans. When he was about twenty yards from the enemy, an American soldier levelled his piece at Drummond and fired, knocking him over, apparently dead. Soldiers from the 104th closed in, bayoneted the man, and then turned to see to Drummond. As they began lifting his body from the ground, Drummond grunted out, "tis not mortal, men, I can move my legs." Then, getting to his feet, the badly bruised officer cried out, "Charge on Men!"[41] Drummond owed his good fortune to his epaulettes, which were backed by a metal plate tucked into his pocket and had taken the force of the round that struck him.[42]

Baynes now divided his force into two groups. The main column, consisting of the 1st, 8th, 100th, and Newfoundlanders under Colonel Robert Young, advanced toward the naval dockyard using the shore road; a second group, commanded by Drummond, with the four companies of the 104th under Major Moodie, a company from the Glengarry Light Infantry, two companies of the Voltigeurs Canadiens under Major Frederick Heriot, and First Nations warriors, took a route that lay further inland to Young's right. The two artillery pieces could not be unloaded from the merchant-man, so artillery support was limited to fire from the gunboats and the schooner *Beresford*, whose captain ordered the use of sweeps to propel his vessel into the inlet.[43]

The movement of Drummond's column was hampered by the close country and the abattis until his scouts located a path through the densely packed brush along which they could continue, clearing it of enemy strag-glers. The Voltigeurs experienced similar difficulties, and were forced to move through the bush in sections. About an hour later, both columns reunited in line, with Young on the left and Drummond on the right. Before them were American troops arrayed in front of three barracks build-ings that formed the main enemy position.[44]

After quickly surveying the American dispositions, Baynes ordered "an impromptu attack"[45] against the barracks, but it was beaten back "with heavy loss."[46] By this time, Colonel Young, who had been ill when he embarked at Kingston, was unable to continue and returned to the landing site. Major Drummond, who was rallying the troops, then suffered a second wound, but continued leading his element. By now, support from the British gunboats ended when a rise in the ground masked their fire. Baynes was now in a difficult position: he faced a strong, entrenched enemy with clear fields of fire and artillery support, while his infantry were in the open with no artillery support; moreover, by this time, his force had been reduced to some three hundred men.[47]

Prevost now intervened and ordered a second attack. The right of the British line faced overwhelming fire and was rebuffed, but the troops on the left, who now included the 8th, 100th, and 104th Foot, cleared one of the barracks buildings. Lieutenant George Jobling from the Light Bobs made a dash for the American battery with half of the light company and promptly lost half of them. Another group of soldiers from the 104th momentar-ily took possession of one of the American field pieces. As Lieutenant Le Couteur, Major Moodie, and Private Cornelius Mills began turning a mortar they had taken on the blockhouse near Fort Tompkins, Mills was "slightly hit in five places"[48] and Moodie was wounded. A dash by another group to cross the open space to the adjacent barracks was met by heavy fire, and more casualties were suffered. Among the wounded was Major Thomas Evans, commanding the companies from the 8th Foot. Another key officer, Captain Andrew Gray, the acting deputy quartermaster general for Upper and Lower Canada, who had helped plan the landings, was killed. Believing the outcome hung in the balance, Major Drummond obtained Prevost's permission to take a message under a flag of truce to the Americans demanding their surrender, which they refused. Baynes, who had limited command experience, was uncertain about what to do next, and when he consulted Prevost, the commander-in-chief intervened a second and final time, ordering the force to withdraw and re-embark.[49]

It was the correct decision. The British attack force had been ashore for five hours, and while they had advanced inland over 1,200 yards nearly unmolested and were now at the last obstacle before the dockyard, their progress proved deceptive. Approximately 30 percent of the infantry were casualties and three of the key officers, Young, Evans, and Drummond, were unable to continue. Moreover, the attackers could not break through the main defensive position, where the protected defenders enjoyed artillery support, and many soldiers were running around aimlessly. The situation also seemed confused: to some it appeared that the Americans were fleeing from Fort Tompkins, while other witnesses believed the columns of dust near the village signalled the approach of enemy reinforcements. The bewildering state of the battle was so complete that, as the British order to withdraw was given, Lieutenant Wolcott Chauncey, the commodore's brother, on the *Fair American* near Fort Volunteer, sensing that the dockyard was about to be overrun, raised a pre-arranged signal for American marines ashore to torch the storehouses and burn the new ship in the stocks.[50]

At this critical moment, Prevost directed his attention toward the stationary British squadron and the question of where the American fleet might be. If Chauncey's squadron arrived, it would be disastrous — the combined British force might be captured in its entirety or intercepted as it returned to Kingston. In the event of a naval engagement, the British squadron would have difficulty manoeuvring against the trimmed enemy vessels, as the British decks would be filled with soldiers and equipment. At no time, however, did Yeo express any concern; rather, he left his squadron, and instead of supervising naval support for the operation, went ashore and was seen "running in front of and with our men ... cheering our men on."[51] The result was that most of the squadron—and its powerful guns—remained several miles away and out of the battle; the only British vessels to participate in the battle were gunboats armed with a single 24-pounder carronade each and the 12-gun schooner *Beresford,* and they did so on the initiative of their commanders, not because of an express order from Yeo.

Fortunately, Prevost's fears of a sudden appearance by Chauncey were never realized—in fact, the American commodore did not learn of the raid until May 30. He departed from the Niagara on the morning of May 31 and, upon arrival at Sackets Harbor, decided, after a period of "mature reflection,"[52] to remain there to await the completion of the *Pike,* which would give him command of Lake Ontario. The new ship, which had emerged from the fire unscathed, would not be ready until mid-July, however, giving Yeo control of the lake for two months. Within days, Prevost exploited this turn of events by directing Yeo to deliver 220 men of the 8th Foot, along with much-needed supplies, to Vincent's army at Burlington Bay.[53]

Although Prevost had been right to call off the action, this would have provided little comfort to the troops of the 104th. Le Couteur called the raid "a scandalously managed affair."[54] He had every right to be bitter. After being confined in the cramped spaces of the ships, boats, and bateaux for nearly two days, enduring rain, and then landing on enemy territory with no real idea of how far distant their objective lay, the four companies of the 104th "went into action admirably, formed and advanced as on a field day."[55] Enduring both friendly fire and heavy resistance from their opponents, they withdrew just as their objective appeared to be within reach.

It comes as no surprise that, in contributing nearly a third of the men to the raid on Sackets Harbor, the 104th Foot also suffered the highest losses: seventy-eight dead, wounded, and missing, or nearly one-third of the total British and Canadian losses.[56] Among the officer casualties were Major William Drummond, Captain Richard Leonard, Captain George Shore, Lieutenant Andrew Rainsford, Lieutenant James DeLancey—who would

West of the memorial to the 104th Foot (see page 162) is a memorial to the Crown Forces who fell during the Battle of Sackets Harbor. Twenty of the fifty names on the memorial are those of soldiers from the 104th Foot.

Photograph by author

die from his wound on December 11 at Kingston — and Lieutenant Fowke Moore. Two sergeants, one corporal, and seventeen privates were killed outright and six men later died of wounds. It is estimated that another fifty-one men were wounded or missing. The raid was one of the costliest actions the British conducted in the northern theatre, and the casualties suffered were greater than those at Queenston Heights, York (losses to the regular troops only), Stoney Creek, Châteauguay, or Crysler's Farm. Of the nine hundred men who sailed on May 27, forty-nine were killed in action, 195 wounded, and sixteen missing.[57]

The 104th Moves to the Niagara Peninsula

By late May, the Americans' ambitious offensive plans to exploit their control of Lake Ontario by attacking York, Fort George in the Niagara Peninsula, and Kingston had begun to unfold. The campaign season had opened in April with their attack on York, which proved only partially successful. In May, the Americans landed in the Niagara Peninsula and, following the retreat of Brigadier-General Vincent's Centre Division to Burlington Heights at the head of Lake Ontario, they took Fort George. However, with the lake now in British hands due to Chauncey's decision to remain at Sackets Harbor, the plan to attack Kingston was put off. Moreover, Prevost was preparing to send Yeo, along with reinforcements and supplies, to join Vincent at Burlington Heights.[58] As a result, the Niagara now became the principal theatre of operations.

The strategically important Niagara Peninsula was one of the most fertile and heavily populated areas of Upper Canada. This rectangular block of land, about thirty miles wide and fifty miles long, is bounded by water on three sides: on the north by Lake Ontario, to the south by Lake Erie, and in the east by the Niagara River. The peninsula straddled the important communications route that connected the British supply line from Lake Ontario to Lake Erie. Soldiers, ordnance, supplies, and equipment were moved by boats using the Niagara River. The falls of Niagara and the gorge below it rendered that part of the river impassable, so a portage around the falls was established between Queenston and Chippawa. Fortifications were also placed near the source and mouth of the river, and at both ends of the portage. Fort George lay at the northeast end of the peninsula. More of a stockaded garrison site than a fort, this post also served as the British headquarters in the region. The town of Newark, also known at Niagara, at one time the capital of Upper Canada, was adjacent to the fort, and had a population of five hundred. Fort Erie was near the confluence of Lake Erie and the Niagara River. Built and rebuilt since the 1760s, it was in dilapidated condition when the war began.

Minor fortifications mounting ordnance were also placed at both ends of the portage route.

In spring 1813, the American fixed defences along the Niagara Frontier included Fort Niagara, on the opposite side of the river from Fort George. Originally built by the French in the seventeenth century, the fort was transferred to Britain following the Seven Years' War and later to the United States. About two miles upstream from the falls, at the end of the American portage around the falls, lay Fort Schlosser, and smaller battery positions and supply depots were established at other locations along the river as required.

The American occupation of Fort George and Newark had cut the British line of communication between Lake Ontario and Lake Erie. Unable to make use of the Niagara River, British forces in the Western District and Detroit found their supply situation worsened, as supplies and men now had to be transported from Lake Ontario across the Niagara Peninsula by cart and then reloaded onto vessels on Lake Erie. Outnumbered and with few defendable points between Fort George and Burlington Heights, British commanders considered completely evacuating the Niagara Peninsula, and perhaps moving as far as York should the US Navy regain ascendency on Lake Ontario. The British attempted to rebalance the situation by shifting units and supplies from Kingston to reinforce the 1,500 men currently serving in the Niagara. In the aftermath of Vincent's withdrawal to Burlington Heights, the British began moving regular, fencible, and provincial units to the Niagara.

In early June, units along the St. Lawrence were hurried westward, including a detachment of the Canadian Fencibles that departed immediately for Burlington Bay. At Prescott, the Voltigeurs Canadiens, Glengarry Light Infantry, and the 100th Regiment were grouped into a brigade of light infantry and sent to Kingston.[59] The flank companies of the 104th Regiment were brought up to a strength of sixty men each and, with a company from the Glengarry Light Infantry and detachments of the 8th and 49th Regiments, were also concentrated at Kingston, where they were to be "kept in perfect readiness to proceed from Kingston to the Head of the Lake."[60] On June 6, eleven bateaux were prepared to ferry these troops, along with ten days' provisions, camp equipage, and all the militia clothing remaining in stores. Two days later, the gunboats *Thunder* and *Black Snake* were readied to escort the bateaux. On 8 June, the flank companies of the 104th Foot and a company from the Glengarry Light Infantry departed Kingston for Burlington Bay. Later that same afternoon, news arrived at Kingston of Vincent's attack on the American camp at Stoney Creek and the Americans' withdrawal toward Fort George.[61]

On June 11, the remainder of the 104th Foot, consisting of the four line companies under Major Moodie, were instructed to "proceed by water to join the forces under Brigadier General Vincent."[62] To bring them up to strength, "[a]ll of men of the 104th Regiment fit for field service" at Quebec were "to be sent forward to join the 1st and 2nd divisions of their regiment."[63] Furthermore, "all of the 104th Regiment fit for field service" from the two companies en route from New Brunswick to Quebec were to be "sent forward by detachments as they arrive."[64] On the morning of June 20, "all men of the [104th] fit for field service" and two companies of the 1st Foot under the command of Colonel Archibald Stewart embarked in bateaux for "the head of the Bay of Quinte, from thence they are to march at York, where they will receive further orders."[65] This detachment was delayed another two weeks, however, before they were finally loaded into bateaux for the journey to the Niagara Peninsula.

Among the staff at Kingston that oversaw the assembly of this large force of men, along with rations and equipment, as well as the collection of supplies for Vincent's army and arrangements for the bateaux to transport them, was the newly promoted Lieutenant-Colonel Drummond, who was appointed acting deputy-quartermaster general to coordinate the great number of military, naval, commissariat, and civilian personnel needed for this large-scale movement to the Niagara. Personnel shortages required the militia to provide crews for the bateaux and their escorting gunboats, while gunners from the Royal Artillery were assigned to work the guns and a pilot was secured for navigation.[66]

The journey between Kingston and the Niagara Peninsula was difficult and dangerous. Not only were the men subject to the elements, including rain, wind, and cold, which weakened the men's health and damaged their weapons and equipment, but they also faced threats from the enemy, whose warships were patrolling the lake. In most cases, the bateaux took the troops as far as York, from whence the journey continued on foot along poor roads that stretched around the head of the lake to Burlington Heights and continued along the south shore of the lake to the Niagara Peninsula. The soldiers of the 104th had already experienced long marches, however, and would have found this journey more pleasant than their trek from New Brunswick to Upper Canada, despite the potential threat they now faced from the enemy.

The movement of such a large number of "Troops and Stores up the Lake" was not missed by the Americans. In mid-June, Commodore Chauncey sent the schooner *Lady of the Lake* to "cruise close in with the enemy's shore" west of Kingston and intercept any bateaux "passing up or down" the shoreline, while Major-General Henry Dearborn, the American commander in the northern theatre, reported the arrival of "about 500 men of the 104th regiment"[67] to the Niagara Peninsula. On June 16, the American warship "captured the Schooner *Lady Murray* from Kingston bound to York with an Ensign and 15 non-commissioned officers and privates belonging to the 41st and 104th regiments, loaded with provisions, powder, Shot, and fixed ammunition."[68] Among the prisoners were the six-man crew of the schooner, an ensign and five privates from the 41st and nine privates from the 104th—William Drayton, John English, Henry Kane, Joseph Larencell, Thomas McGrierson, Malkam McKinsey, William G. Stewart, Joseph Wall, and Francis Xavier. The American patrol was resumed following the delivery of the prisoners to the naval base at Sackets Harbor, where they provided Chauncey with important intelligence on naval construction at Kingston.[69]

In response to the threat of the US Navy on the lake, the British undertook additional precautions to protect the bateaux convoys, including adding to the number of bateaux to increase the flow of troops to their destination. Regular troops, rather than militia, were now used to crew the bateaux, such as the "one sergeant and 12 men of the 104th Regiment" who were placed under the command of Captain Peter Chambers of the quartermaster general staff. Those selected for this arduous task were chosen from among "strong, healthy men who understand the management of boats."[70] An additional gunboat was also based at Gananoque to protect reinforcements moving from Prescott to Kingston. The continual shortage of manpower meant that desperate measures were necessary. Dr. Macaulay, a physician at Kingston, was instructed to select from the "convalescents of the 104th Regiment" men to join the gunboat patrol at Gananoque. Once at Gananoque, the men were to be issued with "arms, equipment, accoutrements and necessaries,"[71] and then placed under the charge of Lieutenant Andrew Rainsford (spelled "Rangeworth" in the order), a son of the receiver general for New Brunswick, aboard the gunboat *Retaliation*.

The transfer of the 104th from Kingston to the Niagara Peninsula continued throughout the summer. In late June, "[o]ne captain, two sub-alterns, one sergeant and 11 privates embarked to join their regiment with the army under Brigadier-General Vincent."[72] The men received six days' field rations for their journey. The captain in charge in all likelihood was Richard Leonard, the brigade major at Kingston, who had been released from his duties and allowed to return to the regiment. In early July, four bateaux carrying one officer, two sergeants, and twenty-two rank and file left Kingston to deliver stores to the Niagara. The 104th contributed one sergeant and eight soldiers to this duty, the rest being drawn from the 8th Foot. Upon arriving at their destination, these men would find that, although the British position in the Niagara had become more stable than in June, the situation was still serious.[73]

At his headquarters on Burlington Heights, Vincent approved a plan put forward by Lieutenant-Colonel John Harvey to attack the Americans at their recently established camp at nearby Stoney Creek, from where the enemy intended to descend on Burlington Heights. During an action on the night of June 5-6, seven hundred British troops confronted over three thousand Americans, captured their two generals, and left the defenders in disarray. On June 7, the Americans withdrew eastwards to Forty Mile Creek. By this time, Yeo had arrived and worked out a plan with Vincent to cut off the American force, but Dearborn, the American commander at Fort George, fearing this might occur, ordered his troops to withdraw to Fort George, a movement that was hastened by pressure from First Nations warriors, British infantry, and bombardment by Yeo's squadron.

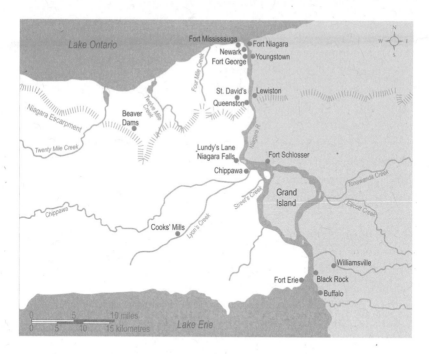

The eastern end of the Niagara Peninsula, showing where
the 104th Foot fought in 1813 and 1814. MB

By the second week of June, all American forces in the peninsula had
withdrawn to Fort George.

Encouraged by these successes, the British commodore ranged around
Lake Ontario, ferrying troops, bombarding shore installations, landing
raiding parties, and even preparing for another assault on Sackets Harbor
—although it was cancelled once surprise was lost—before anchoring
off Kingston and ending his cruise in late June.[74]

This turn of events allowed Vincent to advance closer to Fort George,
and in mid-June he moved his headquarters from Burlington Heights to
The Forty (now Grimsby). From there, he established, under the overall
command of Lieutenant-Colonel Cecil Bisshopp, a triangular network
of forward outposts that harassed the enemy and ringed the American

positions. Vincent selected Balls Falls at the mouth of Twenty Mile Creek as the headquarters for the advance force. His forces also reoccupied a large, two-storey house known as DeCou's, seven miles to the southwest, that had been used as a depot for stores and ammunition and general rendezvous for troops prior to the capture of Fort George. A third outpost was established at Twelve Mile Creek (modern Port Weller) on the shore of Lake Ontario to the east of Bisshopp's headquarters. These locations enjoyed good communications as they were linked by roads built on former First Nations trails extending westwards from Queenston and Newark. The three outposts were approximately seven miles apart, allowing them mutual support in an emergency.

Vincent stationed the two hundred men from the flank companies of the 104th and the light company of the 8th Foot at the mouth of Twelve Mile Creek under the command of Major Peter V. De Haren of The Canadian Fencibles, and a light company of the 49th Foot under Lieutenant James Fitzgibbon at DeCou's. An embodied troop of militia cavalry, The Provincial Light Dragoons, and eventually a troop of the 19th Light Dragoons, were also active in the area. First Nations warriors, whose confidence was restored by the victory at Stoney Creek, were based at Beaver Dams, just east of DeCou's, with another detachment at Forty Mile Creek. They were soon joined by a reinforcement of nearly eight hundred tribesmen arranged by agents of the Indian Department from the Seven Nations around Montreal who arrived in the Niagara around the same time. Three hundred of the Caughnawaga (Kahnawake) warriors joined De Haren's force at Twelve Mile Creek. Despite these new arrivals, Vincent was still outnumbered by the enemy, who occupied a fortified position.[75]

British patrols that penetrated as far as Fort George and even crossed the Niagara River helped to limit the reach of the American forces, reported on enemy activity, and harassed them whenever possible. On June 8, one patrol reported that the Americans were quickly withdrawing, and provided an estimate of their strength at Fort George. Whereas two days earlier Vincent had faced "3,500 men, 8 or 9 field pieces and 250 cavalry"[76] at Stoney Creek, now that the Americans were withdrawing to Fort George, fresh reports indicated they had "4 to 5,000 men," although many were considered to be "in a sickly condition."[77] These reports boosted Vincent's confidence, and he believed that, with the cooperation of Commodore Yeo, he could "push forward and retake Fort George."[78] Unfortunately, the unresolved struggle to gain superiority on Lake Ontario made the commodore reluctant to commit his warships, and Vincent would have to continue with the blockade of the fort. Both armies also began raiding one another's positions, often seizing supplies and food for their own use.

This semi-guerrilla war of patrols conducted between the British and American lines intensified as the weeks passed. In the course of one sharp skirmish, a detachment from the 104th light company was cut off from the main body of troops. Seeing the Americans through the trees, the Light Bobs set an ambush, and when the enemy responded by manoeuvring to surround them, they dashed into the woods and made their way back to their lines.

Over time, the Americans began to fix their attention on DeCou's house, the base from which this aggressive patrolling originated and a lucrative depot filled with supplies. At Fort George, Major-General Dearborn and Brigadier-General John Parker Boyd agreed that the capture or destruction of that outpost would disperse the British and ease the harassment they faced from British patrols. They assigned this task to Lieutenant-Colonel Charles Boerstler and a force of six hundred men and two field pieces. Unfortunately, the Americans lost the element of surprise when, on June 21, two officers openly discussed the plan while dining at the home of James and Laura Secord in Queenston. With her husband still recovering from wounds he had received at Queenston Heights, Laura departed the next day to deliver this important information to the British. That evening, following an arduous seventeen-mile journey by foot, she reached DeCou's, where she passed the details on to Lieutenant Fitzgibbon, who immediately sent out a party of First Nations warriors in search of Boerstler's column and ordered the supplies and weapons stored at the house to be hidden.[79]

Boerstler left Fort George on June 23 and halted overnight at Queenston. His column pressed on the next day, and at St. David's the advance guard skirmished with warrior scouts. Just before 9:00 a.m., as they were nearing their objective, the Americans walked into an ambush at a point selected by

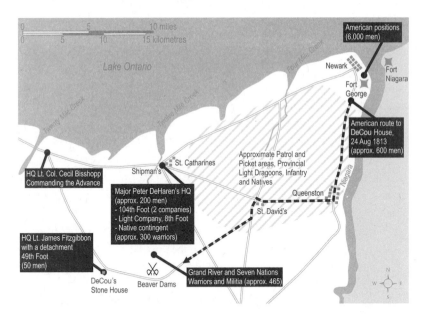

The deployment of British advance positions in the Niagara Peninsula
in June 1813, and the movements of the US Army prior to the
Battle of Beaver Dams. MB

Captain François Ducharme, the senior officer of the Indian Department
present, and held by 465 Seven Nations and Grand River warriors and local
militia. The initial volley created much disorder, but Boerstler regrouped his
men and attempted to push through to DeCou's. As the fighting erupted,
Ducharme sent word to the other patrol bases to come to his aid.[80]

As the struggle continued, British reinforcements converged on Beaver
Dams. Major De Haren immediately mustered both flank companies
of the 104th and the light company from the 8th, and had them march
southward to the sound of battle. As the column came within the sound of
the musketry, De Haren ordered Lieutenant Le Couteur to ride forward to
learn what he could. It took fifteen minutes for the young officer to reach
the battlefield, where he immediately joined Fitzgibbon and his company
from the 49th, which had just arrived. At the same time, a "flag of truce
was sent in with an offer to surrender to a British force."[81]

In the time it took the reinforcements to reach Beaver Dams, the struggle gradually had turned in favour of the First Nations forces, with the Americans suffering heavy casualties in a vain attempt to dislodge the warriors from their positions. They struck at the Americans repeatedly, and as noon approached Boerstler concluded that, with many of his men dead or wounded, the ammunition nearly expended, and his force surrounded, he was unable to continue the action or withdraw. With great reluctance, he sent forward a flag of truce offering to surrender. It was at this moment that the first reinforcements under Fitzgibbon arrived and, for reasons that are unclear, many of the Seven Nations warriors left the field.[82]

When the American artillery continued to fire on the redcoats, though ineffectively, Fitzgibbon attempted to convince Boerstler of the hopelessness of his situation by posting his men in plain view along the line of retreat, and then went forward to discuss terms with the American commander. Whatever reluctance Boerstler might have had in surrendering to the small force of British regulars present and whatever fears Fitzgibbon had that his ruse might fail ended when the companies belonging to the 8th and 104th arrived some twenty minutes later. De Haren "ratified the treaty which Fitzgibbon had entered"[83] on behalf of Lieutenant-Colonel Bisshopp, and 512 American officers and men were taken into captivity. Another thirty men lay dead on the field and seventy were wounded. As the British troops maintained guard over the prisoners, De Haren placed Le Couteur in charge of Boerstler and the senior American officers. Later that day, as the 104th's grenadier and light companies prepared to return to their patrol base, orders arrived instructing them to move to St. David's, where they would be joined by the regiment's four line companies, currently en route from Kingston. British forces were about to close in on the Americans occupying Fort George.[84]

Chapter Three

The Blockade and Reconnaissance of Fort George and Return to Kingston, July-December 1813

Able to repel any force which the enemy may be able to bring against us.

— *Kingston Gazette*, October 9, 1813

In early July 1813, the British advanced their lines closer to Fort George following the First Nations' victory at Beaver Dams. By this time, Major-General Francis de Rottenburg, the recently appointed commander of Upper Canada, had arrived in the Niagara Peninsula and assumed control of operations. He had determined that the uncertain naval situation on Lake Ontario and the stalemate around Fort George warranted increasing the garrison of the stronghold at Burlington Heights against a *coup de main*, while pickets maintained watch over the fort.[1]

De Rottenburg complained to Lieutenant-General Prevost that "everything is unhinged" in Upper Canada. Disappointed that lack of cooperation from the Navy — had it been provided, he claimed, "Fort George would have fallen" — now forced him to establish a blockade of the fort, which would require many more men. The needed reinforcements from Kingston, including the "104th[,] are not yet arrived" due to the poor condition of the roads, "the worst" de Rottenburg "ever saw anywhere."[2]

Nonetheless, fortune smiled on the British, and de Rottenburg was able to tighten the noose around the American foothold on the peninsula. A blockade of the mouth of the Niagara River and the capture of merchant vessels by the naval squadron under Commodore Yeo, and raids against supply depots along the Niagara River and the south shore of Lake Ontario by naval personnel, British and Canadian troops, and First Nations warriors left the Americans under Major-General Dearborn relying on a tenuous line of communication to Buffalo. A probe of the American lines at Fort George on July 8 by British troops and warriors led to a vicious skirmish that allowed the British to extend their blockade close to the village of Newark, and British patrols continually harassed the defenders.[3]

Following the conclusion of the encounter at Beaver Dams, the grenadier and light companies of the 104th relocated to St. David's, where de Rottenburg had moved his headquarters. The arrival of reinforcements, including the 104th's line companies, still left him with too few men to lay siege to Fort George, but de Rottenburg believed his force strong enough to blockade the Americans and reduce "the enemy to the ground he stands upon, and prevent his getting any supplies from our territory."[4] Occupation of the new positions commenced on July 17.

The blockade extended from the mouth of Four Mile Creek, south to St. David's, and then east to the Niagara River. The Lake Road, running from Stoney Creek to Newark, ran parallel to the shoreline, and was intersected by the Black Swamp Road near Newark, which ran south, crossing Two and Four Mile Creeks. The bridges over the creeks on both roads were protected by fieldworks. The blockade was maintained using units posted well forward. The British left, commanded by Colonel Robert Young, rested on Servos's Mills, near the mouth of Four Mile Creek, where there was a secure shelter for the supply boats. The artillery was also located here and supported by the two flank and four line companies of the 104th under the command of Major Moodie. Pickets, each between twenty-four and sixty men strong, were established nearly a mile in advance on the Lake Road. The centre, consisting of the 8th Foot, a detachment of the 100th, and all of the warriors, under Lieutenant-Colonel Francis Battersby, was based on the Swamp Road where it crossed Four Mile Creek, with pickets thrown out at Ball's farm. The 1st Foot and the Glengarry Light Infantry held the ground between St. David's and Queenston, placing their pickets well forward. A strong observation post was also established on Queenston Heights. Unfortunately for Major Drummond, who had just arrived in the Niagara and was to have taken command of a force of light infantry, orders sent him back to Kingston, from where he would take command of the garrison at Gananoque.[5]

Across from the British positions, Dearborn had departed, and Brigadier-General John Parker Boyd was appointed to temporary command of Fort George. He found himself in a difficult position. All was not well within the fort: many of the five-thousand-man division were recent recruits, and foul weather, "having been extremely unfavourable to health,"[6] brought widespread illness, leaving a thousand men unfit, and causing Boyd to consider withdrawing his men to Fort Niagara—although, because the naval issue on Lake Ontario remained unresolved, such a plan could not be executed. Given these circumstances, in early July Boyd was instructed to "pay the utmost attention to instruction and discipline of the troops, and engage in no affair with the enemy, that can be avoided."[7]

The division Boyd commanded consisted of a large detachment of artillery, a regiment of light dragoons, a regiment of riflemen, ten regiments of infantry, and warriors. Since early June, they had been busy erecting fieldworks and placing artillery in battery positions. Records are unclear as to the total ordnance mounted in the defences, but it might have included six 18-pounders and "about" fifteen 6-pounder field pieces. The Americans positioned their outposts around the perimeter of farm houses running along Two Mile Creek. From the north, these outposts were identified as: "Crooks" (No. 1), "Secord" (No. 2), "John Butler" (No. 3), "Thomas Butler" (No. 4), "McClellan" (No. 5), and "Fields" (No. 6).[8]

British raids in July against Fort Schlosser, located across the Niagara River from Chippawa, and Black Rock, near Buffalo, helped to isolate Boyd's command, and his only support now came from across the river at Fort Niagara. Despite receiving instructions not to attack the British, Boyd did not remain complacent. In late July, he arranged with Commodore Chauncey an amphibious attack against Burlington Heights to compromise de Rottenburg's line of communication. The force, five hundred men from Fort George, was unable to negotiate the heights, however, and re-embarked on Chauncey's warships. The Americans then headed for York, where they secured a large quantity of supplies, before returning to Fort George and continuing to improve the works. A similar operation, planned to take place a few days later, was called off because of unfavourable winds. Boyd's confidence improved in August with the arrival of reinforcements that allowed him to reinforce his outposts, which were now facing daily attacks from the British and Canadian forces and their First Nations allies.[9]

In this war of outposts, the two sides tested the mettle of their opponents. Day and nighttime raids became the norm, wearing out the men, as they were almost continually under arms or called out by nearly endless alarms. Losses also mounted. In one incident on July 17, elements drawn from the 8th, 49th, 104th, and the Glengarry Light Infantry advanced to the intersection of the Black Swamp Road and the Four Mile Creek Road, known as the "Crossroads" (now Virgil, Ontario), where, in a sharp skirmish, they succeeded in driving back an American picket. The next day, American riflemen, supported by Oneida warriors, attacked the advance picket, killing two men and wounding five others. The artillery often supported these attacks or conducted its own harassing fire against the enemy.

In July, de Rottenburg complained about the increasing rate of desertion in the Centre Division, which was a "growing evil in this army."[10] One sergeant from the 104th, Thomas Chase, deserted, no doubt due to "cowardice,"[11] as Lieutenant John Le Couteur saw it.[12] Desertion, the absenting of a member of the regular army without permission, was a serious crime in the British Army that, upon conviction, was punishable by death or other punishment "as may be inflicted."[13] Increasingly, however, as the war continued, the need to preserve manpower brought a decline in the use of capital punishment, and soldiers convicted of desertion were often returned to the ranks. Although desertion received scant attention in official papers, it was a leadership challenge that all officers and NCOs dealt with at one time or another. The reasons a soldier would abandon the Army were complicated, and could be attributed to low morale and the conditions of service, including lack of pay, poor lodging, inadequate rations, and strict discipline, as well as the effects of combat and physical discomfort caused by climatic conditions.

The rate of desertion in regular units serving in British North America during the War of 1812 was the second highest the British Army faced

During the summer and autumn of 1813, the 104th Foot participated in
the blockade of American-occupied Fort George; in August, it took part
in the reconnaissance of the defences, coming within visual sight of the fort.
The following summer, the grenadier and light companies marched past
the ruins of Fort George as they advanced south to meet the Americans at
Lundy's Lane. (LAC C-000026)

anywhere during the Napoleonic Wars. The desertion rate between 1812
and 1815 amounted to four men per thousand, accounting for two thousand five hundred men. This situation mirrored British experience during
the Seven Years' War and the American Revolutionary War, when desertion
rates were higher in North America than in any other theatre. This was
because the largely English-speaking colonies provided a society that was
easier for a deserter to meld into and offered them a new life. It should not
come as a surprise, then, that many units raised in British North America,
including fencible and provincial regiments, experienced a high rate of
desertion; the 104th alone lost forty men from this cause during its stay
in the Niagara in 1813.[14]

Major James Fulton, an aide-de-camp to Prevost, noted that the desertions "from this Army" in the Niagara "lately have been very great." He cited "no less a number than fifteen men from the 104th Regt" as having deserted, six of whom came from the flank companies. Fulton explained that, in consequence of "the shameful conduct of this Corps [the 104th]," the 1st Foot had to "relieve them"[15] of some of their duties. To put an end to this disturbing trend, de Rottenburg made an example of five men belonging to the 104th who had abandoned their posts at St. David's and headed for the enemy's lines, only to be apprehended when they decided to return. At a general court martial at de Rottenburg's headquarters at Twelve Mile Creek, all of them, as well as another soldier from the 1st Foot, were found guilty. Prevost confirmed the finding, but decided to show clemency. On July 21, only two privates from the 104th, James Bombard and John Wilson, and the man from the 1st Foot were "shot for examples sake." The others — Privates William Jackson, Daniel Lee, and Sawyer Ruby[16] — were conditionally pardoned and transported for life to Australia. Unfortunately, the problem would persist into the autumn as the inclement weather worsened morale.[17]

In August, changing circumstances caused Prevost once again to consider attacking Fort George. By this time, the British had 2,800 men surrounding the fort and nearby Newark, but still faced almost twice as many Americans. On August 21, Prevost reached the British lines, his visit prompted by the worsening situation on Lake Erie and at Detroit, where reinforcements and supplies were desperately needed. Since he had taken command of his flagship *Queen Charlotte* at Amherstburg, Commander Robert Barclay had struggled to obtain materiel to outfit his squadron and sufficient seamen to complete his crews. Prevost, anxious to re-establish the flow of supplies to both Barclay and Major-General Henry Procter, the commander of the Right Division of the Army of Upper Canada, wanted to eject the enemy from Fort George in order to free up troops to reinforce Procter and provide manpower for the Lake Erie squadron. Before he ordered a general assault, however, Prevost deemed it necessary to determine the extent of the "enemy's position and strength,"[18] and ordered a reconnaissance of the enemy's defences.[19]

Prevost appointed de Rottenburg overall commander of the operation, while Brigadier-General Vincent would oversee its execution. The brigade under Colonel Robert Young, which held the line along the Four Mile Creek, would form "two columns of equal strength"[20] of approximately a thousand men each. The left column, consisting "principally of light troops" of the 8th and 104th Foot and companies from the Voltigeurs Canadiens under the command of Lieutenant-Colonel James Ogilvie, was to move eastward along the shoreline and then "surprise and cut off"[21] the enemy's pickets on Two Mile Creek at the outposts identified as "Crooks" and "Secord" (Nos. 1 and 2). To their south, the second column, consisting of a demi-brigade commanded by Lieutenant-Colonel Francis Battersby, with his 8th Foot, and the 49th Foot commanded by Lieutenant-Colonel Charles Plenderleath, with one 3-pounder gun, would advance northeast of St. David's and attack the four pickets on Four Mile Creek at outposts "John Butler" (No. 3), "Thomas Butler" (No. 4), "McClellan" (No. 5), and "Field" (No. 6). Dismounted light dragoons and four companies of the 1st Foot would support the attack by feigning movement against the McClellan picket. A reserve of sixty men and one gun stood ready to guard the post at St. David's, while another detachment guarded Queenston. First Nations warriors were to participate as well. Both columns would attack simultaneously, with the "commencement of a heavy fire"[22] being the signal to advance.

At daybreak on August 24, a barrage announced the opening of the attack. Joining Ogilvie's column on the left were 326 men from the 104th commanded by Major Moodie, a detachment of Ogilvie's 8th Foot, and three companies of the Voltigeurs Canadiens under Major Frederick Heriot. Instructed to move carefully under cover as they approached their two objectives, Moodie "was hotly pressing the American picquets," when Le Couteur arrived with instructions from Prevost, who was observing the attack, only to feel out the pickets and "not to expose Himself"[23] to the enemy's guns at Fort George. For his part, Moodie was upset with the limited scope of the attack. Having cleared one picket and the enemy from the nearby woods and gone forward with Colour Sergeant Benoni Avery[24] and bayoneted an American sentry, Moodie felt that, given the ease

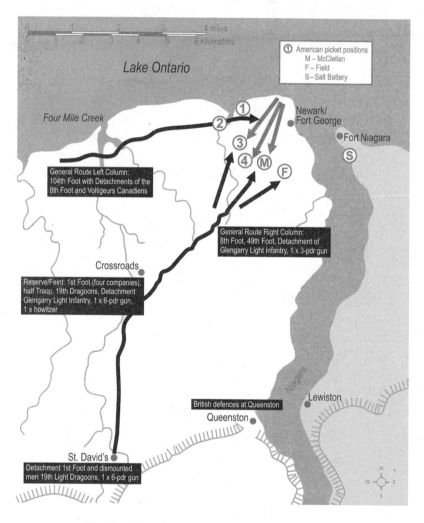

The Fort George Reconnaissance, August 24, 1813. MB

with which the pickets fell and the occupation of a portion of Newark, the "defence was quite feeble" and "the place [Fort George] could be taken by a *coup de main*."[25]

The notion that the reconnaissance made by British, Canadian, and First Nations warriors was sufficient to have taken the fort and avoided the destruction of Newark in December has made its way into the literature of the War of 1812. British officers had carefully surveyed the main defences, however, and determined that a complicated plan, requiring a battering train of artillery and the cooperation of Yeo's squadron, would be needed to take the fort. In addition, a second attack would have to be directed simultaneously against Fort Niagara, across the Niagara River and within supporting range of Fort George. As well, Yeo was unwilling to expose his squadron until Chauncey had been defeated. In late August, Prevost studied the American defences from the deck of one of Yeo's warships and, once again, concluded that a successful attack on Fort George was impossible until the British had secured naval control of Lake Ontario. At the cost of several men killed and wounded, the reconnaissance revealed that Fort George could not be taken under existing conditions, and the British continued with an "economy-of-force" operation to contain a large American army on an insignificant part of British soil to prevent its being employed elsewhere.[26]

The 104th's reconnaissance of Fort George cost the regiment Privates Edward Mitchell and John Thom, both from Lower Canada, killed; and Privates James Nicholson and John Reed captured. As well, on August 28, Private William Garths, a veteran of The New Brunswick Fencibles, died of wounds received in the attack. On August 25, the 104th reported an "effective strength" — those men present for duty — of 156 men, a considerable reduction from the 422 rank and file who were available in June. The remaining men were "on command" — that is, employed away from the unit.[27]

By the end of the summer, more than 3,200 British troops were distributed among two brigades and three smaller commands between Burlington Heights and the Niagara River. As impressive as these forces appeared, however, the approach of autumn and the cooler, damp weather worsened the conditions for the men living in the open, and the spread of disease reduced their numbers. By mid-September, 525 men were reported as sick, and with more men succumbing to disease every day, de Rottenburg secured permission to move the Centre Division to a healthier location at Burlington Bay.

Then, after learning of the shift of American troops from Fort George to Sackets Harbor, which indicated that the next likely threatened point would be the important naval base and logistical installation at Kingston, de Rottenburg began moving a considerable portion of his force there. Before heading to Kingston himself in early October, he left instructions for Major-General Vincent to concentrate the remainder of the forces in the Niagara Peninsula against Fort George and to be ready to withdraw to Burlington Heights should he be threatened by Americans advancing from the Western District of Upper Canada.[28]

Learning of their pending departure from the Niagara, the officers and men of the 104th "thoroughly rejoiced."[29] It's possible none were happier than the 251 men occupying the pickets between Four Mile Creek, and the "pestiferous and noisome marsh"[30] of the Black Swamp between Six and Eight Mile Creeks. Other detachments of the 104th were farther west and included 3 men at St. David's, 65 between Ten and Twelve Mile Creeks, and, at another post, located between Ten and Twelve Mile Creeks and commanded by Lieutenant Andrew Playfair, were 26 of men from his company and 2 members of The Provincial Light Dragoons. Another 46 men were at Burlington Heights. The poor weather contributed to lowering the men's morale, leading to another 20 desertions during September. As well, in mid-September, 62 of the 391 men present were reported as sick and another 79 were absent.[31]

In early October, the 104th, 49th, and three companies from the Voltigeurs Canadiens departed the Niagara for Burlington Bay, where they embarked on boats for York. Moving quickly out of Burlington Bay on October 3, the flotilla sailed through the line of warships of the Royal Navy squadron commanded by Yeo that had anchored there on September 28 following a sharp engagement with the Americans. The squadron had just completed repairs and was about to sail. From their bateaux, the soldiers of the 104th and their comrades gave the sailors "three Jolly cheers"; the sailors returned the compliment by manning the yards.[32] Made wet and miserable during their voyage by the rain and high waves that crashed into the bateaux, and often out of sight of the other boats, thirty men of the 104th reached Kingston in the early afternoon of October 7, with the remainder of the convoy arriving the following day.[33]

The arrival of these reinforcements, amounting to nearly eleven hundred men, was welcome news to the citizens of Kingston and was reported in the local newspaper:

> We are happy to announce the arrival of Lt. Col. Drummond with the first detachment of the 104th Regiment from Burlington Heights. This Regiment with the 49th and the corps of Voltigeurs may be expected here in the course of to-day or to-morrow. These three gallant Regiments together with our brave Militia who are pouring in from all quarters and have already assembled in considerable numbers will be a sufficient reinforcement and with our present respectable garrison will be able to repel any force which the enemy may be able to bring against us.[34]

The 104th now joined the Left Division, a geographical command responsible for the defence of the important line of communication that extended from Kingston to Montreal and commanded by Major-General de Rottenburg, lately replaced as commander of Upper Canada by Lieutenant-General Gordon Drummond.[35]

Meanwhile, fears that Kingston would be attacked proved unfounded, as the Americans instead began their largest offensive of the war, against Montreal. In October, a four-thousand-strong division under Major-General Wade Hampton invaded Lower Canada from eastern New York, followed by an army of seven thousand three hundred men under Major-General James Wilkinson that proceeded down the St. Lawrence River. Hampton posed the most direct threat to Montreal, but on October 26, 1,770 Canadian soldiers and warriors under the command of Lieutenant-Colonel Charles de Salaberry defeated the Americans at the Châteauguay River, causing Hampton to withdraw back across the border.[36]

Attention then shifted to Wilkinson's army advancing on Montreal. Based on Prevost's earlier orders, six hundred men under Lieutenant-Colonel Joseph Morrison left Kingston to pursue Wilkinson, while Yeo detached two schooners and seven gunboats under Captain William Mulcaster in support. Wilkinson's advance by boat down the upper St. Lawrence was slowed by British and Canadian troops, who enjoyed good intelligence and communications, while his logistical situation only worsened. The campaign ended in November following the British victory at Crysler's Farm, 18 miles west of Cornwall. With the rear of his column hounded by British troops, his rations running low, and facing a large garrison defending Montreal, the strength of which was "equal, if not greater than our own,"[37] Wilkinson went into winter quarters at French Mills, now Fort Covington, New York, ending the last major enemy offensive of the year.[38]

During this crisis, the 104th Foot contributed to the defence of the Kingston area. Most of the regiment was concentrated in Kingston, with a detachment under Lieutenant-Colonel Drummond at Gananoque. In late October, American intentions were still unclear, and the garrison of Kingston was subject to many alarms, all of which proved false. Then, on November 7, as the 328 boats carrying Wilkinson's army came into view on the St. Lawrence River at Prescott, Brigadier-General Duncan Darroch at Kingston ordered the light company of the 104th to the spot. The Light Bobs reached their destination in just a few hours, only to be told to return to Kingston.[39]

The abandonment of the American offensive ended the campaign season and the troops moved into winter quarters. Attention now turned to the more agreeable tasks of rest and recuperation and a much-needed opportunity to bring in replacement personnel and replace kit and necessaries. The soldiers looked forward to the opportunity of spending some of the pay owed to them in arrears in happier pursuits than could be obtained from the suttlers and in the taverns. The officers enjoyed the more pleasant aspects of civil society, including balls, dinners, and mixing with the fairer sex. In the meantime, training also began as the regiment drilled on the ice of the frozen harbour.

In November, the officers and soldiers became "entitled to share in the captures made by the Centre Division upon the Niagara Frontier in the Summer of 1813."[40] Payment of the shares of prize money provided a welcome supplement to their income. As in the Royal Navy, Army practice was to offer cash payouts to the troops for all public property they had had a hand in taking. The funds paid were determined by the assessed value of the materiel or goods captured, and were distributed in shares based on the recipient's rank. The thirty shares that Major Moodie, the senior officer present from the 104th, was entitled to resulted in a payout of £9 7s and 6d. Each captain received £5 7s 6d, while lieutenants received £2 10s 6d, sergeants 12s 6d, and corporals 9s 4½d. Lewis Lock, a private man, received a single share of 6s 3d, more than six days' wages.[41] The £200 15s 7½d in prize money Noah Freer, the prize agent to the Army in the Canadas, allocated to the 104th was divided by regulations into 642½ shares to allow its proper distribution to the twenty-two officers, twenty-nine sergeants, twenty-nine corporals, fourteen buglers, and 297 private men eligible. Unfortunately for volunteer gentleman John Winslow, his status meant that no prize money could be granted to him.[42]

The end of the year also brought some personnel changes to the 104th Foot. During 1812, British authorities had augmented the defences of New Brunswick with another fencible regiment. When this news reached Upper Canada, a handful of the serving officers, NCOs, and men from the 104th requested transfers to the newly raised New Brunswick Regiment of Fencible Infantry. Among them was Robert Moodie, whose application to be the commanding officer found favour with Prevost. In early 1814, Moodie, who had been in the Army since 1795, handed command of the 104th over to Lieutenant-Colonel Drummond and departed to take up his new command at Fredericton. Joining Moodie was Colour Sergeant Peter Smith,[43] who had commenced his service in 1804 as a private in the old New Brunswick Fencibles and who was now appointed an ensign, a rare distinction for this period.[44]

As the officers and men of the 104th Foot settled into winter quarters, they likely took stock of their experiences since arriving in Upper Canada that spring. In six months of active campaigning, four companies had participated in the amphibious assault on Sackets Harbor, followed by the transfer of all six companies stationed at Kingston to the Niagara Peninsula, where they occupied the forward defences, participated in the closing stages of the action at Beaver Dams, and then took part in the blockade of Fort George. In that time, they had lost fifty-two men dead from all causes and a number of wounded. At least forty men had also deserted during the year. As they reminisced about these events, their thoughts likely turned to the coming spring and what the new campaign season would bring.[45]

Chapter Four

Kingston, the Upper St. Lawrence River, and the Flank Companies on Detached Service in the Niagara Peninsula, January-December 1814

[E]verything that could be required in a soldier.
— Surgeon William Dunlop

In early 1814, William Drummond discovered that, despite his appointment as commanding officer of the 104th Foot, Lieutenant-General Gordon Drummond, the commander of Upper Canada, had other plans for him. In April, while Lieutenant-Colonel Drummond was still the acting deputy quartermaster general, General Drummond sent him to Fort George to assist the newly arrived commander of the Right Division, Major-General Phineas Riall, in ensuring "matters" within his command "assume an aspect of more promise than they have hitherto done as far as regards the Works of Defence ordered to be erected upon that line."[1]

As was the case with other competent senior officers serving on the staff, Drummond also received an opportunity for further field command, and in March 1814, following the British defeat at Longwoods in the Western District of Upper Canada, he was "entrusted with the command of the force advanced towards the mouth of the Thames"[2] that was to oppose the Americans should they continue their advance eastward. Instead, the enemy withdrew to Detroit, and Drummond returned to his duties in the Niagara, where, in early May, he learned he was to return to Kingston. He undoubtedly was pleased with the publication of the General Order on May 9, 1814, stating that, upon his "delivering over the charge of the [quartermaster general's] department" to Lieutenant-Colonel Christopher Myers, recently paroled from having been a prisoner of war, he was, finally, to "assume command of the 104th Regiment."[3]

Drummond found the sickness that had plagued the regiment during the winter had reduced it to the point where it was "so much afflicted by the intermittent fever as to be extremely ineffective."[4] The 104th was well below strength, numbering just 384 men in April. Recruiting parties that had been sent to Montreal during the winter under Captain Andrew Rainsford found only seven men to serve in the ranks. In late June, believing the root of most of the illness was the damp and miserable conditions at Kingston, Drummond secured approval to move the 104th to Fort Wellington, at Prescott, and "select[ed] from it a detachment of the most effective for Cornwall."[5]

Drummond also continued with the intensive program of training he had initiated earlier in the year. His goal was to prepare his men for the rigours of fighting in the wooded terrain of Upper Canada. As Lieutenant John Le Couteur recalled, the day began early: "Up at five for a Muster. Our Colonel is an early bird with a Vengeance."[6] Drummond "amused Himself," Le Couteur noted, "by teaching us to load on our backs," drill that the light company "did not at all enjoy scratching their nice bright pouches and dirtying their Jackets."[7] At the end of June, the regiment was inspected by Major-General Richard Stovin, commander of the Centre Division, followed by a review of all regimental books, barracks, and kit.[8]

In addition to their training, on June 4 the men also found reason to celebrate when they observed King George's seventy-sixth birthday. The officers and men also rejoiced when the "great and glorious intelligence [was] received of the dethroning of Bonaparte and the restoration of the Bourbons to the throne."[9] Hopes now grew that, with the war in Europe over, reinforcements would be sent quickly to join the troops in North America and end the war there.

During the spring, Lieutenant-General Prevost, Lieutenant-General Drummond, and Commodore Yeo considered a number of schemes for attacking enemy installations. One proposal was to assault the American naval base at Sackets Harbor with a much larger contingent than had been used in 1813. Of the three thousand troops selected to take part, the

104th was to have contributed two hundred and fifty, but the plan was never approved. Instead, in May, nine hundred soldiers and Royal Marines drawn from the Kingston garrison attacked the American supply depot at Oswego, an operation in which the 104th did not take part.[10]

The 104th did play a brief role, however, in the struggle for naval supremacy on Lake Ontario. In March, construction began at the naval dockyard of a new warship that would "look down all opposition."[11] Once launched, the first-rate warship would be the largest naval vessel to serve on the Great Lakes. Assembling all the material needed to complete the new warship placed a great strain on the upper St. Lawrence supply line, and this delayed the delivery of necessary equipment and postponed the launch date from early summer to September. As well, insufficient personnel were available to sort through the tons of stores arriving at Kingston and to build the new ship. More men accordingly were hired for the task, and units from the Kingston garrison joined in the work. In mid-June, the "*whole* of the" 104th Foot was ordered to "work at the new Line-of-Battle Ship, 104 guns." Unfortunately for the regiment, musings that, "in compliment to our number of course she sh[oul]d be called the 104th,"[12] never transpired; instead, the ship was commissioned that autumn as HMS *St. Lawrence*.[13]

As these activities continued into July, reinforcements steadily flowed into Kingston. On July 6, news arrived that the Americans had struck again in the Niagara Peninsula, this time sending a division under Major-General Jacob Brown across the Niagara River against Fort Erie. The next day, part of the 89th Foot, which had just returned to Kingston, was sent to York, while other units in Kingston prepared to reinforce British troops in the Niagara Peninsula. On July 9, Lieutenant-Colonel Drummond was informed that the flank companies of the 104th were to concentrate at Kingston and then embark in bateaux, destined once again for the Niagara.[14] The remainder of the regiment was to be sent to Fort Wellington as planned.[15]

Earlier in the summer, the British had received evidence of a build-up of American troops near Buffalo. Lieutenant-General Drummond decided the large concentration indicated that he would be facing the main American offensive of 1814. As Prevost read these reports and began sending reinforcements to Drummond, he expressed concern about whether it would be possible to provide enough supplies while the Americans controlled Lake Ontario. By the early summer, the British had four thousand men deployed as the Right Division, under Major-General Phineas Riall, between York and Fort Erie. Reports indicated the Americans had amassed four thousand five hundred men, ironically styled the Left Division of the Army of the United States, under Major-General Jacob Brown. Riall proposed leaving garrisons at Forts George and Niagara and concentrating the balance of his troops in a field force that would meet the Americans in the open. The flaw in this assessment was that Drummond and Riall believed they would face poor-quality troops similar to those encountered during the previous winter. The first encounter, at Chippawa in July, revealed, however, that Brown's troops were well trained and that the Right Division would require reinforcements. Prevost's fears regarding his ability to provide adequate support to Drummond quickly became reality.[16]

On July 10, Drummond advised Prevost of Riall's defeat at Chippawa and of the reinforcements he was sending to the Niagara. The 6th and 89th were on their way to York, and he had placed the "two flank companies of the 104th, completed to 60 men each, under Lieut. Colonel Drummond, for the purpose of acting with the Indians in that direction."[17] As in the summer of 1813, Kingston was denuded of troops and supplies as the regular regiments departed, accompanied by the Glengarry Light Infantry Fencibles, the Incorporated Militia of Upper Canada, and the Regiment de Watteville, until the 104th became the only regular unit left there. The other units "were pushed on"[18] by boat or overland march to an assembly area at Burlington, where they were to be met by Lieutenant-General Drummond, who was planning to assume command of the army in the Niagara Peninsula. Following three days' rest at York, the reinforcements' journey continued to Burlington Bay, where a final check was made of their health and the serviceability of their equipment before they were sent on to the Niagara Peninsula.[19] The flank companies of the 104th commanded by Captains Richard Leonard and George Shore were part of this move, but only as far as York, where Lieutenant-Colonel Joseph Morrison, commanding officer of the 89th Foot, ordered them to halt. On July 20, Riall requested Drummond to order the "flank companies detained at York" and the 89th to "be pushed forward with all despatch."[20] These movements reduced the size of the Kingston garrison, and in a short time the line companies of the 104th became the only regulars left there.

Meanwhile, the American campaign plan had fallen apart. Learning that Commodore Chauncey was ill and unwilling to cooperate with his division, Major-General Brown developed a new plan. Beginning on July 20, Brown tried to coax the garrison of Fort George into the open or to lure Riall, who had withdrawn the remainder of his force to the west, into a general action. Neither scheme worked. Two days later, Brown ordered his division back to Queenston to consider his options. Early on July 24, he concluded that the supply state of his division would be improved by shortening his line of communication from Buffalo, and ordered his men to break camp and move to Chippawa.[21]

That evening, Lieutenant-General Drummond arrived at York. Based on intelligence given him by Riall, he planned to make use of the fresh units now gathered there to attack an American battery being erected at Youngstown, to the south of Fort Niagara, which was thought to threaten Fort George. With British naval forces under Yeo now in command of Lake Ontario, on July 23 Drummond instructed the four hundred-strong 89th Foot to proceed to Fort Niagara — which the British had occupied in December — in two ships, with Lieutenant-Colonel Drummond and the one hundred and twenty men of the 104th to follow the next day.[22]

The attack on the American battery was scheduled to take place on July 25. Fifteen hundred men, divided between two forces and a naval contingent, were to advance south along each bank of the Niagara River. On the Canadian side, Lieutenant-Colonel Morrison would threaten Queenston with his 89th Foot, while Lieutenant-Colonel John Tucker, the commander at Fort Niagara, would proceed along the American bank of the river and then attack the enemy battery thought to be near Youngstown. Lieutenant-Colonel Drummond and the flank companies of the 104th were attached to Tucker's command, which also included three hundred men from the 41st, two hundred from the 1st Foot, and a contingent of First Nations warriors.[23] Before the operation began, Lieutenant-General Drummond decided to "ascertain the accuracy of the intelligence respecting the enemy's force and of his preparations on the [American] side of the river."[24] In the meantime, instead of joining Tucker's advance, the 104th's Drummond was assigned to the reconnaissance of the Canadian side of the river, while the flank companies of the 104th were allocated to a brigade in Riall's Right Division.[25]

On July 24, two reconnaissance parties left Fort George to learn more of the enemy's disposition. Drummond and First Nations leader Captain John Norton led one party, while a detachment of The Provincial Light Dragoons commanded by Captain William H. Merritt made up the other. By this time, the American Left Division had broken camp and was retiring on Chippawa. At St. David's, Norton learned of the withdrawal from a deserter and immediately sent a messenger with this information to Riall, which set in motion a new series of moves.[26]

Riall had reorganized his scattered command into two main forces, each with a mix of regular, fencible, and embodied militia commanded by Lieutenant-Colonel Hercules Scott and Lieutenant-Colonel Thomas Pearson, and a reserve based on the 1st Foot. Upon learning about the American withdrawal, Riall ordered Pearson with 1,200 men to maintain contact with the Americans. Meanwhile, at Fort Niagara, Tucker also informed Lieutenant-General Drummond, who had just arrived from York that morning, of the American withdrawal to Queenston. Drummond ordered Tucker to continue with the attack on the Youngstown battery, while he would accompany Morrison on his advance along the Canadian bank of the river. Tucker's men quickly cleared the Americans' battery, and his mission completed, he was instructed to return to Fort Niagara. Meanwhile, Drummond and Morrison halted at Queenston, where Drummond told Riall to bring up Scott's force.[27]

Scott received Riall's message at his camp at Twelve Mile Creek. Anticipating that a move would take place that day, Scott had had his men ready since 3:00 a.m., but, as nothing had happened, he let his men rest. Among the recent arrivals at Twelve Mile Creek was Captain Richard Leonard, in overall command of the 120 men of the two flank companies of the 104th. His own Grenadier Company and Captain George Shore's Light Company were assigned to Scott's 1st Brigade, which also included the 8th

Foot under Major Thomas Evans, the 103rd commanded by Major William Smelt, and three 6-pounder brass guns, with forty personnel, commanded by Captain James Mackonochie. In reserve were the four-hundred-strong 1st Foot and the 2nd Militia Brigade commanded by Lieutenant-Colonel Christopher Hamilton that included men drawn from five militia regiments. With orders to move in hand, the column of troops immediately marched to join Lieutenant-General Drummond.

The day had grown quite warm by the time Scott's force set off from Twelve Mile Creek, and the troops kicked up clouds of dust as they marched. Their route took them by way of Beaver Dams toward Lundy's Lane, a road leading east to the Niagara River. When they were three miles from the intersection with Portage Road, which ran parallel to the Niagara River, a messenger arrived with orders from Riall to retire on Queenston. Scott retraced his route up the Beechwoods Road, which ran along the escarpment to Queenston. After covering four miles, another message arrived ordering Scott to move to the junction of Lundy's Lane and Portage Road as quickly as possible. With the evening coming on and frustrated by these countermarches, Scott now heard artillery fire coming from the south, and had his men increase their pace to double time.[28]

Movements by the enemy had caused the need to countermarch. Earlier, around 2:00 p.m, when reports of the British advance had reached his headquarters at Chippawa, Jacob Brown, concerned that his supply base at Fort Schlosser was threatened, sent Brigadier-General Winfield Scott north to Queenston to report on the situation there. Three hours later, the four regiments of Hercules Scott's 1st Brigade, accompanied by artillery and cavalry, crossed the bridge over the Chippawa River toward their objective. For his part, Riall, who had not yet recovered his nerve following his defeat at Chippawa, concluded that he was facing the entirety of Brown's army, and ordered the forces commanded by Scott and Pearson to converge on Queenston, where he hoped to fight the enemy on more even terms.[29]

When Lieutenant-General Drummond, who had been following Morrison's force, learned of the American advance, he quickly rode ahead until he found Pearson, who was now about two miles north of Lundy's Lane, and ordered him to return to his earlier position on a high feature

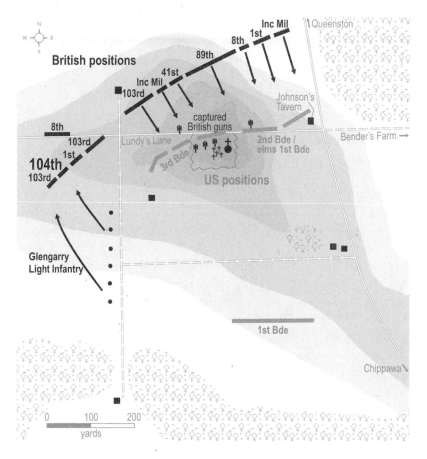

The positions of American, British, and Canadian troops during the final phase of the Battle of Lundy's Lane, July 25, 1814. MB

on Lundy's Lane that had a commanding view of the Portage Road. Pearson and Riall arrived at the hill at Lundy's Lane around 7:00 p.m., where they found Lieutenant-Colonel William Drummond and Captain Norton,[30] who had gone forward together to observe the American advance. Having found the position atop the hill abandoned, Drummond and Norton had decided to remain there after noticing dust clouds from the north that signalled the approach of a British column. No sooner were

Pearson's twelve hundred men and five artillery pieces deployed along a thousand-yard-long line centred on a hill on the east-west ridge running along Lundy's Lane than the American Winfield Scott arrived with his brigade, having made their approach from Chippawa using the Portage Road. Within minutes, the opening shots were fired, and the Battle of Lundy's Lane was under way.[31]

Meanwhile, in the late afternoon, Morrison, his men having been rested and fed, continued toward Lundy's Lane. It had been a long and difficult day for the flank companies of the 104th. Marching, countermarching, and now at the double, the men were hot, thirsty, and exhausted, having marched twenty miles. They approached Lundy's Lane from the west and moved onto the battlefield around 8:30 p.m. By then, the battle had been raging for over an hour. Despite a determined attack by the Americans that nearly broke the militia on the British left flank, the line was intact, and a lull in the fighting gave Lieutenant-General Drummond time to realign his position and incorporate Hercules Scott's men into the line.[32]

Directed onto the field by a member of Drummond's staff, the 1st Foot and the flank companies of the 103rd and 104th were placed to extend the "front line on the right," where Drummond "was apprehensive of the enemy outflanking" him.[33] The 1st Foot was in extended line, flanked by the light and grenadier companies of the 103rd Foot, with the flank companies of the 104th under Leonard and Shore in a skirmish line on the extreme right. The smell of powder and the cries of wounded men filled the air, and the bodies of dead and wounded men and horses were strewn about.

As night approached, and amid sporadic firing, the men found it difficult to adjust their eyes to the fading light.[34] Within minutes of taking up their position, the men of the 104th saw a "black line rising" to their front, and they "poured a rolling volley on them."[35] The response came from a voice shouting "We're British!"[36] and other cries that the troops who were approaching were not American. The 104th ceased fire immediately, but the 103rd grenadier company unleashed one more volley before the situation was understood. The victims of the friendly fire in the fading light proved to be the Glengarry Light Infantry, who, having been sent forward earlier to engage the Americans in the flank, were now moving back into the main line.[37]

Leonard was then instructed to move both companies of the 104th to the northern edge of the hill to form a reserve behind the rear of the 89th Foot, who occupied the centre of the British line. Although the men were sheltered by a split-rail fence, the officers, hoping to reduce casualties from the persistent enemy fire, instructed them to lie down. One soldier belonging to the light company, Private Nathaniel Nickerson, who was also servant to Captain Shore, ignored the shots whizzing around him and the repeated orders of the officers to stay down, and remained standing. The young private explained that the heroism of his commanding officer, Lieutenant-Colonel Drummond, "sitting on that great horse, up there amongst all the balls,"[38] inspired his reckless behaviour. How could anyone, Nickerson cried, "not admire the fellow's generous heroism!"[39] Drummond was indeed an inspiration to all who saw him. Le Couteur shared Nickerson's sentiment at the sight of their commanding officer "seated on his war horse like a knightly man of valour as He was exposed to a ragged fire from hundreds of brave Yankees who were pressing our brave 89th [Foot]."[40]

By this point, the battle had been raging for over two hours. The British had started well, but Riall had been wounded and taken prisoner, and the American Brown, who had been reinforced by another brigade, chose not to outflank Drummond from the west, but instead struck at the British centre and left. The American attack succeeded in capturing the eight guns lining the crest of the hill and forcing the British off the ridge. Regrouping in the low ground to the north of Lundy's Lane, Drummond readied his men to recapture his artillery.[41]

The 104th's Lieutenant-Colonel Drummond described the next phase of the battle as "the most desperate attempts to regain the hill."[42] With the "confusion of the columns rencontering [sic] in the dark" and the "ridiculous mistakes which could only occur fighting an army speaking the same language,"[43] it took the British general and his staff thirty minutes to sort out the mass of men and prepare for the counterattack. The British commander's plan was to form his men into line, and then

The Battle of Lundy's Lane was the largest engagement in the northern
theatre during the War of 1812. Both flank companies of the 104th Foot
were present, as were Lieutenant-Colonel William Drummond, who was
on detached service, and Lieutenant Henry Moorsom, who died during the
battle while serving on the staff. LAC C000407

advance silently up the slope, retake the guns, and regain the hill. As the
British line was assembling, staff officers, including Lieutenant Henry
Moorsom of the 104th, rode up and down the ranks, passing on details
for the attack and ensuring ammunition was being redistributed and the
line properly arrayed.[44]

With three thousand men, the Right Division was still an imposing
force, and Lieutenant-General Drummond formed it into a single line
divided in two wings and a reserve. The regular troops and incorporated
militia of the eastern wing would attack from the Portage Road to the
slope of the hill. Fifty yards to the west and extending for another two
hundred yards was the western wing, arranged in a line consisting of half
of the 103rd Foot, seven companies of the 1st, the flank companies of the
104th, and the grenadier company of the 103rd. The Glengarry Light
Infantry, some of the sedentary militia, and a group of First Nations warriors remained in forward positions near the centre of the western wing.

Five companies of the 8th Foot, other sedentary militia, and more warriors were placed in reserve to the west along Lundy's Lane.[45]

At 10:00 p.m. came the order to advance, but, for reasons that remain unclear, Drummond held the western wing in place. Nevertheless, anticipating that the Americans might attack the British right, the 104th's William Drummond had his men drag dead horses into a line forming a breastwork from which they could return fire under cover. To their left, the eastern wing began moving up the hill, halting and firing as they went. What followed was a confusing, intense action lasting nearly thirty minutes, and ending with the British and Canadians retiring down the hill. Fifteen minutes later, Lieutenant-General Drummond repeated the attack, which proved "more severe" and "longer continued than the last."[46] As musketry fire was poured into them, the Americans began to waver, but, as the British were unable to press the attack, the firing gradually died down, and Drummond's eastern wing again disappeared into the low ground.[47]

Shortly before 11:30 p.m., despite the intensity of the fighting, the British launched a third attack. Drummond continued to enjoy superior numbers over Brown, who had no more than eighteen hundred troops remaining, and the British commander chose to attack his opponent head on. Once more, the British closed with the Americans, this time meeting with success and recapturing their artillery. Drummond's men, now completely spent and unable to continue, retreated into the darkness, and he withdrew the Right Division westward along Lundy's Lane for half a mile to the Lundy farmhouse, where they spent the night. The British commander hoped to renew the action the following day.[48]

Both armies had fought to a standstill in one of the largest and hardest fought actions of the War of 1812. Nearly 6,400 troops were committed to the battle, and each army suffered nearly 900 casualties.[49] The arrival of the 104th's grenadier and light companies following the opening stage of the battle, and their limited involvement in the effort to regain the hill, spared them heavy losses. The official return of casualties for the Right Division, compiled shortly after the battle, listed the 104th's losses as one soldier killed and five missing. Subsequent research paints a slightly different picture. Private B. John Martinette was the sole casualty from Captain

Leonard's grenadier company, captured in the latter stages of the fighting. In Captain Shore's light company, Privates Joseph Blanchard, Jean Baptiste Bourgignon, John B. Fayette, Moses Holmes, and Ednor Lock also became prisoners of war. Captain Robert Loring, an aide-de-camp to Lieutenant-General Drummond and described by one Canadian militia officer as "[c]ool and determined in the field,"[50] was wounded and taken prisoner as he was delivering orders.[51] The only member of the 104th to be killed in the battle was Lieutenant Henry Moorsom, who fell early in the action while "[c]heering on the Royals [1st Foot]." He had served on Lieutenant-General Drummond's staff as deputy assistant adjutant general since August 1813, and as Lieutenant Le Couteur noted afterward, the loss of their "excellent friend" was very troubling to his brother officers, especially as Moorsom was "the last of four or five brothers killed in the Service."[52]

At first light the next morning, the Right Division returned to the battlefield expecting the action to continue, only to find that the Americans were gone. Before them was a field littered with dead, dying, and wounded men, and so began the process of taking the wounded from both sides to farmhouses, where the regimental surgeons established field hospitals, and disposing of the dead. As the local hospitals were quickly overwhelmed with casualties, some of the wounded were evacuated to Fort George. The Right Division men also did what they could to comfort the dying. In one act of compassion, Le Couteur came across the mortally wounded Captain Abraham Hull, a company commander in the 9th US Infantry, and offered the American brandy and water, and promised to deliver several personal items to his family.[53]

For over a week after the battle, the two armies remained out of contact. Lieutenant-General Drummond kept his division at Queenston, where he contemplated his opponent's next move while dealing with the threat that the appearance of Chauncey's naval squadron on Lake Ontario posed to his line of communication and to the forts at the mouth of the Niagara River. Toward the end of the month, following reports from a reconnaissance party he had sent forward to regain contact with the Americans, Drummond decided it was time to advance closer to the enemy and reorganized the Right Division into an advance body of two brigades of infantry, a reserve, and an artillery park. To cover the advance of the division, William Drummond was given command of a "flank battalion" consisting of the light companies of the 89th and 100th Foot and the flank companies of the 41st and 104th.[54]

For the Americans, the pause allowed a period of consolidation. At the end of July, Major-General Brown's Left Division mustered 2,125 men fit for service, but there was a serious shortage of officers. Brown himself had sustained a wound during the battle that forced him to transfer command to Brigadier-General Eleazar Ripley. Following the withdrawal to Chippawa, however, Ripley had proposed quitting Upper Canada altogether and returning to the United States. Brown overrode the suggestion and instead ordered Ripley to withdraw to Fort Erie. The Left Division arrived at the fort on July 28 and began improving the fortifications. By now, Brown had little confidence in Ripley and decided to replace him. On August 4, Brigadier-General Edmund Gaines arrived and took command of the Left Division.[55]

While the regiment's flank companies campaigned in the Niagara Peninsula, the five line companies of the 104th had remained at their posts along the St. Lawrence River at Gananoque, Prescott, and Cornwall. The 181-mile-long corridor of the upper St. Lawrence, stretching from Montreal to Kingston, was integral to the defence of Upper Canada, acting simultaneously as a front, a flank, and the lifeline for the British forces in Upper Canada.[56] As well, nearly half the province's population of 77,000 lived along the river. During the first six months of the war, American forces had mounted predatory raids aimed at disrupting river communications and securing supplies. In early 1813, the British succeeded in chasing the last group of American regulars from Ogdensburg, on the American side, and except in November, when the American army under Major-General James Wilkinson moved downriver in its unsuccessful offensive toward Montreal, the British maintained control of the river until the end of the war.

Beginning in early 1813, the need to maintain uninterrupted communication between Montreal and Kingston led to the construction of fortifications at several points along the river. Work started on a blockhouse at Prescott, where open navigation for bateaux moving to Kingston began. This defensive work grew to become a fort, which, in July 1814, was named in honour of the Duke of Wellington. Also located at Prescott were a number of gunboats—vessels of forty to sixty feet in length, armed with one or two artillery pieces, and crewed by a mix of regular soldiers, Royal Navy seamen, and militia.[57]

Records do not indicate the disposition along the St. Lawrence of the individual line companies of the 104th, but we know that in the Kingston area were No. 3, commanded by Captain William Bradley, No. 5 under Captain Edward Holland, No. 6 under Captain Andrew George Armstrong, and No. 8 under Captain Charles Jobling. The identity of a fifth company and its commander cannot be confirmed, although it was either No. 7 or No. 10, both having moved to Lower Canada in the late spring of 1813, but only one of them being sent to Kingston. The movements of the individual companies are also difficult to trace. In June 1814, they were distributed between Fort Wellington and Cornwall, but by July they were concentrated at Kingston, with a detachment at Gananoque; later that month, the line companies returned to Fort Wellington, where they remained for the remainder of the year.[58] With Lieutenant-Colonel William Drummond's detached service to the staff, Major Thomas Hunter was appointed acting commanding officer in January 1814, and continued in that role following Drummond's departure for the Niagara Peninsula in July.[59]

In addition to their regular garrison duties, the companies of the 104th often provided detachments to crew the gunboats. During the summer of 1814, gunboats and larger naval vessels from both sides routinely skirmished on the river between Prescott and Kingston. In a typical incident on May 14, a subaltern and ten men from the 104th and an equal number of Voltigeurs Canadiens set off from Gananoque under the command of Lieutenant John Majoribanks of the Royal Navy in pursuit of an American sloop. Losing sight of their quarry, the party landed at Cape Vincent, New York, where they destroyed a blockhouse and barracks and took several prisoners before returning to Kingston. In June, American gunboats took the crew of *Black Snake*, commanded by a militia officer; in response, a

British gunboat was dispatched to pursue the Americans. Its commander, Lieutenant Alexander Campbell of the 104th, and crew of eighteen men "fell in with [the enemy and] in a most gallant manner" and after only firing "a few shot"[60] from their single carronade, obliged the enemy flotilla of one gunboat and four other vessels "to abandon and scuttle their prize." Unfortunately, the enemy escaped with his prisoners, but the gun and stores from the scuttled British gunboat were recovered.[61]

Other duties were less arduous and included providing escorts for American prisoners of war. In January 1814, for example, Lieutenant Frederick Shaffalisky took charge of a party of two corporals and twenty privates from the Glengarry Light Infantry to escort prisoners of war, en route to Montreal, on the leg from Kingston to Prescott.[62] Farther to the east, the small detachment of the 104th at Cornwall, which earlier in the year had served as a base for raiding enemy depots across the river, found that, with the threat from the Americans largely eliminated, their task was mostly limited to protecting the supply bateaux moving along the river.[63]

The relative quiet in this theatre also provided an opportunity to see to the interior economy of the regiment. Sickness and injury took a greater toll on the troops than did combat, and often left men unfit for regular service but still capable of employment. The end of each campaign season left the regiment with a pool of men declared unfit for active service, and the Royal Veteran battalions provided a means of using these men to garrison fortified points, such as Fort Wellington, and freeing up regular units for field operations. Accordingly, in 1812, one man was transferred to the 10th Royal Veteran Battalion, in 1813 another eight followed, and in 1814 another thirty-two men left, the majority of them departing in November following their return from the Niagara Peninsula.[64]

Meanwhile, in the Niagara Peninsula, the Right Division had moved to within six miles of Fort Erie. Reports from First Nations scouts indicated that the Americans had retired to Fort Erie, where they had begun to expand the works to house the entire Left Division. Lieutenant-General Drummond concluded that, lacking the manpower, supplies, and ordnance to conduct a prolonged siege of Fort Erie, he would threaten the American line of communications at Black Rock and Buffalo and, by the "destruction of the Enemy's Depot of Provisions,"[65] force the Americans from the fort. To achieve this goal Lieutenant-Colonel John Tucker was given command of a light brigade of six hundred men divided into three groups. The main body consisted of four line companies and the two flank companies from the 41st Foot under Lieutenant-Colonel William Evans; the second group was formed from the grenadier and light companies of the 104th and the light companies of the 89th and 100th Foot, commanded by Lieutenant-Colonel William Drummond; and the third group was a detachment of artillery. Once Tucker had succeeded in taking his objective, a party of sailors was to capture enemy naval vessels moored nearby.[66]

At 11:00 p.m. on August 2, Tucker's light brigade began crossing the Niagara River; by midnight, they were all across. Although he was only two miles from Black Rock, Tucker halted for four hours to await daylight before continuing toward his objective. Then, instead of employing one of the light companies as an advance guard, a task for which the Light Bobs were most suited, Tucker sent Evans and the 41st Foot forward. In his journal, Lieutenant Le Couteur criticized Tucker, whom he called "Brigadier Shindy," meaning he considered Tucker to be unsteady in action. William Drummond also had little regard for Tucker's professional acumen, but chose to withhold his criticism as it was "no business of his."[67]

Around 4:30 a.m., as Evans's force approached the bridge over Conjocta Creek, just north of their first objective at Black Rock, they came under heavy fire from the enemy. Although numbering no more than 240 men, they had learned of the British advance and were entrenched on the opposite bank. With the element of surprise lost, the six companies of the 41st fired a volley, broke, then fled to the rear. The flank companies from the 89th, 100th, and 104th remained steady, however, and the grenadier and light companies of the 104th returned fire as Drummond rushed forward to where Captain Shore had deployed the light company and ordered Le Couteur to take Sergeant Peter (Pierre) Roy and a detachment of Light Bobs and see what lay ahead.[68]

Meanwhile, order was restored among the 41st, and once reformed, Tucker sent its companies back to the bridge. There was a ford about a mile upstream, but rather than attempt a flanking move, Tucker opted to continue the firefight around the bridge. The action continued for nearly three hours as the Americans — rifle armed, which allowed them more accurate fire at a greater range, albeit with a slower rate of fire than the musket-equipped British — held off the attackers. Then, in the afternoon, thinking the Americans were about to stage a large counterattack, Tucker broke off the engagement and ordered his men back across to the Canadian side of the Niagara River.

The action had achieved nothing, and cost thirty-three casualties: twelve killed, seventeen wounded, and four missing. In his report, Tucker stated that, from the 104th, one sergeant and five men had been killed in the action, one man had been wounded, and another four were missing, although the records reveal only a single death in the regiment, that of Sergeant Pierre Roy, killed when the reconnaissance party under Le Couteur came under enemy fire. Four privates, all of them from the light company, were also missing.[69]

Disappointed with the results and furious with Tucker, Lieutenant-General Drummond now had to contemplate establishing a siege of Fort Erie. On August 3, as the lead elements of the Right Division pushed back the American pickets, Drummond was finally able to see his objective and to study the improvements the Americans had made to the fort. In short order, they had reinforced and expanded the original fortification, a stone fort consisting of two demi-bastions — two-sided angular works made of brick and sod that projected outwards — connected by an earthen curtain wall on their west side, and two stone buildings on the east. A low wall connected the northeast demi-bastion to the shore of Lake Erie, while the curtain wall was extended nearly nine hundred yards to the south to a sand mound known as Snake Hill, which was also fortified. Inside were twenty-eight hundred men and eighteen pieces of ordnance, distributed between the northeast bastion and along the entire line to Snake Hill. A dry ditch surrounded the outer walls of the stone fort, and abattis had been placed along the perimeter. Batteries across the river at Black Rock provided additional fire support, and three naval schooners on Lake Erie guaranteed uninterrupted communication with Buffalo. The enemy position was

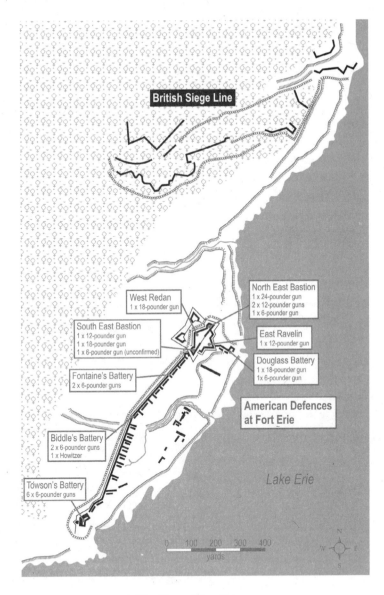

The following labels appear on the map:

British Siege Line

West Redan
1 x 18-pounder gun

North East Bastion
1 x 24-pounder gun
2 x 12-pounder guns
1 x 6-pounder gun

South East Bastion
1 x 12-pounder gun
1 x 18-pounder gun
1 x 6-pounder gun (unconfirmed)

East Ravelin
1 x 12-pounder gun

Fontaine's Battery
2 x 6-pounder guns

Douglass Battery
1 x 18-pounder gun
1x 6-pounder gun

American Defences at Fort Erie

Biddle's Battery
2 x 6-pounder guns
1 x Howitzer

Towson's Battery
6 x 6-pounder guns

Lake Erie

0   100   200   300   400
yards

N
W — E
S

The Siege of Fort Erie. MB

formidable, and when Le Couteur saw it he remarked that it was "an ugly Customer for" the Right Division's "fifteen hundred men to attack."[70]

Drummond would have to satisfy a number of conditions before he could assault the fort. First was the denial of supplies and reinforcements to the enemy, which would be achieved by cutting their line of communication to Buffalo. Second, in accordance with siege doctrine, batteries would have to be established to wear down the enemy's morale and to batter the walls to create one or more breaches through which the attackers would assault. Finally, a large number of men would be necessary to take the fort by attacking it at several points.

Lacking the resources, ordnance, and manpower to isolate Fort Erie, the best Drummond could achieve was to erect a single five-gun battery. An officer of the Royal Engineers supervised the construction of the gun platforms and works, while the infantry provided the labour. Members of the flank companies of the 104th contributed work parties and also manned the pickets that were thrown forward to provide warning and protection from any enemy threat against the British siege line. Skirmishes between the British and American picket lines became part of the daily routine as the Americans attempted to hamper the working parties at the battery. First Nations Warriors, militia, and regulars, often commanded by the 104th's William Drummond, routinely ventured out to clear American patrols from the neighbouring woods.[71] As the days passed, the casualty toll rose, and in the first two weeks of August, the 104th lost five men killed, three missing, three taken prisoner of war, and one desertion.[72]

On August 12, the enemy sent out eighty riflemen to determine whether the British were erecting a second battery. In the course of their reconnaissance, the Americans attacked several pickets manned by the 104th. Lieutenant Le Couteur described this sharp action in his journal: "The enemy made a desperate attempt to turn our flank but after an hour's hard fighting they were driven back with serious loss, leaving many of their dead and rifles along our front."[73] Three privates from Captain Leonard's Grenadier Company[74] died in the attack and one man was missing. Some good news came later that day from Lake Erie, where a detachment of sailors commanded by Commander Alexander Dobbs captured two American

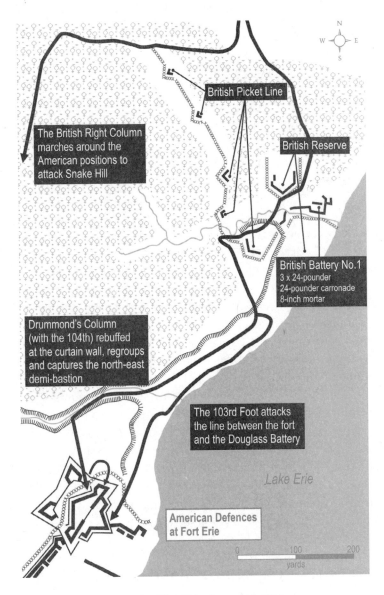

The British Picket Line

The British Right Column marches around the American positions to attack Snake Hill

British Reserve

British Battery No.1
3 x 24-pounder
24-pounder carronade
8-inch mortar

Drummond's Column (with the 104th) rebuffed at the curtain wall, regroups and captures the north-east demi-bastion

The 103rd Foot attacks the line between the fort and the Douglass Battery

Lake Erie

American Defences at Fort Erie

0   100   200
yards

The Assault of Fort Erie, August 15, 1814. MB

schooners from their anchorages off Fort Erie following a fierce hand-to-hand struggle with the American crews.[75]

After all the hard work, however, the sole British battery was found on completion to be nearly eleven hundred yards from the stone fort — too far away to be effective. Regardless, believing that the two-day bombardment that had begun on August 13 had produced "a sufficient impression" on the "works of the enemy's fort,"[76] on August 14 Lieutenant-General Drummond issued orders for the assault, which was to take place on the following morning.

Drummond's plan was ambitious. While a group of warriors and soldiers made a diversionary demonstration from their pickets at the American centre, three columns were to make the assault at different points. Beginning at 2:00 a.m., a fifteen-hundred-man column commanded by Lieutenant-Colonel Victor Fischer was to seize the southern end of the defences between Snake Hill and the lake. This was to be main attack. Once Fischer had penetrated the American line, the left column, seven hundred men from the 103rd Foot under Lieutenant-Colonel Hercules Scott would seize the enemy's northern entrenchments between the fort and the lakeshore. To Scott's right, a second column commanded by Lieutenant-Colonel William Drummond would attack the fort itself. A reserve force under Lieutenant-Colonel Gordon of the 1st Foot would be ready to exploit any success.[77]

Drummond's column numbered 340 men and included the flank companies of the 41st (one hundred and ten men) and 104th (seventy-seven men), one officer and a dozen men from the Royal Artillery, and a contingent of ninety seamen and fifty Royal Marines under Commander Alexander Dobbs of the Royal Navy. In accordance with the established doctrine for an assault against a fort, Captain William Barney of the 89th Regiment was nominated to guide the lead elements of Drummond's column to their assault position, from where he would then point out the route to their objective.[78]

Both Drummond and Scott had uneasy feelings about the attack, each having premonitions of death. Scott wrote to his brother that "I have little hope of success for the manoeuvre;"[79] in Drummond's case, "something whispered" to him as he observed the artillery fired on August 14 "that this would be his last day."[80] On the morning of the attack, Drummond breakfasted with several officers, including his friend William Dunlop, the surgeon of the 89th Foot, who later recalled:

> We sat apparently by common consent long after breakfast was over. Drummond told some capital stories, which kept us in such a roar that we seemed more like an after dinner than an after breakfast party. At last the bugles sounded the turn-out, and we rose to depart for our stations; Drummond called us back, and his face assuming an unwonted solemnity, he said, "Now boys! we never will all meet together here again; at least I will never again meet you. I feel it and am certain of it; let us all shake hands, and then every man to his duty, and I know you all too well to suppose for a moment that any of you will flinch it." We shook hands accordingly, all round, and with a feeling very different from what we had experienced for the last two hours, fell into our places[81]

The disaster was far greater than either Drummond or Scott reckoned. Lieutenant-General Drummond had ordered the men of the Regiment de Watteville, advancing on the far right, to remove their flints to avoid any chance of losing the element of surprise by the accidental discharge of a musket. They were then held up by trees felled to block their route, causing several of the companies to move toward Snake Hill. An attempt to get into the battery position failed when the scaling ladders thrown up against the parapet were found to be too short. The enemy poured artillery and musket fire into the men crowded below the battery, causing many to break and run. A combined effort by the light companies from the Regiment de Watteville and the 8th Foot — the latter allowed to retain their flints — to outflank the American position also failed. The remainder of the 8th Foot, coming behind them, fared no better and, unable to continue with the attack, Fischer's column fell back.[82]

To the north, the feint by warriors and troops from the picket positions against the enemy's centre also went wrong. Scheduled to begin before

Fischer's assault, the First Nations contingent moved to the north, where it joined Drummond's assault on the fort, while one picket made a long-delayed demonstration against the enemy's centre. Despite the failure of this portion of the overall assault, the Americans perceived the threat was great enough to prevent the units manning that portion of their line from moving elsewhere.[83]

At around 2:45 a.m., sentries inside the fort heard sounds in the distance. It was Drummond and Scott, moving their columns from the British camp along the lakeshore toward their objectives. As they neared the fort, Scott moved closer to the lakeshore, while Drummond aimed his directly at the fort. Scott had his men moving in a mass about forty ranks deep and fifteen wide. Their route, however, brought them directly in front of two American artillery pieces and 180 armed men. The Americans opened up with a devastating fire that halted the column about 150 yards away, forcing it to retire into the darkness. After regrouping, Scott launched two more attacks that also were repulsed by heavy fire.[84]

Meanwhile, during the final approach to the fort, Drummond was able to shield his column from the effect of the guns in the northeast demi-bastion by using dead ground, largely provided by mounds of earth strewn about the field. Captain William Barney was in the lead, guiding the "forlorn hope"—the detachment, made up mainly of sailors carrying scaling ladders, that would make the first assault on the fort—to its attack position. Colour Sergeant Richard Smith of the 104th, who had joined The New Brunswick Fencibles in 1805, was in command of the forlorn hope; if he survived the action, his reward would be a commission as an ensign.[85]

Le Couteur described the next stage of the attack by Drummond's column. Once the forlorn hope "got to the ditch" that surrounded the curtain wall on the northwest face of the fort, they "jumped in, reared the Scaling ladders and," turning towards the remainder of the column, "cheered us as they mounted"[86] the ladders. Inside, the soldiers of the 19th US Infantry withheld their fire until Drummond's men appeared above the parapet. As the forlorn hope and other members of the column, including soldiers from the 104th, worked their way up the ladders and pushed their way in, a terrific melee took place on the small gun platform

Following the rebuff at the curtain wall, William Drummond's column succeeded in storming the northeast demi-bastion by escalade using ladders thrown up against the wall. Photograph by author

inside the wall. The Americans momentarily pushed the British back, but, after regrouping, the redcoats made a second and then a third charge. Unable to break through the defenders, however, the column withdrew and readied still another attempt.[87]

The survivors of the two columns felt their way along the edge of the fort until they met near the northeast demi-bastion. Drummond took control of both groups and, seeing that they appeared to be in a blind spot in the defences, ordered another assault aimed at the northeast demi-bastion.[88] Once again ladders were thrown up against the wall, and Drummond himself was the first up. The thirty American artillerists manning four

The interior of the northeast demi-bastion as the American defenders would have seen it. Heavy fire covered the narrow defile into the fort, and it was during one of the charges that Lieutenant-Colonel William Drummond fell, somewhere near the door of the cookhouse on the right.

Photograph by author

guns inside were so completely taken by surprise that the bastion fell within minutes. Drummond, now joined by members of his 104th Foot, regrouped his men and led them toward the seven-foot-wide passageway that provided access from the demi-bastion into the fort itself. Major William Trimble, the American commander in the stone fort, had noticed the British officer leading the assaults who had "advanced as far as the Door of the mess house," a stone building adjacent to the entranceway to the demi-bastion, and when Drummond rushed forward again, Trimble gave his men the "order to kill him."[89] Seconds later, Lieutenant-Colonel William Drummond fell from the concentrated fire of the defenders.[90] The men from Drummond's regiment among the two or three hundred packed into the bastion might have been inspired by the death of their commanding officer to press home the attack; instead, however, the momentary pause following Drummond's death took the impetus out of the assault.[91]

It was now about 4:00 a.m., and reinforcements from both sides rushed to the passageway as Captain Joseph Glew, commander of the light company from the 41st, took charge. The action turned into a stalemate as neither side could gain an advantage over the other in the narrow defile. Then, a detachment from the Royal Artillery who had made their way into the demi-bastion swung one of the guns round and opened fire on the Americans. Suddenly, there was a massive tremor as the demi-bastion exploded, blowing men, guns, and equipment into the air and landing as far as three hundred yards away. Le Couteur was climbing a ladder into the bastion when it blew up. Knocked unconscious, he later recorded what he saw once he recovered from the shock a few minutes later,

> lying in the ditch fifteen or twenty feet down where I had been thrown by a tremendous explosion of gunpowder which cleared the Fort of three hundred men in an Instant. The platform had been blown over and a great beam had jammed me to the earth but it was resting on the Scarp. I got from under it with ease, bruised but otherwise unhurt. But what a horrid sight presented itself. Some three hundred men lay roasted, mangled, burned, wounded, black, hideous to view. On getting upon my legs, I trod on poor L[ieutenan]t. Horrens [Le Couteur likely meant Captain S.B. Torrens of the 1st Foot] broke leg of the 103rd, which made me shudder to my marrow. In placing my hand on Captain [George] Shore's back to steady myself from treading on some other poor mangled person, for the ditch was so crowded with bodies it was almost unavoidable, I found in my hand a mass of blood and brains — it was sickening.[92]

As the survivors from both sides regained their senses, the Americans recommenced firing on the attackers, who were left with no option but to withdraw. From the battery position in the rear, the British guns tried to provide covering fire as the survivors made their way back. Regaining the British lines, Le Couteur was called over by Lieutenant-General Drummond, who asked him: "Do you know anything about Y[ou]r Colonel?" For his part, shaken by what he had experienced, Le Couteur "could not articulate for grief. 'Killed, Sir.' 'Col. Scott?' 'Shot thro' the head, Sir, Your Grenadiers are bringing Him in, Major Leonard & Maclauchlan wounded & Capt. Shore a prisoner.' The General felt for me and said 'Never mind, Cheer up. You are wanted here. Fall in any men of any regiment as they come up, to line our batteries for fear of an attack.' Duty instantly set me to rights and I was actively employed cheering & ranging the men as they came in. Our men behaved."[93]

The approaching daylight revealed the carnage on the field. Bodies dotted the landscape, and as officers and men struggled to reach the British lines, the Americans continued firing on them. From an assault force of 3,073 men, Lieutenant-General Drummond reported 57 dead, 309 wounded, and 539 missing, for a total of 905 casualties. For the survivors of the explosion that destroyed the northeast demi-bastion, no cause for the detonation of the powder magazine located under its platform could be determined, and since then no evidence has been found offering a convincing explanation of this mystery.[94] The grenadier and light companies of the 104th Foot had suffered grievously in the attack. Sergeant John McEachern and sixteen privates were dead; Captain Richard Leonard, commander of the grenadier company, Lieutenant James McLaughlin, and twenty-seven other ranks were wounded. One man was missing and five were prisoners of war. Discrepancies in the returns make it difficult to be precise, but of the seventy-seven men from the flank companies who were fit for duty on the morning of the assault, between forty-seven and fifty-four of them had become casualties. Colour Sergeant Smith, commander of the forlorn hope, had survived unscathed, but as the assault had failed, he did not receive a commission.[95]

Surgeon William Dunlop described Lieutenant-Colonel Drummond, the much respected and beloved commanding officer of the 104th, as having "everything that could be required in a soldier; brave, generous, openhearted and good natured," and "a first-rate tactician."[96] The enemy found his body in front of the mess building inside the fort at a point farther than any other attacker had penetrated the defences. The Americans stripped his corpse to the shirt and displayed it for the rest of the day. The double-barrelled gun Drummond customarily carried and the beads a group of warriors had presented him were found on the field by Le Couteur.

Despite the failure of the assault and the heavy losses to the Right Division, Lieutenant-General Drummond decided to continue with the siege, and ordered the construction of a second battery about seven hundred yards from the fort. Commodore Chauncey's intermittent blockade

Monument dedicated in 1904 to the officers and men who fell during the siege of Fort Erie. Originally placed in the ruins of the fort, the monument was moved to its current location in the late 1930s during the restoration of the fort. Beneath the monument are the remains of 150 British and three American soldiers discovered during the restoration.

Photograph by author

of the mouth of the Niagara River plagued the reinforcement of Drummond's army and further construction, however, as the flow of supplies was reduced to a trickle. Nonetheless, work on the battery continued, and by the end of August it began firing on the Americans.[97]

The survivors of the 104th manned the pickets, where they routinely came under enemy fire, and under the supervision of engineering officers, they also formed work parties to construct the battery. Royal Engineer Lieutenant George Philpotts, who was supervising this activity, complained that the infantry provided only small work parties for this task, reflecting the dire state of manning in the Right Division, where the grenadier and light companies of the 104th were now down to "Eight officers to Eighteen men."[98] The only reinforcements to arrive were officers, as Captain George Jobling, Lieutenant René-Léonard Besserer, Lieutenant Waldron Kelly, and Lieutenant Thomas Leonard joined the "debris" from the two companies in early September. As Captain George Shore was placed in charge of invalids at Fort George, command of this group fell to Jobling.[99]

As work parties toiled on a third battery, Drummond considered making another assault in early September, but then changed his mind. Then, on September 17, the Americans attacked the British batteries, resulting in another five hundred casualties to each side. The 104th was not in the line that day and suffered no casualties.

Tragically, Drummond had already concluded nothing further could be achieved, and with the season growing late, the absence of Yeo on the lake, dwindling ammunition supplies, persistent food shortages, near constant rain, and sagging morale that created the "smells of retreat,"[100] he had ordered the guns to be withdrawn from the batteries on September 16, and on September 21 he withdrew the Right Division to Chippawa, and then redistributed his units. The forwardmost group was positioned between Frenchman's Creek and Chippawa, a battalion was placed at Chippawa, and another at Lundy's Lane. The flankers of the 104th were moved to Queenston, where, along with the 89th Foot, they assisted with the movement of supplies on the Niagara River. These dispositions allowed Drummond to remain in contact with the enemy, while masking a potential flanking movement he was considering along the American side of the river. The siege was over, but the campaign was not.[101]

In October, a large American reinforcement arrived at Fort Erie from its base at Plattsburgh, New York. Major-General George Izard, now commanding the American Left Division, also took command of the fort and began offensive operations against the British. His plan was to draw the British from their entrenchments north of the Chippawa River and into open battle. For his part, when Drummond learned of Izard's arrival, he thinned out his troops between Frenchman's Creek and the Chippawa River, ordered the works at Chippawa to be improved, and sent the 100th Foot, a troop of the 19th Light Dragoons, and two guns to join the 104th and 89th at Queenston, forming the whole into a mobile reserve under the command of Lieutenant-Colonel The Marquess of Tweeddale. Unable to draw Drummond from his defences, Izard then sent a one-thousand-man detachment under Brigadier-General Daniel Bissell to Cook's Mills, on Lyon's Creek, to threaten the British right flank and seize supplies believed to be stored there.[102]

On October 18, Drummond sent Lieutenant-Colonel Christopher Myers with the Glengarry Light Infantry and a seven-company detach-

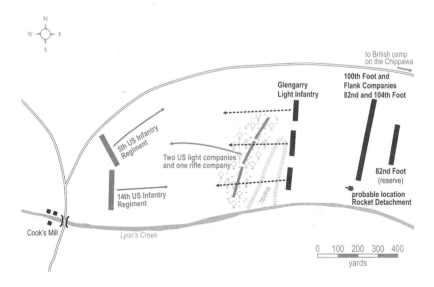

The Action at Cook's Mills, October 19, 1814. MB

ment of the 82nd Foot to determine what the Americans were doing. Drummond also sent a second force farther inland to destroy a bridge over the Chippawa River, fearing the Americans might use it to outflank him. After receiving reports of upwards of two thousand Americans advancing against Cook's Mills, Drummond sent Tweeddale, with the 100th Foot, the flank companies of the 82nd and 104th Foot, a 6-pounder gun, and a rocket detachment to reinforce Myers. Additional units were held at readiness should they be required. Tweeddale, whom Le Couteur described as "something like our dear [William] Drummond,"[103] met up with Myers about three miles to the east of Cook's Mills, where they established camp for the night. Myers sent the Glengarries forward to observe the American position, and during the night they skirmished with American pickets.[104]

On the morning of October 19, Myers deployed his seven-hundred-and-fifty-man force on the north side of Lyon's Creek, about a thousand yards east of Cook's Mill. His position was bounded by the creek on the left and a ravine to his front that ran perpendicular to the creek, beyond which stood a small wood and the Americans. East of the ravine was Tweeddale with the 100th Foot, the 6-pounder gun, and the rocket detachment. The Glengarries were ahead in skirmish order, followed by the 100th Foot and the flank companies of the 82nd and the 104th. The remainder of the 82nd was in reserve. Myers's aim was to establish the Americans' strength and intentions without becoming decisively engaged with the enemy. Before moving into their positions, the Glengarries treated the men of the 104th to "a hearty breakfast that saved" them "from famishing."[105] For now, Bissell kept the main body of his force near a bridge on the other side of the creek, while a rifle company and two light companies occupied the wood on the north side of the creek.

Myers opened the action by ordering the Glengarries to advance in two groups. The first headed directly for the ravine, while the other swung north to outflank the Americans. The American commander responded by sending two regiments across the bridge; one to deal with the Glengarries advancing directly across the ravine, and the second to sweep around the British right. Now outnumbered, Myers ordered his skirmishers back through the woods and the ravine, where they joined Tweeddale's men. The Americans pursued, halted before the British line, presented their arms, and fired. A hot firefight ensued, which was joined on the British left by the lone artillery piece and four rockets under Lieutenant Thomas Carter. The few remaining Light Bobs of the 104th were in extended line covering the artillery. As pressure from the enemy mounted, the Light Bobs charged ahead to the ravine until forced to withdraw. The light company from the 82nd then came up in support, but as Tweeddale's brigade was unable to force the Americans back, Myers withdrew from the field, leaving pickets behind to observe the enemy, who now turned their attention to destroying bushels of grain before returning to their camp. Myers then marched his men six miles to the east before they halted for the night, wet, weary, and hungry.[106] The Americans reported seventy-seven casualties, Myers, thirty-six. Three men from Captain Shore's company, Corporal Charles Lahore and Privates Isaac Church and William Lindsay, were killed in the action.[107]

The skirmish at Cook's Mills proved to be the last battle in this long and

Cairn erected in 1977 to commemorate the action at Cook's Mills.
The plaque describes the action and lists the units involved, including the
flank companies of the 104th Foot. Photograph by Donald E. Graves

gruelling campaign, and the final action of the 104th Foot. With the enemy
still present on Canadian territory, Drummond reorganized his effective
units into two brigades, the first based at Chippawa and the second farther
to the south at Street's Creek, near the site of the Battle of Chippawa. After
two major engagements, a minor battle, a siege, a great many skirmishes,
and the effects of disease, the Right Division was a spent force. To ease the
logistical situation in the division, all battalions or detachments that were
seriously below strength or surplus to the new divisional structure were to
be withdrawn. Among the worn units that were designated to depart were
the flank companies of the 104th, the strength of which, between July 25
and October 18, had been reduced to a fraction of its original strength.[108]

On October 21, the surviving members of the 104th's grenadier and
light companies were ordered to Fort George, where they camped in an
open field without "blankets, the fire out and frost on the ground."[109]

Drummond, meanwhile, urged Yeo "to apply his ships to the only service which they could render to"[110] his army by returning these companies and the 1st Battalion of the 8th Foot to Kingston. The following day, the two flank companies and the 8th Foot boarded the ship *Niagara*; they sailed on the twenty-third. The next day, the crowded conditions onboard became more comfortable when the men of the 8th were transferred to the *Princess Charlotte*. At noon on the twenty-fifth, Kingston came into sight, but the men's hopes of going ashore quickly were dashed when they were told they could not land that evening. Finally, at 6:00 a.m., the following morning, the exhausted survivors of the flank companies marched off the ship and into quarters at Kingston.[111]

The Americans in the Niagara Peninsula, meanwhile, concluded that nothing could be gained by continuing the occupation of Fort Erie, and on November 5, as their last elements withdrew across the Niagara River to Buffalo, charges were detonated, destroying what remained of the fort. The 1814 campaign in the Niagara was over.

Military operations during 1814 were far from restricted to the Niagara Peninsula. That year, British forces lay siege to Plattsburgh, New York, occupied Washington, attacked Baltimore, and occupied Maine. The Americans raided the Western District of Upper Canada, failed in an attempt to recapture Fort Mackinac, and were defeated at Prairie du Chien, in what is now Wisconsin. In August, peace talks to end the war opened at Ghent. As the British and American commissions argued the finer points of diplomacy, it became clear that the war was becoming a stalemate, and both governments instructed their commissions to come promptly to an agreement. The signing of the peace treaty on Christmas Eve 1814 did not end the war, however, as the British commissioners insisted the treaty be ratified by both governments before it came into effect. Their rationale was that, on three previous occasions, the US government had reneged on treaties. Until this was concluded, the war dragged on.

As these events unfolded, the 104th Foot was concentrated at Kingston, with Major Thomas Hunter now in command following the death of Lieutenant-Colonel Drummond. In early November, the regiment reported its strength at one major, seven captains, eighteen lieutenants, thirty-eight sergeants, nineteen drummers, and three hundred and seventy other ranks fit for duty. Another thirty-two men were in hospital. At the end of the month, thirty-six men who were deemed unfit for continued service in the line were transferred to the 10th Royal Veteran Battalion, and another twenty were discharged and sent to England.[112]

Meanwhile, the remaining two companies of the 104th that had remained in the Maritimes were ordered to Lower Canada. Captain William Procter's company from Prince Edward Island moved in two detachments, the first departing the island in August, and by October, the company was complete in Quebec. The following month, the company from Sydney joined them in Quebec.[113]

As well, two groups of boys belonging to the regiment were in Kingston and Three Rivers. Ten boys between ten and fifteen years of age and taken on strength between 1807 and 1811 were at Kingston; one, David Macintosh, was serving as a paymaster clerk. The second group of forty-four boys between ten and sixteen years old were at Three Rivers, and had also joined the 104th between 1807 and 1813. Of the total, twenty-four boys had fathers, uncles, or brothers serving in the 104th; the fathers of seven of these boys had been killed in action or died of wounds, and three boys had also lost brothers during the war. Sergeant Hugh McLauchlan, the father of twelve-year-old Alexander McLauchlan, had been killed at Sackets Harbor, and Hugh's brother John had passed away in September 1813. Ten-year-old Dennis Smith lost his brother William, who died of wounds in June 1813, while his father passed away in September.[114]

Although the routine of training and garrison duty was broken by the occasional alarm, the situation in the Kingston area was relatively peaceful as the year ended. The town now had formidable defences. During the course of the war, the Kingston garrison had grown from 100 men in 1812 to 3,500 in the autumn of 1814. An elaborate system of defensive works protected the town, the naval base at Point Frederick, and the encampment at Point Henry. Le Couteur was confident the town was safe from a "coupe de main" even if the fleet were absent.[115]

Rain, snow, dysentery, and other diseases made conditions uncomfortable for the men of the 104th, although, at Cataraqui, Captain William

Bradley oversaw the construction of new barracks.[116] In February 1815, word of a possible peace treaty boosted spirits, but these were soured by the news of the British defeat at New Orleans. In the meantime, the Prince Regent had ratified the Treaty of Ghent at the end of December, followed, on February 17, 1815, by its ratification by President Madison. The war was over. News of the peace was welcomed at Kingston within a few days of its proclamation by a series of public and private celebrations. Jubilation spread among the ranks of the 104th, and for all there were many questions, including about the regiment's future and the disposition of the men, boys, and their families.[117]

Chapter Five

The End of the War of 1812 and the Disbandment of the 104th Foot

The 104th Regiment will be Disbanded at Montreal.
— General Order, Quebec, April 19, 1817

While the American and British commissioners at Ghent were seeking a negotiated end to the war, military leaders from both sides in North America began planning for the next campaign season, which was to commence in spring 1815. A pressing problem for British leaders was how to ensure an adequate flow of supplies into Upper Canada on the important line of communication between Montreal and Kingston. The arrival of a significant number of reinforcements in Upper Canada and the expansion of the Royal Navy establishment on Lake Ontario required a corresponding increase in the capacity of the bateaux service that provided the primary means of moving men and materiel into the province. An idea of the importance of the bateaux service is given by its growth, from 1,315 men and 165 bateaux on the upper river, with a handful of boats and men on Lake Ontario in 1812, to the expectation that, in 1815, 700 bateaux and 150 Durham boats (a variation of the bateau) would be needed, operating from eleven stations from Three Rivers to Niagara and requiring 4,250 men to crew them.[1] Commissary General William Henry Robinson, who was responsible for supplying the forces in the Canadas, had little faith in the current measures, however, and proposed "the immediate detachment of one thousand men, to be taken from the embodied militia."[2]

In February 1815, a Board of Officers chaired by Major-General Edward Baynes, the adjutant general, investigated the mechanics of improving the transportation system. Among the board's recommendations was to have the 4th Battalion Select Embodied Militia, a Lower Canadian militia unit, assume control of the Commissariat Voyageurs, the unruly group of men who currently operated the bateaux. To allow for further expansion of the service, it was also proposed to attach the 104th Foot and the Nova Scotia Fencibles to the river transportation service. Before these measures could be implemented, however, the peace treaty was promulgated and the war was over.[3]

Although no decision had yet been made about the disposition of the Army in British North America, following the confirmation of the peace treaty, some units were moved from Upper to Lower Canada, mainly to ease the demand for rations and other supplies due to reductions in the bateaux service. The 104th was ordered, first, to Quebec City, and from there its 44 officers, 632 NCOs and men, and 2 boys were posted to Drummond Island, Coteau-du-Lac, Île-aux-Noix, Lacolle, Lachine, and the Cascades. In August 1816, the regimental headquarters was moved to Montreal.[4]

In March 1815, Lieutenant-Colonel Robert Moodie, who had taken command of the New Brunswick Regiment of Fencible Infantry, was appointed commanding officer of the 104th upon Sir George Prevost's recommendation; Moodie took up his new appointment in April. In August, James Sampson, lately of the Royal Newfoundland Fencible Infantry, replaced Surgeon William Thomas, who, for health reasons, had returned to England.[5]

As the strength of the 104th Foot was still below its authorized limit of nine hundred men, recruiting parties began their work in Lower Canada. In autumn 1815, parties were also sent to New Brunswick. Both groups succeeded in gathering another one hundred men — not enough, however, so Moodie petitioned London for permission to recruit in Britain and Ireland. Instead, the British government, unconvinced of any immediate difficulty with the United States, issued orders in January and February 1816 for the reduction of the regular establishment and authorized the disbanding of several regular and provincial corps in British North America. The government also ordered a hold on defensive measures there, and rejected proposals from Lieutenant-General Gordon Drummond, who had replaced Prevost as captain general and governor-in-chief of British North America, to establish new fortifications in Upper Canada until "His Majesty's Government shall have decided upon some general plan for the future defence of the Province."[6]

In response to the unit reductions, Drummond proposed to London that advantages "would be derived from retaining"[7] the 104th Foot, the Glengarry Light Infantry Fencibles, and The Canadian Fencibles in New Brunswick, Upper Canada, and Lower Canada. London remained unmoved, however, and the reductions proceeded. Whereas, in December 1814, the strength of the Army in the Canadas and the Maritime provinces had numbered nearly thirty-eight thousand regulars, within five years it was reduced to fewer than six thousand men.[8]

The modern reader might find the association of a regular line regiment with a colony in British North America as a sound reason for its retention. Despite its origins, however, the 104th Foot was not a colonial force, but a unit of the British Army and subject to the establishment set by the government in London, which was determined to reduce expenditures after nearly twenty-two years of war. Seniority was now the sole criterion used to determine which units would be retained, which meant that the wartime regiments, including the overseas fencible regiments and foreign corps, would be the first to go. The Army's peacetime establishment was set at ninety-three regiments of the line, and the fate of the 104th Foot, the most junior of all the regular infantry regiments, was sealed.[9] Meanwhile, the 104th carried on with the routine of peacetime soldiering. Soldiers being soldiers, many of the men used the period between the end of the war and the decision about the regiment's future to find innovative ways of getting into trouble. Disciplinary problems increased as men tired of the army and wanting to return to their homes or find better paying employment created mischief. In one incident, at La Prairie in February 1817, five men in uniform fired on a sleigh carrying soldiers from the 19th Light

Dragoons, wounding one of the cavalrymen in the arm. An investigation revealed that the culprits were most likely five deserters from the 104th Foot, who, though chased, were never apprehended.[10]

In early 1817, the Horse Guards informed Lieutenant-General Sir John Sherbrooke, now governor of British North America, that the "104th Regiment has been ordered to be Disbanded,"[11] and the following General Order was published in Quebec City on April 19, 1817:

> The 104th Regiment will be Disbanded at Montreal on the 24th May next under the Superintendence of such officer as may be appointed.
>
> His Royal Highness the Prince Regent having been pleased to signify His Pleasure in Testimony of the sense which His Majesty's Government entertains of their faithful Services that such of the Officers and men of the 104th Regiment as may prefer continuing in British North America, and who may avail themselves of the Gracious offer should be allowed Grants of land in proportion to their respective Ranks, either in Canada or in any other of His Majesty's North American Possessions — and to whom the same facility will be afforded in regard to advance of Pay and Rations as was extended to the other settlers from the Retired Colonial and Foreign Corps; the wishes of the Officers and Men are therefore to be ascertained on this point without delay and nominal Returns of them specifying the settlement or place of their choice are to be transmitted to this office and to that of the Deputy Quarter Master General as soon as possible in order that the necessary arrangements may be made by the Departments concerned.
>
> The portion of the Regiment who may not accept of Settlements but who may wish to remain in the Colony are to receive Two Months full pay from the period of the Reduction

of the Corps, and the Natives of New Brunswick, Nova Scotia will be furnished with passages to proceed to their Homes by the first opportunity after their arrival at Quebec.

The officers having permanent Rank are entitled to Half Pay to commence from the Dates to which their Full Pay shall have been paid.

Each non-commissioned Officer, Drummer and Private Man is to be permitted to carry away with him, his Knapsack, and his proper Regimental Clothing for the Year 1817. The Great Coats in wear will also be allowed to be taken away by the Non-commissioned Officers and Men if they shall have been actually worn for the space of two years but if not they are to be carefully packed up and delivered over to the Storekeeper General's Department.[12]

The work of closing down a unit is never pleasant, and involves the writing of numerous reports accounting for expenditures and equipment. Ten of the paragraphs in the original handwritten order dealt with such matters as regimental accounts, pay, benefits, travel allowances, arms, ammunition, camp equipment, and the equipment that each solider was allowed to retain. These administrative details were struck from the text of the General Order, as they would be administered "under the superintendence" of Lieutenant-Colonel Donald McBean of the 99th Foot, the senior officer in the Montreal District, whose appointment to head these inquiries was announced in May 1817.[13]

Over the next several weeks, the regimental staff officers, assisted by the district staff, completed the tedious work of settling accounts, returning stores, sorting out discrepancies in the regimental books, compiling returns, and calculating the men's final pay. Missing pieces of equipment had to be accounted for, and in one case, a board of three officers from the Montreal District met to "Investigate Certain Charges made by the Commissariat Department for Necessaries furnished to the 104th Regiment." At issue

When The New Brunswick Fencible Infantry became the 104th Foot in 1810, the centre of the existing Regimental Colours was altered to include the numeral "104," reflecting the regiment's new designation.

New Brunswick Museum 33 485-2

was the accounting of shoes, stockings, and canteens issued to the regiment in 1813 for which there appeared to be no record. The matter was resolved when Lieutenant-Colonel Moodie produced signed receipts for the stockings, while he reminded the board that the canteens were field issue and required no accounting. Testimony from Sergeant Alexis Lemery resolved the matter of the shoes. At the time, Lemery was in Kingston, from where he forwarded supplies to the regiment in the Niagara Peninsula. He testified under oath that he never saw the shoes in question, and the matter was closed.[14]

At the end of May 1817, McBean reported that, "in obedience to General Orders of the 17th Instant, the Reduction of the 104th Regiment was effected under my Superintendence on the 24th May, having previously satisfied myself by particular inquiry that not any of Claims existed among the Men against the Regiment, or His Majesty's Government."[15] At this time, 578 NCOs and privates received two months' advance pay. Most of

Military General Service Medal, issued in 1847 to surviving veterans of the Napoleonic Wars and the War of 1812, although no one from the 104th Foot received it. Only three of the twenty-nine authorized clasps commemorating engagements from these conflicts were for actions from the War of 1812. The medal shown here is named to Lieutenant (later Major) Thomas Moses of the 7th Foot, and the bars are for actions in Iberia between 1810 and 1812: Badajoz, Ciudad Rodrigo, Albuhera, and Busaco. Moses later emigrated to New Brunswick, where he became a Collector of Customs in Charlotte County.

New Brunswick Museum 1944.335(1)

the veterans chose to remain in the Canadas: 102 of them went to Upper Canada, 349 settled in Lower Canada, 30 went to Nova Scotia, and 100 returned to New Brunswick. The group heading for New Brunswick was transported by sail from Montreal to Saint John. There, about half of them were taken by bateaux up the St. John River to Presqu'Ile, where they were issued with lots in the military settlement. In 1818, another group of forty to fifty veterans of the 104th and The New Brunswick Fencibles were placed in a military settlement between St. Andrews and Fredericton. Other veterans chose to go to Britain, and in July 1817, an unspecified number of men under the charge of Lieutenant George Croad, who had fought at Fort George in 1813 and was now on half-pay, proceeded by the brig *Harmony* for England.[16] Another twenty-nine men classified as invalids — discharged as no longer fit for service — including Sergeant Major Joseph Haynes, received pensions of between 1s and 2s 3½d.[17]

Following the disbandment of the 104th Foot, the Regimental Colours were presented to Lieutenant General Martin Hunter, who had played such a key role in the formation of The New Brunswick Fencibles and its being taken into the line. Hunter kept the Colours in his residence at Coldstream, Scotland. In 1939, the family donated them to the New Brunswick Museum, and in 1940, in a ceremony held in Saint John attended by Murray MacLaren, lieutenant governor of New Brunswick, and Allison Dysart, the provincial premier, the Colours were laid up.

Between 1815 and 1826, the British government acknowledged the service of the Army during the Great War, as the conflict fought against Revolutionary and Napoleonic France between 1793 and 1815 was called, by issuing Battle Honours to commemorate service around the globe. Five Battle Honours acknowledged engagements during the War of 1812.[18] In November 1815, the *London Gazette* announced the granting of the Battle Honour "Niagara"[19] to the 104th, as follows:

> His Royal Highness the Prince Regent has been placed, in the name and on behalf of His Majesty, to approve of the Flank Companies of the 104th Regiment being permitted to bear on their appointments (in addition to other badges or devices which may have been heretofore granted to the 104th Regiment), the word "Niagara," in consideration of the gallantry and good conduct evinced by those Companies in the action at Lundy's-Lane, near the Falls of Niagara, on the 25th July 1814, and during the whole of the campaign on the Niagara Frontier in the year 1814.[20]

The 104th Regiment of Foot, the only regular British regiment to be raised in North America during the Napoleonic Wars, enjoyed a brief existence lasting from 1810 to 1817. Liable for service anywhere the Army desired to send it, the 104th remained in North America, and in 1813, in response to the American threat around Lake Ontario, it was sent to Upper Canada. During that year, the regiment moved between Kingston, the upper St. Lawrence River, and the Niagara Peninsula, often with its companies dispersed to different locations. The 104th Foot saw its first action in May 1813, when it provided a large contingent for the raid on the American naval base at Sackets Harbor, on Lake Ontario. Thereafter, the 104th was sent to the Niagara Peninsula, where it contributed to the blockade of Fort George. In 1814, as the line companies protected the important communications route between Montreal and Kingston, the grenadier and light companies returned to the Niagara Peninsula, where they fought in the Battle of Lundy's Lane, the action at Conjoncta Creek, the siege and assault on Fort Erie, and, finally, at Cook's Mills. The officers, NCOs, and men involved in these actions, and in a great many other skirmishes, were a microcosm of the Empire, drawn from the Canadas, New Brunswick, Nova Scotia, England, Ireland, Scotland, and other countries. Together, they contributed to the defence of New Brunswick, Cape Breton, and Prince Edward Island and helped defeat the enemy's designs on Upper Canada. By their efforts, the men of the 104th contributed to the successful defence of British North America in the War of 1812. Although their regiment did not survive long after the peace, veterans of the 104th Foot settled in and contributed to the post-war development of Britain's North American colonies.

For the men of the 104th, wartime service brought many perils, including battle, sickness, and death. Disease, indeed, was deadlier than the enemy, and often responsible for painful, lingering deaths.[21] Determining the 104th's total losses is difficult, given incomplete and inaccurate records, while changes to the status of the missing, prisoners of war, and wounded were not always recorded. Nonetheless, it is estimated that, between its first action in May 1813 and its last in October 1814, the 104th suffered eighty-two deaths due to battle, missing and not returned, wounded, or prisoners of war, as follows:

- the raid on Sackets Harbor, May 29, 1813: twenty-one killed and five dead later of wounds;
- the reconnaissance of Fort George, August 24, 1813: two killed;
- the Battle of Lundy's Lane, July 25, 1814: one killed, six prisoners of war;
- the siege of Fort Erie, August 3-September 21, 1814: four killed, three missing, three prisoners of war;
- the assault on Fort Erie, August 15, 1814: sixteen killed, twelve missing, six prisoners of war;
- the action at Cook's Mills, October 19, 1814: three killed.

To the Memory of

Lieutenant Colonel WILLIAM DRUMMOND
of the 10 4th Regiment.
Who fell while gallantly leading on a
Column, at the Attack on FORT ERIE,
on the Morning of the 15th August 1814.

As a small testimony of their Esteem for his Qualities as a Friend
and respect for his Character as a Soldier.
The Officers of the 10 4th Regiment,
have placed this Tablet.

Following the War of 1812, the officers of the 104th Foot erected this plaque in St. Anne's Chapel of Ease, Fredericton, to honour Lieutenant-Colonel William Drummond, who fell at Fort Erie. Courtesy of Brent Wilson

The remains of these men, including casualties from other causes, rest on or near the fields where they fell or where they succumbed to sickness or injury, in York, Kingston, Montreal, Quebec City, and other locales, but their memory shall live for evermore.

The Soldier Cut Down in His Prime[22]

As I was a-walking down by the Lock Hospital,
Dark was the morning and cold was the day,
When who should I spy but one of my comrades,
Draped in a blanket and cold as the clay.

Then beat the drums slowly and play the fifes lowly,
Sound the "Dead March" as you carry me along,
And fire your muskets right over my coffin,
For I'm a young soldier cut down in his prime.

Had she but told me when she did disorder me,
Had she but told me about it in time,
I might have got salts and pills of white mercury,
But now I'm cut down in the height of my prime.

Got six of my comrades to carry my coffin,
Six of my comrades to carry me on high,
And each of them carry a bunch of white roses,
So no-one may smell me as we pass them by.

On top of his tombstone these words they are written,
"All you young fellows take warning by me,
Keep away from them flash girls who walk in the city,
The girls of the city was the ruin of me."

Appendix 1

Monthly Returns for the 104th Foot

During the Great War of 1793 to 1814, every unit or independent detachment of the British Army was required to provide a complete return once a month. Until June 1809, the monthly return was to be completed on the first of the month; thereafter it was changed to the 25th. Completed returns were sent to the general officer under whose command the unit served and to the adjutant general at the Horse Guards, the headquarters of the British Army.

The monthly return was useful in a number of ways. In the case of the Canadas, the return provided the commander-in-chief of British North America with a timely appreciation of two important pieces of information: the strength and fitness of the units under his command. This information could influence a regiment's employment in operations — revealing, for example, the need for additional training — and signal the need for reinforcements by transferring units from another, quieter garrison, by calling up additional militia, or, if manpower was becoming acute, by applying to England for more men.

The monthly returns of the 104th Foot presented in Tables 1 and 2 are drawn from two sets of returns for British North America. Table 1 shows the regiment's strength while it was based in New Brunswick and reported to Nova Scotia Command. The Nova Scotia returns encompassed the forces based in Nova Scotia, New Brunswick, Newfoundland, Cape Breton, Prince Edward Island, Bermuda, and, in 1814 and 1815, troops engaged in operations against Maine. Table 2 provides the regimental returns from its service in the Canadas between May 1813 and July 1815. Although Canada Command began reporting on the 104th in May 1813, Nova Scotia continued to submit figures for a detachment that remained in New Brunswick until September 1814. These returns are for the rank and file only; officers were reported in a separate return, which I have not included. Finally, the return was only as accurate as the information entered into it. The adjutants, staff officers, and clerks who compiled the information and completed the forms were always short of time and often focussed on immediate operations. Sometimes they were lazy and occasionally careless in their work.

Table 1: Nova Scotia Command Returns, 104th Regiment of Foot, January 1812-September 1814

Date	Effective	Effective (%)	Sick	Sick (%)	On Command	Total Other Ranks	Dead since Last Return	Deserters	Sent Home
Jan 1812	663	77.73	29	3.40	161	853	2	0	0
Feb 1812[a]	851	94.24	52	5.76	0	903	3	0	0
Mar 1812	666	78.08	24	2.81	163	853	0	0	0
Apr 1812	655	76.97	36	4.23	160	851	0	0	0
May 1812	850	96.81	28	3.19	0	878	4	2	0
Jun 1812	881	97.13	26	2.87	0	907	2	10	0
Jul 1812	862	95.25	43	4.75	0	905	1	1	0
Aug 1812	796	88.84	60	6.70	40	896	2	1	0
Sep 1812	859	95.98	36	4.02	0	895	2	3	0
Oct 1812[b]	859	95.98	36	4.02	0	895	0	0	0
Nov 1812	859	95.87	37	4.13	0	896	0	7	0
Dec 1812	855	95.32	42	4.68	0	897	2	0	0
Jan 1813[c]	851	94.24	52	5.76	0	903	3	0	0
Feb 1813	354	91.95	31	8.05	0	385	0	0	0
Mar 1813	354	91.95	31	8.05	0	385	0	0	0
Apr 1813	357	93.46	25	6.54	0	382	0	0	0
May 1813	153	100.00	0	0.00	0	153	0	0	0
Jun 1813	153	100.00	0	0.00	0	153	0	0	0
Jul 1813	161	100.00	0	0.00	0	161	0	0	0
Aug 1813	156	96.89	5	3.11	0	161	0	0	0
Sep 1813	156	96.89	5	3.11	0	161	0	0	0
Oct 1813	156	96.89	5	3.11	0	161	0	0	0
Nov 1813	156	96.30	6	3.70	0	162	0	0	0
Dec 1813	156	96.30	6	3.70	0	162	0	0	0
Jan 1814	162	100.00	0	0.00	0	162	0	0	0
Feb 1814	152	95.60	7	4.40	0	159	0	0	0

Mar 1814	152	95.60	7	4.40	0	159	0	0	0
Apr 1814	152	95.60	7	4.40	0	159	0	0	0
May 1814	159	100.00	0	0.00	0	159	0	0	0
Jun 1814	159	100.00	0	0.00	0	159	0	0	0
July 1814	159	100.00	0	0.00	0	159	1	0	0
Aug 1814	153	97.45	4	2.55	0	157	0	1	0
Sep 1814	74	92.50	6	7.50	0	80	0	0	0

Note: "On command" identifies personnel, whether as individuals or a detachment, who were employed away from the unit.

a One member also shown as being on furlough.

b Three members also shown as being on furlough.

c One member also shown as being on furlough.

Sources: United Kingdom, National Archives, Kew, War Office 17/2259-2263, Office of the Commander in Chief: Monthly Returns to the Adjutant General Nova Scotia, January 1812 to December 1815; and WO 17/1516-1519, Office of the Commander in Chief: Monthly Returns to the Adjutant General Canada, January 1812 to December 1815.

Table 2: Canada Command Monthly Returns, 104th Regiment of Foot, March 1813-July 1815

Date	Effective	Effective (%)	Sick	Sick (%)	On Command	Total Other Ranks	Dead since Last Return	Deserters	Sent Home
Mar 1813	489	53.85	14	1.54	405	908	1	0	0
Apr 1813	304	33.52	46	5.07	557	907	3	2	0
May 1813	422	47.26	67	7.50	404	893	18	0	0
June 1813	422	47.26	67	7.50	404	893	0	0	0
July 1813	422	47.26	67	7.50	404	893	0	0	0
Aug 1813	156	19.31	10	1.24	642	808	6	5	0
Sep 1813	146	19.29	147	19.42	464	757	8	20	0
Oct 1813	282	38.06	200	26.99	259	741	9	3	0
Nov 1813	352	48.55	95	13.10	278	725	18	1	0
Dec 1813	389	54.33	66	9.22	261	716	9	0	0
Jan 1814	393	72.51	57	10.52	92	542	10	0	0
Feb 1814	379	69.54	49	8.99	117	545	6	0	0
Mar 1814	380	54.91	48	6.94	264	692	4	0	0
Apr 1814	386	56.27	65	9.48	235	686	5	0	0
May 1814	344	51.04	47	6.97	283	674	7	4	14
June 1814	327	48.81	45	6.72	298	670	4	0	1
July 1814	201	30.32	35	5.28	427	663	2	6	1
Aug 1814	191	29.52	7	1.08	449	647	9	1	0
Sep 1814	203	32.58	12	1.93	408	623	24	2	0
Oct 1814	154	24.02	62	9.67	398	641	7	3	0
Nov 1814	361	61.82	80	13.70	143	584	4	6	20
Dec 1814	423	72.56	33	5.66	127	583	1	0	0
Jan 1815	427	74.65	42	7.34	103	572	7	0	0
Feb 1815	393	72.78	25	4.63	122	540	1	1	0
Mar 1815	467	85.53	19	3.48	60	546	2	1	0

Apr 1815	396	74.02	65	12.15	74	535	2	0	20
May 1815	438	84.39	17	3.28	64	519	1	16	0
July 1815	432	85.38	17	3.36	57	506	1	13	0

Sources: United Kingdom, National Archives, Kew, War Office 17/2259-2263, Office of the Commander in Chief: Monthly Returns to the Adjutant General Nova Scotia, January 1812 to December 1815; and WO 17/1516-1519, Office of the Commander in Chief: Monthly Returns to the Adjutant General Canada, January 1812 to December 1815.

Appendix 2

The New Brunswick Regiment of Fencible Infantry, 1812-1816

In the opening months of the War of 1812, concerns about the potential threat to New Brunswick and aspirations to resurrect a fencible regiment in the province inspired Lieutenant-General John Coffin, a distinguished veteran of the American Revolutionary War and member of the provincial assembly, who exercised great influence within the province, to petition the Prince Regent to form a new regiment there. Accordingly, on October 12, 1812, the Prince Regent authorized the raising of "a Regiment of Fencible Infantry in New Brunswick for the immediate service in that province and Nova Scotia,"[1] with the possible "extension of Service in case of necessity to any of His Majesty's Dominions in North America."[2]

Organizationally, the New Brunswick Regiment of Fencible Infantry had ten companies, each of sixty rank and file, for a total of 673 all ranks. Half of the officers above the rank of ensign were to be drawn from regiments of the line, while Coffin had authority to nominate the remaining officers from those "gentlemen in the country who from their local interest may be most likely deemed to complete the regiment."[3] The pay offered to men agreeing to serve anywhere in British North America was higher than for those willing to serve only in New Brunswick and Nova Scotia. The regiment was given authority to recruit men in Nova Scotia, New Brunswick, and Upper and Lower Canada.[4]

Captain Henry Cooper, described as "an active, zealous, diligent officer"[5] and adjutant of the 2/8th Foot, was appointed commanding officer and served in that capacity until early 1814, when Major Robert Moodie replaced him. Moodie held command of the Fencibles until spring 1814, when he was appointed commanding officer of the 104th Foot. Command thereafter devolved to Major Tobias Kirkwood, a veteran of the 101st Foot and son-in-law to Lieutenant-General Coffin.[6]

Recruiting proceeded slowly, as efforts to man other units had reduced the number of suitable men. Rumours of irregularities, such as the enlistment of unfit men, prompted

Lieutenant-General Sherbrooke to order Major-General Sir Thomas Saumarez, the acting administrator and commander-in-chief of the province, to inspect the unit. Saumarez found a number of problems, but was generally pleased with what he found. The "Men of this Corps are in general very stout and make a respectable appearance under Arms," but the detachment of many of the men on duties around the province during the summer allowed little time for training. Saumarez expected some improvement to be made over the winter as the recently arrived adjutant had "fitted up a large Drill Room" for daily training. A delay in the arrival of clothing from England was overcome by drawing uniforms from militia stores, much of which were new.[7]

From what he saw of the men, Saumarez believed that the "Recruiting Instructions or the Letter of Service for raising" the regiment had "not been strictly adhered to."[8] In his report, he cited sixteen cases where the physical condition or health of new recruits made it impossible for them to go on active service, or whose age or height made them ineligible to serve. By this time, recruits were indeed difficult to find, prompting the recruiting parties to accept less than satisfactory men to meet their quotas. Difficulties persisted in filling the ranks, and by the end of 1813 only three hundred men had been recruited.[9]

In May 1815, Major-General George Smyth, who had replaced Saumarez as the administrator and commander-in-chief of New Brunswick, conducted another inspection of the regiment. From an establishment of 570 personnel, 357 rank and file were considered effective. Nearly half of these were British, 21 were foreigners, and 172 were listed as British Americans, proportions similar to those in the fencible regiments previously raised in the province. Unlike in earlier recruiting efforts, however, few men with extensive military experience were found: only one private had ten years' previous service, while the majority had one year or less in the ranks. The NCOs were "as good as can be expected," given how recently many of them had been recruited. With this collective lack of experience and the majority of the officers absent on duty elsewhere, disciplinary problems resulted, and the men were found to be "not respectful of their officers and non-commissioned officers." As a result, between late September 1814 and late May 1815, sixty-eight NCOs and men were convicted of various crimes, including the theft of food and supplies, absence from duty, desertion, insubordination, and "unsoldierlike conduct." The sentences included corporal punishment — the average penalty was one hundred lashes, although there were three sentences of seven hundred; most of these sentences were reduced in number — a stoppage in pay, solitary confinement, or reduction in rank. These difficulties aside, Smyth found the privates to be "a fine, active and serviceable body of men," and despite their having "little opportunity for instruction in military drill," he concluded that the Fencibles were "very efficient for the service of the colonies."[10]

During its brief existence, the New Brunswick Regiment of Fencible Infantry garrisoned outposts at Fredericton and Saint John, provided work parties to build roads and improve fortifications, and manned gunboats on the St. John River. Officers also served on detached service in the Canadas, New Brunswick, and Prince Edward Island. The regiment was disbanded on February 24, 1816.[11]

Appendix 3

The March of the 104th Foot in Canadian Military History:
A Comparative Overview

The bicentenary of the War of 1812 has brought much attention to the story of the epic march of the 104th Foot from New Brunswick to Upper Canada. In the winter of 2013, a group of volunteers re-enacted this seven-hundred-mile journey of the original six companies from Fredericton to Kingston, joined at various stages along the route by soldiers from militia regiments in New Brunswick, Quebec, and Ontario. The culmination of this historic re-enactment occurred in Kingston on April 12, 1813, in a special concluding ceremony on the grounds of the Royal Military College of Canada.

As with other themes developed for the bicentenary, the "March of the 104th Regiment" has taken on a mythological status. A published study of the march concluded that it was "one of the more significant feats accomplished during the War of 1812,"[1] and suggested it was on par with the greatest marches in history. Military history, in fact, is replete with lengthy and difficult marches. In 218 BC, Hannibal took sixteen days to cross the Alps to Italy. In 1704, the Duke of Marlborough moved 14 battalions of infantry, 39 squadrons of cavalry, and 1,700 wagons pulled by 5,000 draught horses 250 miles from the Spanish Netherlands to Bavaria in five weeks. Napoleon lived up to his maxim that "marches are war" and, in 1805, moved 210,000 men in seventeen days from the Rhine River to meet his opponent east of the Danube. One could go on, but what distinguished these marches was the large number of soldiers, horses, and guns involved and that, following the ordeal, whether distance, pace, weather, topography, or a combination thereof, the forces involved were fit enough to fight and defeat their enemy.

Canadian military history also has its share of marches, many of which occurred in the western reaches of the country, although it must be pointed out that none of these "marches" was conducted entirely on foot, but incorporated other means of transportation, including waterborne craft, horse-drawn transport, and rail.

In 1870, British Colonel Garnet Wolseley led a 1,200-man expedition from Collingwood, on Georgian Bay, to Upper Fort Garry, in Manitoba, travelling by boat, canoe, and overland through difficult marsh and swamp to their objective 870 miles distant; the march was completed remarkably free of injury or disease. Then, in 1885, the eight-thousand-strong North West Field Force travelled from eastern and central Canada to points as far west as Calgary before leaving the rail line and marching north across the prairie toward their objectives. Gaps in the still-incomplete Canadian Pacific Railway required the troops to march portions of this route through difficult conditions, giving the Canadian government impetus to complete the project. It should also be remembered that, in New France, expeditions of various sizes were mounted from communities on the St. Lawrence River to attack First Nations and English settlements in New York and New England.[2]

A lesser-known march took place in May 1846, when the British responded to threats of American encroachment into the northwest by sending infantrymen of the 6th Foot, gunners, and engineers — a force totalling 347 men — accompanied by 17 women, 19 children, and 4 pieces of artillery, to the Red River Colony. They used a northern route, via Hudson Bay, the Hayes River, Lake Winnipeg, and the Red River, a distance of over nearly seven hundred miles, to reach their destination. Most of the voyage was conducted using boats and canoes, and lengthy portages were common. Unlike the route taken by the 104th Foot, which was marked by settlements, villages, and towns, the men, women, and children of the 1846 column moved through desolate territory, where little help, virtually no refuge, and few supplies could be found. Norway House was the sole outpost between Fort York on Hudson Bay and Fort Alexander near the southern end of Lake Winnipeg. As many soldiers, women, and children would experience, getting anywhere in British North America involved difficult travel over long distances.[3]

As for the War of 1812, the 104th Foot was not the only unit to make the overland journey from New Brunswick to the Canadas — artillerists, infantry, and even sailors also covered this route. In February 1814, five companies of the 2nd Battalion of the 8th Foot made the journey, while the Royal Navy also made use of it to move reinforcements to Kingston. In December 1813, Commodore Sir James Yeo sent Lieutenant John Scott, who had travelled by the route from Saint John the previous spring with Commander Robert Barclay, to make an appeal for seamen to Vice-Admiral Sir John Warren, the naval commander at Halifax. Eventually, two hundred and ten officers and men from four ships were collected, and in January 1814, with the band of the 8th Foot playing in their honour, the contingent began what in the annals of naval history must be a unique and difficult trek that took the sailors part way through New Brunswick by sleigh and thereafter on foot in a fashion similar to the march of the 104th Foot. The men were issued with snowshoes and one toboggan for every four men. Not as well versed with living in field conditions as soldiers would have been, the sailors often slept in the open, getting what warmth they could from campfires; frostbite reduced their numbers along the way. Once at Rivière-du-Loup, sleighs carried the sailors to Quebec City, from where they completed the journey to Kingston on foot.[4]

Finally, although only a portion of the 1,900-mile trek of the 203-strong Yukon Field Force from Vancouver to Dawson in 1898 was covered on foot, it involved a back-breaking journey through very rough terrain.[5]

Public interest in the winter march of the 104th Foot was resurrected in 1862, when, in response to the claim made by the Duke of Wellington that the march of the 43rd Light Infantry from Fredericton to Quebec in 1837 was the only "military achievement performed by a British officer that he really envied,"[6] Andrew Playfair, the "last officer on the half-pay list of the late 104th Regiment," reminded readers of the more difficult conditions faced by the 104th than those experienced by the 43rd twenty-four years later. After comparing the myriad differences in equipment, transportation, and conditions, including the more primitive conditions found in the countryside of New Brunswick, Playfair offered advice on the "safest means of reinforcing" Canada "after the St. Lawrence is closed." "So long as we are at peace with the United States,"[7] Playfair continued, "the best and shortest route for troops coming from the British Isles to Canada…is by the Port of St. Andrew's, in the Bay of Fundy."[8]

Attempting to rank these marches by level of difficulty is moot, however, especially in light of the tremendous physical stamina and determination of those involved and the different conditions each group faced. The march of the 104th Foot was a significant event in that it achieved Sir George Prevost's goal of reinforcing Upper Canada, and provided him additional forces with which to respond to the American assaults on the province. It is unfortunate that the emphasis given to the winter march in the recent bicentenary literature has reduced the service history of the 104th Foot on the upper St. Lawrence River and in the Niagara Peninsula to a paragraph-long narrative that is unsatisfying not only for its brevity but also for the many errors therein. It was at Sackets Harbor, Beaver Dams, Fort George, Kingston, Gananoque, Prescott, Cornwall, Lundy's Lane, Fort Erie, and Cook's Mills that the 104th Foot defended British North America from foreign invasion, and it is a pity that, in comparison with the march, these actions have been reduced to near-insignificance.

On August 3, 2013, a ceremony commemorating the bicentenary of the Battle of Sackets Harbor included the unveiling of a memorial to the 104th Foot, located near the place where the lead elements of the regiment landed in 1813. Photograph by author

Acknowledgements

A great many individuals assisted in the preparation of this history of the 104th Foot. I offer my sincerest appreciation to J. Marc Milner and Brent Wilson, both of the University of New Brunswick, for commissioning me to prepare this book.

Donald E. Graves, the doyen of War of 1812 scholars, has for more than a decade served as my mentor and close friend. His unparalleled knowledge of archival holdings and understanding of the complex intricacies of the British Army of the Napoleonic Wars and the War of 1812 has been most helpful in preparing this book.

Special thanks also to Andrew Bamford, René Chartrand, Dr. Gary Gibson, and Robert Henderson for their generosity in providing documents and advice. Lieutenant-General Jonathan Riley, CB, DSO (late Royal Welch Fusiliers) provided insights into the organization, training, and employment of British Napoleonic infantry regiments; Michael Bechthold of the Laurier Centre for Military Strategic and Disarmament Studies at Wilfrid Laurier University, in Waterloo, Ontario, prepared the maps; and Julie Scriver of Goose Lane Editions oversaw the design of this book. Freelance copy editor Barry Norris ably applied his professional skills and, in his role as "friend to the reader," enhanced the style of the manuscript. The online collection of War of 1812 documents available through the Library and Archives Canada website was an extremely valuable resource. The staff of Massey Library at the Royal Military College of Canada in Kingston, Ontario, assisted with securing material from their special collections and from other libraries. Overseas in England, the staff at The National Archives was helpful as always.

Lastly, I must give loving appreciation to my wife Helga and our children, Sylvia, Karl, and Natasha, who, through the preparation of this title and others, have been an unending source of support, while they gained a greater—and sometimes unexpected—appreciation of the War of 1812, or so they tell me. Without their support, this book would never have been completed.

Compiling the story of a regiment involves many complexities; regiments are living organisms, and their stories centre on the men who served in them and the families that marched with them. The heroes, cowards, and ordinary people that make up the regimental family develop their own character and contribute to a unit's identity, which is much more than regimental facings, colours, battle honours, and unit heritage. This character reveals itself as one gets to know the regiment's members, and I have enjoyed getting to know the 104th Regiment of Foot. Any errors or oversights in telling the story of the family of the 104th Foot between 1803 and 1817 are my own.

Endnotes

Introduction

1   Arthur Swinson, ed., *A Register of the Corps and Regiments of the British Army* (London: Archives Press, 1972), 206.

Chapter 1

1   John R. Grodzinski, "They Really Conducted Themselves Quite Well: Canadian Soldiers and the Great War, 1793-1815," in *The Canadian Way of War: Serving the National Interest*, ed. Bern Horn (Toronto: Dundurn Press, 2006), 65, 66, 68, 69.

2   Rory Muir, *Britain and the Defeat of Napoleon, 1807-1815* (New Haven, CT: Yale University Press, 2006), 3, 4.

3   Grodzinski, "They Really Conducted Themselves Quite Well," 68, 69.

4   David Facey-Crowther, *The New Brunswick Militia, 1787-1867* (Fredericton: New Brunswick Historical Society, 1990), 3-4, 9.

5   Ibid., 3, 9-10.

6   Ron McGuigan, "The Forgotten Army: The Fencible Regiments of Great Britain, 1793-1816," *The Napoleon Series*; available online at http://www.napoleon-series. org/military/organization/fencibles/c_fencibles.html, accessed August 19, 2013; Charles Dupin, *A Tour through the Naval and Military Establishments of Great Britain* (London: Sir Richard Phillips, 1822), 86-87.

7   Dundas to Carleton, February 8, 1793, Library and Archives Canada (hereafter cited as LAC) RG 8 I 3241, vol. 718, 1.

8   Ibid.

9   "The King's New Brunswick Regiment, 1793-1802," *Collections of the New Brunswick Historical Society,* 1 (1894): 1; James Hannay, *A History of New Brunswick*, vol. 1 (Saint John: John A. Bowes 1909), 237, 238, 240; Dundas to Carleton, February 8, 1793, LAC RG 8 I 3241, vol. 718, 1; René Chartrand, *British Forces in North America, 1793-1815* (London: Osprey Publishing, 1993), 13-15.

10　"King's New Brunswick Regiment, 1793-1802," 1; Hannay, *History of New Brunswick*, vol. 1, 238.

11　Dundas to Carleton, February 8, 1793, LAC RG 8 I 3241, vol. 718, 1; Hannay, *History of New Brunswick*, vol. 1, 237; Chartrand, *British Forces in North America*, 13-15.

12　"King's New Brunswick Regiment, 1793-1802," 38.

13　Chartrand, *British Forces in North America*, 16-17.

14　In its letter authorizing the formation of this regiment, the War Office named it the "New Brunswick Regiment," whereas the Army List showed it as the "New Brunswick Fencible Infantry." Several secondary sources incorrectly designate the regiment as the "New Brunswick Regiment of Fencible Infantry," which refers to a different regiment that was raised in 1812. For the purposes of this book I use the designation "New Brunswick Fencible Infantry," or the more common "New Brunswick Fencibles." See Yorke to Martin, August 1, 1803, LAC RG 8 I 3241, vol. 718, 20; War Office, *Army List, 1811* (London: Horse Guards, 1811), 388.

15　Yorke to Martin, August 1, 1803, LAC RG 8 I 3241, vol. 718, 20; Roderick MacArthur, "The British Army Establishments during the Napoleonic Wars Part I: The Infantry," *Journal of the Society for Army Historical Research* 87, no. 350 (Summer 2009): 164-166; Royal Warrant, July 20, 1803, quoted in W. Austin Squires, *The 104th Regiment of Foot (The New Brunswick Regiment), 1803-1817* (Fredericton, NB: Brunswick Press, 1962), 30.

16　War Office, *Army List, 1811*, 6, 338; Stuart Sutherland, *His Majesty's Gentlemen: A Directory of British Regular Army Officers of the War of 1812* (Toronto: ISER Publications, 2000), 136, 353, 384; "Thomas Emerson," *Dictionary of Canadian Biography On-Line*, http://www.biographi.ca/en/bio/emerson_thomas_7E.html, accessed August 27, 2013; Martin Howard, *Wellington's Doctors: The British Army Medical Services in the Napoleonic Wars* (Staplehurst, UK: Spellmount, 2002), 12.

17　War Office, *Army List, 1811*, 6, 338; Sutherland, *His Majesty's Gentlemen*, 136, 353, 384; "Thomas Emerson"; Howard, *Wellington's Doctors*, 12.

18　Adjutant General's Office, *General Regulations and Orders for the Army, 1811* (London: Horse Guards, 1811), 65.

19　Ibid.

20　Ibid., 66.

21　For a fascinating exploration of a little-known regular corps of black engineers, see René Chartrand, "The British Army's Unknown, Regular, African-West Indian Engineer and Service Corps, 1783 to the 1840s," *Journal for the Society for Army Historical Research* 89, no. 358 (Summer 2011): 117-138; Squires, *104th Regiment* of Foot, 66, 212; Winston Johnston, *The Glengarry Light Infantry, 1812-1816* (Charlottetown, PEI, 2011), 37.

22   *General Regulations and Orders for the Army, 1811*, 93.

23   Ibid.

24   MacArthur, "British Army Establishments during the Napoleonic Wars Part I: The Infantry," 161; Inspection Return of the 104th Regiment of Foot, 11 June 1812, The National Archives (hereafter cited as TNA) WO 27/226.

25   Royal Warrant, July 20, 1803, quoted in Squires, *104th Regiment of Foot*, 30.

26   Ibid., 31, 37-38, 43.

27   Secretary at War, *Collection of Orders, Regulations and Instructions for the Army* (London: T. Egerton, 1807), 279; Yorke to Martin, August 1, 1803, LAC RG 8 I 3241, vol. 718, 21.

28   Martin was very clear on this point, stating that each man would receive three guineas after being examined and attested, two more guineas following inspection by a general or field officer, half a guinea for necessaries, and the remaining half guinea for the surgical examination and messing. Martin to White, August 14, 1803, LAC RG 8 I 3241, vol. 718, 17.

29   *Collection of Orders, Regulations and Instructions for the Army*, 279.

30   Kevin Linch, "The Recruitment of the British Army, 1807-1815" (PhD diss., University of Leeds, 2001), 129, 130; *Quebec Gazette*, February 24, 1804, reproduced in Squires, *104th Regiment of Foot*, 32; *Collection of Orders, Regulations and Instructions for the Army*, 293.

31   Martin to White, August 14, 1803, LAC RG 8 I 3241, vol. 718, 17.

32   Ibid.; White to Hunter, November 23, 1803, LAC RG 8 I 3241, vol. 718, 18-19; Mann to Green, March 22, 1804, LAC RG 8 I 3241, vol. 718, 30; Squires, *104th Regiment of Foot*, 33-34.

33   Squires, *104th Regiment of Foot*, 40, 45.

34   Yorke to Martin, August 1, 1803, LAC RG 8 I 3241, vol. 718, 24.

35   *London Gazette*, July 12, 1803, no. 13600: 837; *London Gazette*, August 6, 1803, vol. 15608, 922.

36   Squires, *104th Regiment of Foot*, 30, 42-43.

37   Ibid., 74, 75.

38   Francis J. Dunbar and Joseph H. Harper, *Old Colours Never Die: A Record of Colours and Military Flags in Canada* (Oakville: F.J. Dunbar & Associates, 1992), 30, 130; Chartrand, *British Forces in North America*, 177.

39 Muir, *Britain and the Defeat of Napoleon,* 22-25; John Fortescue, *A History of the British Army,* vol. 6 (London: Macmillan and Company, 1910), 64, 64n2; *Caledon Mercury,* September 20, 1806; Wentworth to Castlereagh, January 3, 1808, Public Archives of Nova Scotia (hereafter cited as PANS) CO 217 A 140, 17; Castlereagh to Wentworth, January 24, 1808, PANS CO 217 A. 140: 43; Castlereagh to Prevost, January 24, 1808, PANS CO 217 A. 140, 221; Linch, "Recruitment of the British Army," 105; "Portsmouth, Saturday, May 2," *Hampshire Telegraph and Sussex Chronicle,* May 4, 1807; "Portsmouth, Saturday May 18," *Hampshire Telegraph and Sussex Chronicle,* May 18, 1807; "Portsmouth, Saturday January 23," *Hampshire Telegraph and Sussex Chronicle,* January 25, 1808.

40 John R. Grodzinski, *Defender of Canada: Sir George Prevost in the War of 1812* (Norman: University of Oklahoma Press, 2013), 33.

41 J.C.A. Stagg, *Mr. Madison's War* (Princeton, NJ: Princeton University Press, 1983), 76-78; J. Mackay Hitsman, *The Incredible War of 1812: A Military History* (Toronto: Robin Brass Studio, 1999), 22-23.

42 Squires, *104th Regiment of Foot,* 81.

43 Torrens to Hunter, September 18, 1810, LAC RG 8 I 3241, vol. 719, 6; Squires, *104th Regiment of Foot,* 86; J. Mackay Hitsman, *Safeguarding Canada: 1763-1871* (Toronto: University of Toronto Press, 1968), 74.

44 Andrew Bamford, *Sickness, Suffering, and the Sword: The British Regiment on Campaign, 1808-1815* (Norman: University of Oklahoma Press, 2013), 12.

45 Linch, "Recruitment of the British Army," 25, 25n12.

46 Torrens to Hunter, September 18, 1810, LAC RG 8 I 3241, vol. 719, 6; MacArthur, "British Army Establishments during the Napoleonic Wars Part I: The Infantry," 158, 163.

47 The change of establishment is noted in Torrens to Hunter, September 18, 1810, LAC RG 8 I 3241, vol. 719, 6; MacArthur, "British Army Establishments during the Napoleonic Wars Part I: The Infantry," 156, table 2: "British Infantry Battalion Establishments," 157; Squires, *104th Regiment of Foot,* 83.

48 McCarthy had served in a number of European armies before obtaining a British commission in 1799. He joined The New Brunswick Fencibles in 1804 and left the regiment to take command of the Royal African Rifles. Afterwards he was governor of several British territories. Drummond's seniority in the 60th of March 1807 was changed to reflect the date he joined The Fencibles. War Office, *Monthly Army List, March 1808,* 46; War Office, *Monthly Army List, January 1812,* 51; Donald E. Graves, "William Drummond and the Battle of Fort Erie," *Canadian Military History* 1, no. 1 (1992): 26; Nesbitt Willoughby Wallace, *A Regimental Chronicle*

and List of Officers of the 60th, or King's Royal Rifle Corps (London: Harrison, 1879), 158; Squires, *104th Regiment of Foot,* 185.

49   Roderick Hamilton Burgoyne, *Historical Records of the 93rd Sutherland Regiment* (London: Richard Bentley and Son, 1883), 18, 20-21, 36, 45, 386.

50   Penelope Winslow to Edward Winslow, June 6, 1811, in W.O. Raymond, ed., *Winslow Papers, A.D. 1776-1828* (St. John, NB: Sun Printing Company, 1901), 668.

51   Penelope Winslow to Edward Winslow, November 17, 1810, *Winslow Papers,* 657.

52   Viger to Wife, June 6, 1813, LAC M-8 Viger Papers, vol. 4; *London Gazette*, May 1, 1810, issue 16366, 2.

53   Dennis Carter-Edwards, *At Work and Play: The British Junior Officer in Upper Canada, 1796-1812* (Ottawa, Parks Canada, 1985), 26.

54   Captain A. Suasso, *A Treatise on the British Drill and the Exercise of the Company* (London: W. Clowes, 1816), 5.

55   Ibid., 312.

56   Jenkins is perhaps best known for leading one of the British columns in the successful attack on Ogdensburg in early 1813. During the attack, Jenkins was wounded in both arms. His left arm was amputated at the shoulder, and he could move his remaining arm only partially. Jenkins returned to Fredericton, where he became town major until he was discharged in 1816. In February 1819, Jenkins passed away at Kingsclear, and was buried in the Old Burying Ground in Fredericton. War Office, *Army List for September 1812,* 51; War Office, *Army List for July 1813,* 52; War Office, *Army List for July 1814,* 55; Squires, *104th Regiment of Foot,* 192; Johnston, *Glengarry Light Infantry,* 283.

57   War Office, *Army List, June 1812,* 51; Robert Burnham and Ron McGuigan, *The British Army against Napoleon: Facts, Lists and Trivia, 1805-1815* (Barnsley: Frontline Books, 2010), 130-133; *Monthly Army List, February 1805,* 42; Alan J. Guy, *Oeconomy and Discipline: Officership and Administration in the British Army, 1714-1763* (Manchester, UK: Manchester University Press, 1985), 59.

58   *London Gazette*, July 24, 1810, issue 16390, 2.

59   Extract of a letter from Major Maule, January 6, 1812, LAC RG 8 I 3241, vol. 719, 9; Linch, "Recruitment of the British Army," 130, 132-134, 139; Bartlett, "Development of the British Army," 144.

60   Linch, "Recruitment of the British Army," 133.

61   Ibid., 133, 135, 178.

62   Recruiting Department, Horse Guards to unknown, June 29, 1811, LAC RG 8 I
      3241, vol. 719, 7; Extract of a letter from Major Maule, January 6, 1812, LAC RG 8
      I 3241, vol. 719, 8.

63   Gilpin to Adjutant General, March 30, 1812, LAC RG 8 I 3241, vol. 719, 1.

64   Torrens to Prevost, 6 April 1812, LAC RG 8 I 3241, vol. 719, 4-5.

65   According to the establishment, the recruiting company included one captain,
      two lieutenants, one ensign, eight sergeants, eight corporals, and four drummers.
      MacArthur, "British Army Establishments during the Napoleonic Wars Part I: The
      Infantry," 163.

66   Ibid.; Squires, *104th Regiment of Foot,* 88.

67   Inspection Return of the 104th Regiment of Foot, June 11, 1812, TNA WO 27/226.

68   *Journal of the House of Commons, From November 4th, 1813 to November 1st, 1814*
      (London: House of Commons, 1814), 656, 662.

69   Ibid.

70   Ibid.

71   Ibid.; Squires, *104th Regiment of Foot,* 188-195; Sutherland, *His Majesty's
      Gentlemen,* 404.

72   Inspection Return of the 104th Regiment of Foot, June 11, 1812, TNA WO 27/226;
      Sutherland, *His Majesty's Gentlemen,* 307, 404; Squires, *104th Regiment of Foot,*
      194; "Coun Douly Rankin," *Dictionary of Canadian Biography On-line,* http://www.
      biographi.ca/en/bio/rankin_coun_douly_8E.html, accessed July 8, 2013.

73   Inspection Return of the 104th Regiment of Foot, June 11, 1812, TNA WO 27/226.

74   Prevost to Liverpool, May 18, 1812, Special Collections, Massey Library, Royal
      Military College of Canada (hereafter cited as RMC) CO 42/146, n.p.

75   Donald R. Hickey, *Don't Give Up the Ship: Myths of the War of 1812* (Toronto:
      Robin Brass Studio, 2006), 41.

76   Robert L. Dallison, *A Neighbourly War: New Brunswick and the War of 1812*
      (Fredericton, NB: Goose Lane Editions and the New Brunswick Military Heritage
      Project, 2012), 24.

77   General Order, Fredericton, July 10, 1812, LAC RG 8 I 3520, vol. 1203 1/2/ E, 13;
      unfortunately the index card to the RG 8 series lists the wrong location for this
      document and, as a result, it has not been possible to verify this order; Dallison,
      Neighbourly War, 30, 32.

78   Dallison, *Neighbourly War,* 29, 37.

79 *Salem Mercury,* July 14, 1812.

80 Irvine to James Monroe, March 16, 1814, United States National Archives, RG 92 Commissary General of Purchases, Letters sent, letterbook A.

81 Ibid.

82 Irvine to Wadsworth, March 16, 1814, United States National Archives, Commissary General of Purchases, Letters sent, letterbook C.

83 Ibid.

84 René Chartrand, *A Most Warlike Appearance: Uniforms, Flags and Equipment of the United States Forces in the War of 1812* (Ottawa: Service Publications, 2011), 38-39, 41, 43.

85 Prevost to Bathurst, January 16, 1813, RMC CO 42/150, 19; Prevost to Sherbrooke, April 20, 1813, LAC RG 8 I 3526, vol. 1220, 312; Grodzinski, *Defender of Canada,* 98; Facey-Crowther, *New Brunswick Militia,* 32.

86 W.E. Campbell, "The March of the 104th (New Brunswick) Regiment of Foot" (unpublished manuscript, St. John River Society, June 21, 2011), 2. The author is indebted to the work of Dr. Campbell, whose study of the march of the 104th Foot provides a useful introduction to that portion of the regiment's history.

87 Dallison, *Neighbourly War,* 48; Campbell, "March of the 104th (New Brunswick) Regiment of Foot," 2.

88 Donald E. Graves, ed., *Merry Hearts Make Light Days: The War of 1812 Journal of John Le Couteur, 104th Foot* (Montreal: Robin Brass Studio, 2012), 93.

89 A.W. Playfair, "Comparison Between the March of the 43rd Light Infantry in 1837 and that of the Late 104th Regiment in 1813, from New Brunswick to Quebec," *British Standard,* January 20, 1862, 3.

90 René Chartrand, *A Scarlet Coat: Uniforms, Flags and Equipment of the British in the War of 1812* (Ottawa: Service Publications, 2011), 183; Halkett to Torrens, May 30, 1813, LAC RG 8 I, vol. 2773, 172-173.

91 Chartrand, *Scarlet Coat,* 48-54, 90, 155-156.

92 Charles Rainsford, "Captain Charles Rainsford's Winter March Across Lake Temiscouata: A Thrilling Incident of the War of 1812," *Saint John Daily Sun,* August 23, 1889, no. 202.

93 Chartrand, *Scarlet Coat,* 167, 169, 171-172.

94 De Witt Bailey, *Small Arms of the British Forces in America, 1664-1815* (Woonsocket, RI: Mowbray Publishers, 2009), 44, 46; Blackmore, *British Military Firearms, 1650-1850,* 137-138.

95   The light muskets had the same characteristics as the India Pattern but incorporated components of lighter weight and construction. The issue of this model of the Brown Bess in no way suggests that the 104th, which was established as a colonial line regiment, was to be a light infantry regiment. At least one other line regiment, the 2/82nd, received this version of the Brown Bess without being given any special designation. Bailey, *Small Arms of the British Forces in America,* 286-291; MacArthur, "British Army Establishments during the Napoleonic Wars Part I: The Infantry," 165. On the sergeant's fusil, see Bailey, *Small Arms of the British Forces in America,* 46, 284, 290; Blackmore, *British Military Firearms, 1650-1850,* 137-138.

96   Chartrand, *Scarlet Coat,* 162-163.

97   Campbell, "March of the 104th," 21; Graves, *Merry Hearts,* 95.

98   Playfair, "Comparison."

99   Ibid.

100 Graves, *Merry Hearts,* 95-96.

101 Campbell, "March of the 104th," 13-15.

102 General Order, Quebec, March 13, 1813, LAC RG 8 I 3520, vol. 1203 ½ C, 340; General Order Quebec, March 27, 1813, LAC RG 8 I 3520, vol. 1203½ G, 141; General Order Quebec, March 29, 1813, LAC RG 8 I 3520, vol. 1203½ G, 145; Return of Medical Staff, Lower Canada, March 17, 1813, LAC RG 8 I 2282, vol. 230, 145; Inspectors Office, March 18, 1813, LAC RG 8 I 2864, vol. 290, 18.

103 General Order, Quebec, March 20, 1813, LAC RG 8 I 3520, vol. 1203½ G, 112, 114.

104 Graves, *Merry Hearts,* 102.

105 Prevost to Adjutant General, Horse Guards, March 11, 1813, LAC RG 8 I 3526, vol. 1220, 216.

106 General Monthly Return of Sick of the Forces in Regimental and Detachment Hospitals in Lower Canada, February 25, 1813-March 24, 1813, LAC RG 8 I 3840, vol. 1707, 155.

107 General Order, Quebec, March 27, 1813, LAC RG 8 I 3520, vol. 1203½, 142.

108 Ibid.; Squires, *104th Regiment of Foot,* 143.

109 General Order, March 27, 1813, LAC RG 8 I 3520, vol. 1203½, 142; E.A. Cruikshank, ed., *Documentary History of the Campaigns upon the Niagara Frontier in 1812 to 1814* (Welland, ON, 1896-1908), vol. 5, 137.

110 Authority for the issue of arms was announced in General Order, Quebec, March 26, 1813, LAC RG 8 I 3502, vol. 1170, 140.

111 War of 1812 Casualty Database, available online at http://www.1812casualties. org/casualties_database/advanced_search, accessed August 26, 2013; Campbell, "March of the 104th Foot," 18.

112 *General Regulations and Orders for the Army, 1811*, 255.

113 Welsh had originally joined The New Brunswick Fencibles in 1805. *General Regulations and Orders for the Army, 1811*, 255; Inspection Return of the 104th Regiment of Foot, June 11, 1812, TNA WO 27/226; MacArthur, "British Army Establishments during the Napoleonic Wars Part I: The Infantry," 165.

114 General District Order, March 16, 1813, quoted in Squires, *104th Regiment of Foot*, 137.

115 General Order, Fredericton, March 16, 1813, LAC RG 8 I 3503, vol. 1203½ C, 299.

116 Sherbrooke to Prevost, April 27, 1813, LAC RG 8 I 2822, vol. 229, 67; Freer to Sherbrooke, March 19, 1813, quoted in Squires, *104th Regiment of Foot*, 138.

117 Sherbrooke to Freer, April 27, 1813, LAC RG 8 I 2875, vol. 329, 112-113.

118 Sherbrooke to Freer, June 16, 1813, LAC RG 8 I 3255, vol. 789, 104; Prevost to Adjutant General, Horse Guards, March 11, 1813, LAC RG 8 I 3526, vol. 1220, 215.

Chapter 2

1 Return of Guns and Ammunition in the Batteries and Blockhouses at the Port of Kingston, June 4, 1813, LAC RG 8 I 3232 vol. 688 C, 96; Distribution of Forces in Canada, May 1813, LAC RG 8 I 3840 vol. 1707, 61; General Monthly Return of the Serjeants, Trumpeters, Drummers and Rank and File of the several Corps serving in Canada, May 25, 1813, TNA WO 17/157, 65.

2 Graves, *Merry Hearts,* 108; Jacques Viger, "Reminiscences of the War of 1812-1814," (Kingston, ON: News Printing Company, 1895), 10; Stephen D. Mecredy, "Some Military Aspects of Kingston's Development during the War of 1812" (Masters thesis, Queen's University, 1982), 44, 52n46; LAC Map of Kingston, January 24, 1816, National Map Collection, 22903.

3 Chauncey to Jones, March 18, 1813, in William Dudley, ed., *The Naval War of 1812: A Documentary History,* vol. 2 (Washington, DC: Naval Historical Center, 1992), 431-432.

4 Prevost to Brock, July 31, 1811, in Cruikshank, *Documentary History*, vol. 2, 154; Carl Benn, *Historic Fort York, 1793-2003* (Toronto: Natural Heritage, 1993), 49-50; Robert Malcomson, *Capital in Flames: The American Attack on York, 1813* (Montreal: Robin Brass Studio, 2008), 95.

5   "Robert Roberts Loring," *Dictionary of Canadian Biography Online*, http://www.biographi.ca/en/bio/loring_robert_roberts_7E.html?revision_id=2494, accessed July 8, 2013; Sutherland, *His Majesty's Gentlemen*, 231.

6   Malcomson, *Capital in Flames*, 214, 217, 219.

7   Benn, *Historic Fort York*, 51, 53, 54, 56, 63; C.P. Stacey, "The Battle of Little York" (Toronto: Toronto Historical Board, 1977), 21; Malcomson, *Capital in Flames*, 72; Robert Malcomson, *Warships on the Great Lakes, 1754-1834* (Annapolis, MD: Naval Institute Press, 2001), 45, 100; Chauncey to Jones, March 18, 1813, Dudley, *Naval War of 1812*, vol. 2, 431.

8   Coffin to Halkett, April 29, 1813, LAC RG 8 I 3172, vol. 678, 174.

9   Graves, "William Drummond and the Battle of Fort Erie," 27; Graves, *Merry Hearts,* 110; Viger, "Reminiscences of the War of 1812-1814," 12.

10 Viger, "Reminiscences of the War of 1812-1814," 12.

11 Ibid., 12-13; Graves, *Merry Hearts,* 111-112.

12 General Order, Quebec, April 22, 1813, LAC RG 8 I 3502, vol. 1170, 177.

13 Halkett to Baynes, April 29, 1813, LAC RG 8 I 2773, vol. 165, 178.

14 Ibid., 180; Halkett to Torrens, May 30, 1813, LAC RG 8 I, vol. 2773, 172-173.

15 Halkett to Torrens, May 30, 1813, LAC RG 8 I 2773, vol. 165, 172.

16 Ibid., 174.

17 Prevost to Adjutant General, Horse Guards, March 18, 1813, LAC RG 8 I 3526, vol. 1220, 216.

18 Halkett to Torrens, May 30, 1813, LAC RG 8 I 2773, vol. 165, 175.

19 Ibid.

20 Halkett to Baynes, May 30, 1813, LAC RG 8 I, vol. 2773, 174-175. In 1837, the King conferred upon Halkett the Military Knight Commander of the Royal Hanoverian Guelphic Order; *London Gazette*, March 10, 1837, 124.

21 General Order, Kingston, May 24, 1813, LAC RG 8 I 3521, vol. 1203½ H, 61.

22 Adjutant General's Office, *General Regulations for the Army,* August 12, 1811, 27.

23 Freer to Sheaffe, March 23, 1813, LAC RG 8 I 3232, vol. 1615, 28; Prevost to Bathurst, June 1, 1813, RMC CO 42/150, 175.

24 Prevost to Bathurst, June 1, 1813, RMC CO 42/150, 175.

25 Ibid., 175; Malcomson, *Lords of the Lake*, 129; Graves, "The Attack on Sackets Harbor, 29 May 1813: The British/Canadian Side" (Ottawa: Directorate of History, n.d.). For an overview of Yeo's career, see Malcomson, *Lords of the Lake*, 115-119, 130.

26 Douglas L. Hendry, *British Casualties Suffered at Several Actions during the War of 1812: Queenston Heights, Sacket's Harbor, Stoney Creek, Oswego, Bladensburg, Baltimore* (Ottawa: Directorate of History, Department of Defence, 1994), 12, annex M.

27 Graves, *Merry Hearts*, 113.

28 Elijah Beach was another volunteer attached to the 104th from June 1813 to March 1814. Few details have been located regarding his service other than Squires noting that Beach was "a gentlemen out from England to see the war," and a General Order issued in March 1814 approving Volunteer Beach's "request to withdraw his Services." Why Beach would journey all the way to North America, while a much larger British army was serving in Iberia, is unclear. Squires, *104th Regiment of Foot*, 195; General Order Quebec, March 11, 1814, LAC RG 8 I 3502, vol. 1171, 206; General Order, Quebec, March 11, 1814, LAC RG 8 I 3511, vol. 1023 1/2J, 305.

29 Moodie to Addison, December 30, 1816, LAC RG 8 I 3362, vol. 1026, 77-78.

30 Memorial of John F.W. Winslow, LAC RG 8 I 3362, vol. 1026, 71-73; Sutherland, *His Majesty's Gentlemen*, 382.

31 Graves, *Merry Hearts*, 113-114.

32 Graves, "Attack on Sackets Harbor"; Malcomson, *Lords of the Lake*, 130.

33 Graves, *Merry Hearts*, 115.

34 Baynes to Prevost, May 30, 1813, in Cruikshank, *Documentary History*, vol. 5, 276; Brenton to Freer, May 30, 1813, in Cruikshank, *Documentary History*, vol. 5, 279; Patrick Wilder, "We Will Not Conquer Canada This Year: The Battle of Sacket's Harbor" (unpublished manuscript in the author's possession), chap. 5: 10, 12, 13. Note that the pages are numbered by chapter.

35 Patrick Wilder, *The Battle of Sackett's Harbour, 1813* (Baltimore: Nautical and Aviation Publishing Company of America, 1994), 72, 82; Graves, "Attack on Sackets Harbor."

36 Wilder, "We Will Not Conquer Canada This Year," chap. 3: 10, 14, 18; chap. 4: 18-20.

37 Graves, *Merry Hearts*, 116.

38 Ibid., 115; Wilder, "We Will Not Conquer Canada This Year," chap. 6: 5-6.

39 Wilder, "We Will Not Conquer Canada This Year," chap. 6: 7.

40 Ibid., chap. 6: 9; Bernard Andrès, *La guerre de 1812: Journal de Jacques Viger* (Québec: Presses de l'Université Laval, 2012), 101-102.

41 Graves, *Merry Hearts*, 116.

42 Wilder, "We Will Not Conquer Canada This Year," chap. 6: 14-15; Graves, *Merry Hearts,* 116.

43 Prevost to Bathurst, June 1, 1813, RMC CO 42/150, 175; Graves, "Attack on Sackets Harbor."

44 Wilder, "We Will Not Conquer Canada This Year," chap. 6: 16-17.

45 Graves, "Attack on Sackets Harbor."

46 Baynes to Prevost, May 30, 1813, in Cruikshank, *Documentary History*, vol. 5, 277-278; Graves, "Attack on Sackets Harbor."

47 Prevost to Bathurst, June 1, 1813, RMC CO 42/150, 175.

48 Graves, *Merry Hearts,* 116.

49 Prevost to Bathurst, June 1, 1813, RMC CO 42/150, 281; Baynes to Prevost, May 30, 1813, in Cruikshank, *Documentary History*, vol. 5, 277-278; Brenton to Freer, May 30, 1813, LAC RG 8 I 3829, vol. 1707, 236; Graves, "Attack on Sackets Harbor"; Wilder, *Battle of Sackett's Harbour*, 72, 108.

50 Wilder, *Battle of Sackett's Harbour*, 110; Brenton to Freer, May 30, 1813, LAC RG 8 I 3840, vol. 1707, 236.

51 Graves, *Merry Hearts*, 117; Dearborn to Armstrong, June 8, 1813, in Cruikshank, *Documentary History*, vol. 6, 55; Chauncey to Secretary of the Navy Jones, June 11, 1813, in Dudley, *Naval War of 1812*, vol. 2, 493.

52 Chauncey to Secretary of Navy Jones, June 2, 1813, in Dudley, *Naval War of 1812*, vol. 2, 477-478.

53 Ibid.

54 Graves, *Merry Hearts,* 118.

55 Ibid.

56 See Graves, "Attack on Sackets Harbor."

57 British casualties at Queenston Heights totalled about 105 soldiers and 5 First Nations warriors. The losses at Stoney Creek included 23 killed, 135 wounded, and 55 missing, for a total of 213. At Chateauguay, the British lost 22 men: two killed, 16 wounded, and 4 prisoners of war; 179 casualties were suffered at Crysler's Farm, including 22 dead, 148 wounded, and 9 missing. Total losses at

York, including militia, volunteers, dockyard workers, Provincial Marine, and regular troops were 475, 166 of them regulars. "General Return of Killed Wounded and Missing in an Action with the Enemy Near the Head of Lake Ontario, 6 June 1813," LAC RG 8 I 3172, vol. 679, 35; Robert Malcomson, *A Very Brilliant Affair: The Battle of Queenston Heights, 1812* (Toronto: Robin Brass Studio, 2006), 196; Donald E. Graves, *Field of Glory: The Battle of Crysler's Farm, 1813* (Toronto: Robin Brass Studio, 1999), 109; Sutherland, *His Majesty's Gentlemen,* 121; War of 1812 Casualty Database, available online at http://www.1812casualties.org/casualties_database/advanced_search, accessed August 22, 2013. Overall casualty figures from Graves, "Attack on Sackets Harbor."

58 Grodzinski, *Defender of Canada*, 120.

59 General Order, Kingston, June 10, 1813, LAC Duncan Clark Papers, MG 19, A 39, 68.

60 General Order, Kingston, June 6, 1813, LAC RG 8 I 3522, vol. 1203½ R, 8.

61 General Order, Kingston, June 6, 1813, in Cruikshank, *Documentary History*, vol. 6, 5; General Order, Kingston, 6 June 1813, LAC RG 8 I 3522, vol. 1203½ R, 8; General Order, Kingston, June 8, 1813, in Cruikshank, *Documentary History*, vol. 6, 53-54; Return of the Troops, June 13, 1813, in Cruikshank, *Documentary History*, vol. 6, 73.

62 General Order, Kingston, June 11, 1813, in Cruikshank, *Documentary History*, vol. 6, 69.

63 General Order, Kingston, June 14, 1813, in Cruikshank, *Documentary History*, vol. 6, 84.

64 General Order, Kingston, June 15, 1813, in Cruikshank, *Documentary History*, vol. 6, 87.

65 General Order, Kingston, June 19, 1813, in Cruikshank, *Documentary History*, vol. 6, 99-100.

66 Garrison Order, Kingston, June 22, 1813, in Cruikshank, *Documentary History*, vol. 6, 53.

67 Extract, Headquarters, Fort George, June 20, 1813, *American State Papers, Military Affairs,* vol. 1 (Washington, DC: Gales and Seaton, 1832), 449.

68 Chauncey to Jones, June 18, 1813, in Dudley, *Naval War of 1812*, vol. 2, 495.

69 Chauncey to Jones, June 18, 1813, United States National Archives, Washington, DC, Captain's Letters to the Secretary of the Navy, Record Group 45, 1813, M125 Roll 29, 1813, vol. 4, Item 82.

70 General Order, Kingston, June 23, 1813, in Cruikshank, *Documentary History*, vol. 6, 110.

71　Garrison Order, June 22, 1813, in Cruikshank, *Documentary History*, vol. 6, 104-105.

72　District General Order, June 26, 1813, in Cruikshank, *Documentary History*, vol. 6, 156.

73　Ibid.; District Orders, Kingston, July 4, 1813, in Cruikshank, *Documentary History*, vol. 6, 173; Sutherland, *His Majesty's Gentlemen,* 95.

74　E.A. Cruikshank, *Blockade of Fort George, 1813* (Welland, ON: Niagara Historical Society, 1898), 20. Dispositions based on a map taken from *Niles Weekly Register*, as reproduced in Cruikshank, *Documentary History*, vol. 6, 153; Malcomson, *Lords of the Lake*, 148-151.

75　Benn, *Iroquois in the War of 1812*, 109, 114; Stuart Sutherland, ed., *"A Desire of Serving and Defending My Country": The War of 1812 Journals of William Hamilton Merritt* (Toronto: ISER Publications, 2001), 8; Sutherland, *His Majesty's Gentlemen,* 120-121.

76　Vincent to Prevost, June 6, 1813, LAC RG 8 I 3173, vol. 679, 27.

77　Evans to Vincent, June 8, 1813, LAC RG 8 I 3173, vol. 679, 61-62.

78　Vincent to Baynes, June 14, 1813, LAC RG 8 I 3172, vol. 679, 91.

79　E.A. Cruikshank, *Fight in the Beechwoods: A Study in Canadian History* (Welland, ON: W.T. Swayle, 1895), 10; Graves, *Merry Hearts,* 126-127; Alun Hughes, "Following in Laura's Footsteps," *Newsletter of the Historical Society of St. Catharines* (December 2012): 1, 10.

80　Benn, *Iroquois in the War of 1812*, 115.

81　Graves, *Merry Hearts,* 128.

82　Benn, *Iroquois in the War of 1812,* 117-118.

83　Graves, *Merry Hearts,* 128.

84　Bisshopp to Vincent, June 24, 1813, attachment to Prevost to Bathurst, July 3, 1813, RMC CO 42/151, 52.

Chapter 3

1　Cruikshank, *Blockade of Fort George,* 33, 38.

2　De Rottenburg to Prevost, July 7, 1813, LAC RG 8 I 3173, vol. 679, 202.

3　De Rottenburg to Prevost, July 9, 1813, LAC RG 8 I 3173, vol. 679, 210, 211; Malcomson, *Lords of the Lake,* 149; Benn, *Iroquois in the War of 1812,* 127.

4   De Rottenburg to Prevost, July 20, 1813, LAC RG 8 I 3173, vol. *679*, 264-265; Benn, *Iroquois in the War of 1812,* 124.

5   Cruikshank, *Blockade of Fort George,* 44; Cruikshank, *Documentary History*, vol. 7, Map between 55 and 56; Graves, "William Drummond and the Battle of Fort Erie," 28; Graves, *Merry Hearts,* 130.

6   Extract, Headquarters, Fort George, June 20, 1813, *American State Papers, Military Affairs*, vol. 1, 449.

7   Wilkinson to Boyd, July 7, 1813, John Parker Boyd, *Documents and Facts Relative to Military Events During the Late War* (no publisher, 1816), 17; M. Ian Bowering, *A Study of the Utilization of Artillery on the Niagara Frontier,* Manuscript Report 446 (Parks Canada, March 1979), vol. 2, 243.

8   Cruikshank, *Blockade of Fort George,* 44; Sketch Map of "American Piquets around Fort George, Summer 1813," Cruikshank, *Documentary History*, vol. 7, Map between 55 and 56; John C. Fredricksen, *Green Coats and Glory: The United States Regiment of Riflemen, 1808-1821* (Youngstown, NY: Old Fort Niagara Association, 2000), 38; Bowering, *Study of the Utilization of Artillery on the Niagara Frontier,* vol. 1, 64; ibid., vol. 2, 243

9   Scott to Boyd, August 3, 1813, *American State Papers, Military Affairs*, vol. 1, 450; Boyd to Armstrong, August 12, 1813, *American State Papers, Military Affairs*, vol. 1, 451.

10   De Rottenburg to Prevost, July 7, 1813, LAC RG 8 I 3173, vol. 679, 202.

11   Graves, *Merry Hearts,* 131.

12   Ibid.; War of 1812 Casualty Database, available online at http://www.1812casualties.org/casualties_database/advanced_search, accessed July 16, 2013.

13   Charles James, *Military Dictionary* (London: Military Library, 1805), entry for "Desertion."

14   Bamford, *Sickness, Suffering and the Sword,* 246-247.

15   Fulton to Prevost, July 7, 1813, LAC RG 8 I 3362, vol. 1024, 56.

16   This name appears as Sayer Baby in the General Order of July 18, in Cruikshank, *Documentary History*, vol. 6, 251-252; see also Squires, *104th Regiment of Foot*, 231.

17   De Rottenburg to Brenton, July 18, 1813, RG 8 I 3173, vol. 679, 258; General Order, July 18, 1813, in Cruikshank, *Documentary History*, vol. 6, 251-252; Squires, *104th Regiment of Foot*, 199, 215, 218, 239.

18   General Order, August 23, 1813, LAC RG 8 I 3173, vol. 679, 483.

19   Jones to Chauncey, January 27, 1813, in Dudley, *Naval War of 1812*, vol. 2, 419-420;

Chauncey to Hamilton, January 1, 1813, in Dudley, *Naval War of 1812*, vol. 2, 406-407; Chauncey to Jones, February 16, 1813, in Dudley, *Naval War of 1812*, vol. 2, 426; Jones to Chauncey, June 26, 1813, in Dudley, *Naval War of 1812*, vol. 2, 508; Chauncey to Perry, July, 30 1813, in Dudley, *Naval War of 1812*, vol. 2, 530; Thomas Malcolmson and Robert Malcomson, *The Battle for Lake Erie* (St. Catharines, ON: Vanwell Publishing, 1990), 30, 34, 39.

20　General Order, August 23, 1813, LAC RG 8 I 3173, vol. 679, 483-486.

21　Ibid., 483.

22　Ibid., 484; State of Troops, St. David's, August 22, 1813, in Cruikshank, *Documentary History*, vol. 7, 51.

23　Graves, *Merry Hearts,* 132.

24　Le Couteur makes reference to a "Sergeant Avarne" in his journal. As no such name appears on the regimental nominal role, I assume the reference is to Avery.

25　Graves, *Merry Hearts,* 133.

26　Yeo to Prevost, August 22, 1813, LAC RG 8 I, vol. 3244, 96; State of the Troops, August 22, 1813, in Cruikshank, *Documentary History*, vol. 7, 51; Prevost to Bathurst, August 25, 1813, RMC CO 42/151, 158; *Quebec Mercury*, September 7, 1812, in Cruikshank, *Documentary History*, vol. 7, 59; Malcomson, *Lords of the Lake*, 184; Brian Leigh Dunnigan, *Forts Within a Fort: Niagara's Redoubts* (Youngstown, NY: Old Fort Niagara Association, 1989), 44; Benn, *Iroquois in the War of* 1812, 124.

27　General Monthly Return of Sergeants, Trumpeters, Drummers and Rank and File of the several Corps serving in Canada, August 25, 1813, TNA WO 17/1518; War of 1812 Casualty Database, available online at http://www.1812casualties.org/casualties_database/advanced_search, accessed July 16, 2013.

28　Freer to de Rottenburg, September 7, 1813, LAC RG 8 I 3525, vol. 1221, 45; Darroch to Prevost, October 7, 1813, LAC RG 8 I 3171, vol. 680, 151-152.

29　Graves, *Merry Hearts,* 138.

30　Ibid.

31　Another 22 men of the 104th were at Kingston; see General Weekly Distribution Return of the Troops forming the Centre Division of the Army of Upper Canada, September 15, 1813, LAC RG 8 I 3830, vol. 1708, 50; Morning Sick Report, Centre Division of the Army of Upper Canada, September 15, 1813, LAC RG 8 I 3840, vol. 1708, 42.

32　Graves, *Merry Hearts*, 139.

33　Darroch to Prevost, October 7, 1813, LAC RG 8 I 3171, vol. 680, 151-152; Darroch to Prevost, October 8, 1813, LAC RG 8 I 3173, vol. 680, 159-160; Malcomson, *Lords of the Lake*, 207-208.

34   *Kingston Gazette*, October 9, 1813, in Cruikshank, *Documentary History*, vol. 8, 43.

35   Although William and Gordon Drummond shared the same surname, they were only distantly related. See Graves, "William Drummond and the Battle of Fort Erie," 42n26. The units assigned to the Left Division at this time included 1 Troop, 19th Light Dragoons; two companies of the Royal Artillery; 2nd Battalion, 41st Foot; elements of the 49th Foot; 2nd Battalion, 89th Foot; 104th Foot; the Regiment de Watteville; four companies of The Canadian Fencibles; and four companies of the Voltigeurs Canadiens. Prevost to Bathurst, October 30, 1813, RMC CO 42.151, 291.

36   For an overview of this part of the campaign against Montreal, see Graves, *Field of Glory*; Michelle Guitard, *The Militia of the Battle of the Châteauguay: A Social History* (Ottawa: Parks Canada, 1983); Victor Suthern, *The Battle of the Châteauguay* (Ottawa: Canadian War Museum, 1974).

37   Swift to Armstrong, July 17, 1836, in Benson J. Lossing, *The Pictorial Fieldbook of the War of 1812* (New York: Harper and Brothers, 1869), 655n.

38   Prevost to de Rottenburg, October 12, 1813, LAC RG 8 I, vol. 1221, 179; Prevost to Yeo, October 12, 1812, LAC RG 8 I 3527, vol. 1221, 182; Yeo to Croker, October 14, 1813, in Cruikshank, *Documentary History*, vol. 7, 221; Prevost to Yeo, November 21, 1813, LAC, RG 8 I 3521, vol. 1221, 218; Malcomson, *Lords of the Lake*, 219; Mulcaster to Yeo, November 2, 1813, in Cruikshank, *Documentary History*, vol. 8, 123-124; Prevost to Bathurst, November 15, 1813, RMC CO 42/152, 11; Prevost to Bathurst, October 8, 1813, RMC CO 42/151, 199.

39   Graves, *Field of Glory,* 114-115; idem, *Merry Hearts,* 150.

40   Niagara Frontier: 40 Mile Creek, Burlington Heights, Fort Schlosser, Black Rock, Stoney Creek, Beaver Dams, TNA WO 164/556, 124.

41   As of July 15, 1806, privates earned 1s a day; after seven years of service, their pay increased to 1s 1d, and after fourteen years to 1s 2d. Secretary at War, *Collection of Orders, Regulations and Instructions for the Army on Matters of Finance* (London: Horse Guards, 1807), 39.

42   Niagara Frontier: 40 Mile Creek, Burlington Heights, Fort Schlosser, Black Rock, Stoney Creek, Beaver Dams, TNA WO 164/556, 114-124.

43   Although John Smith appears in the nominal roll of non-commissioned personnel of the 104th in Squires, the closest candidate named Smith in Sutherland's roster of British officers is Jacob, who received a temporary commission as a lieutenant in the New Brunswick Fencibles in March 1814; see Squires, *104th Regiment of Foot,* 233; and Sutherland, *His Majesty's Gentlemen,* 406.

44 Dallison, *Neighbourly War,* 75; Sutherland, *His Majesty's Gentlemen,* 268; Squires, *104th Regiment of Foot,* 174.

45 The records on desertion are incomplete and sometimes contradict one another. The figure provided here is a minimum estimate of desertions. *Journal of the House of Commons, From November 4th, 1813 to November 1st, 1814* (London: House of Commons, 1814), 667.

Chapter 4

1 Drummond to Prevost, April 5, 1814, LAC RG 8 I, vol. 2936, 61.

2 Prevost to Drummond, March 22, 1814, LAC RG 8 I 3527, vol. 1222, 68.

3 General Order, Montreal, May 9, 1814, LAC RG 8 I, vol. 3503, 266; Sutherland, *His Majesty's Gentlemen,* 276.

4 Quoted in Squires, *104th Regiment of Foot,*160.

5 Baynes to Drummond, June 28, 1814, LAC RG 8 I 3527, vol. 1222, 148, 224.

6 Graves, *Merry Hearts,* 163.

7 Ibid., 164.

8 Ibid., 165.

9 Duncan Clark Papers, June 3, 1814, LAC MG 19 A39, 234.

10 Statement of a Force and Means which it is Assumed May be Collected in Upper Canada for the Attack on Sackets Harbor, April 28, 1814, LAC RG 8 I 3174, vol. 688, 65.

11 Yeo to Prevost, April 13, 1813, LAC RG 8 I 3174, vol. 683, 19.

12 Graves, *Merry Hearts,* 164.

13 Malcomson, *Lords of the Lake,* 261-262.

14 Graves, *Merry Hearts,* 166, 172.

15 Drummond to Prevost, July 17, 1814, LAC RG 8 I 3174, vol. 684, 120.

16 Prevost to Drummond, January 5, 1814, LAC RG 8 I 3527, vol. 1222, 15.

17 Drummond to Prevost, 10 July 10, 1814, in Cruikshank, *Documentary History,* vol. 1, 36.

18 "Arrangements for Collecting a Force at Burlington," c. July 13, 1813, in Cruikshank, *Documentary History,* vol. 1, 57.

19   Drummond to Prevost, July 15, 1814, in Cruikshank, *Documentary History*, vol. 1, 59; Drummond to Prevost, July 9, 1814, LAC RG 8 I 3174, vol. 684, 48.

20   Riall to Drummond, July 20, 1814, in Cruikshank, *Documentary History*, vol. 1, 77.

21   Donald E. Graves, *Where Right and Glory Lead: The Battle of Lundy's Lane, 25 July 1814* (Toronto: Robin Brass Studio, 1997), 101-102.

22   Ibid., 102; Harvey to Riall, June 23, 1814, in Cruikshank, *Documentary History*, vol. 1, 82.

23   Harvey to Tucker, July 23, 1814, in Cruikshank, *Documentary History*, vol. 1, 84-85.

24   Harvey to Riall, July 23, 1814, in Cruikshank, *Documentary History*, vol. 1, 82-83.

25   Graves, "William Drummond and the Battle of Fort Erie," 29.

26   Graves, *Where Right and Glory Lead*, 104, 107; idem., "William Drummond and the Battle of Fort Erie," 29.

27   Graves, *Where Right and Glory Lead*, 98.

28   Graves, Merry Hearts, 174; idem, *Where Right and Glory Lead*, 110.

29   Graves, *Where Right and Glory Lead*, 113-114.

30   Norton had great respect for William Drummond and referred to him in his journal as his "gallant friend." As a sign of his respect toward the First Nations, Drummond often wore a string of native beads while in uniform. Carl F. Klinck and James J. Talman, eds. *The Journal of Major John Norton, 1816* (Toronto: Champlain Society, 2011), 343.

31   Ibid., 342.

32   Graves, *Where Right and Glory Lead*, 144-145.

33   Drummond to Prevost, July 27, 1814, LAC RG 8 I 3174, vol. 685, 236. The letter also appears in Prevost to Bathurst, August 5, 1814, RMC CO 42/157, 118.

34   Drummond to Prevost, July 27, 1814, LAC RG 8 I 3174, vol. 685, 236; Richard Barbuto, *Niagara 1814: America Invades Canada* (Lawrence: University Press of Kansas, 2000), 221.

35   Graves, *Merry Hearts*, 176.

36   Johnston, *Glengarry Light Infantry*, 183.

37   Graves, *Merry Hearts*, 176.

38   Ibid.

39   Ibid.

40 Ibid., 175; Johnston, *Glengarry Light Infantry*, 183.

41 Drummond to Prevost, July 27, 1814, LAC RG 8 I 3174, vol. 684, 237-238.

42 Letter, William Drummond, *Edinburgh Annual Register for 1814 vol. Seventh, Parts I and II* (Edinburgh: James Ballantyne and Company, 1816), 334.

43 Ibid.

44 Graves, *Where Right and Glory Lead*, 161-162.

45 Drummond to Prevost, July 27, 1814, LAC RG 8 I 3174, vol. 684, 235.

46 "Testimony of Captain William McDonald," 19th US Infantry, quoted in Graves, *Where Right and Glory Lead*, 174.

47 Graves, *Merry Hearts*, 177.

48 Graves, *Where Right and Glory Lead*, 186.

49 British figures are provided in District General Order, July 26, 1814, in Cruikshank, *Documentary History*, vol. 1, 92-96; American figures come from Barbuto, *Niagara 1814*, 229.

50 Sutherland, *Desire of Serving and Defending My Country*, 59.

51 Return of Killed Wounded, Missing and taken Prisoner of the Right Division … in Action with the Enemy near the Falls of Niagara, July 25, 1814, TNA CO 42/157, 115; War of 1812 Casualty Database, available online at http://www.1812casualties. org/casualties_database/advanced_search, accessed July 16, 2013.

52 Graves, *Merry Hearts*, 177, 179. As for the other Moorsom brothers, Ensign William Moorsom served with the 67th Foot in Iberia and died in October 1812, and three were in the Royal Marines: Nathaniel was a lieutenant-colonel, Henry Nathanial a lieutenant, and William Richard a second lieutenant in the Royal Marine Artillery. The fate of these officers has not been determined. War Office, Army List, 1805, 20, 406, 420, 422; Captain E.A. Challis, "Peninsula Roll Call, also known as the "Challis Index," Napoleon Series, available online at http://www. napoleon-series.org/research/biographies/GreatBritain/Challis/c_ChallisIntro. html, accessed July 25, 2013.

53 Graves, *Merry Hearts*, 177.

54 District General Order, August 1, 1814, LAC RG 8 I 2284, vol. 231, 128; Donald E. Graves, *All Their Glory Past; Fort Erie, Plattsburgh and the Final Battles in the North* (Montreal: Robin Brass Studio, 2013), 26.

55 Austin (ADC to Brown) to Secretary of War, July 29, 1814, in E.A. Cruikshank, ed., *Documents Relating to the Invasion of the Niagara Peninsula by the United States Army, commanded by General Jacob Brown in July and August 1814* (Niagara-on-

the-Lake, ON: Niagara Historical Society, 1920), 51-52; Brown to Secretary of War, August 5, 1814, in ibid., 55.

56   John R. Grodzinski, "The Vigilant Superintendence of the Whole District: The War of 1812 on the Upper St. Lawrence" (master's thesis, Royal Military College of Canada, 2002), 56.

57   Robert J. Burns, *Fort Wellington: A Narrative and Structural History, 1812-1838* (Ottawa: Parks Canada, 1979), 39; Malcomson, *Lords of the Lake*, 331-332.

58   Baynes to Drummond, June 26, 1814, LAC RG 8 I 3527, vol. 1222, 148; Drummond to Prevost, July 9, 1814, LAC RG 8 I 3174, vol. 684, 48; Drummond to Prevost, July 17, 1814, LAC RG 8 I 3174, vol. 684, 120.

59   Most of these officers continued to hold their commands from 1813, except for Jobling, who might have replaced Hunter, who was promoted to major in June 1814. Unfortunately, few of these appointments can be verified. Douglas Hendry, *British Casualties during the Niagara Campaign of 1814* (Ottawa: Directorate of History, Dept. of Defence, 1992), annex P; Sutherland, *His Majesty's Gentlemen*, 200.

60   Drummond to Prevost, June 23, 1814, LAC RG 8 I 3174, vol. 683, 303-304.

61   E.A. Cruickshank, "Record of Services of Canadian Regiments in the War of 1812: III: The 104th Regiment," Canadian Military Institute, Selected Papers 7 (1895-96): 16; General Monthly Return, Canada, July 25, 1814. TNA WO 17/1518, 111.

62   Duncan Clark Papers, January 29, 1814, LAC MG 19 A39, 184.

63   Elinor Kyte Senior, *From Royal Township to Industrial City: Cornwall 1784–1984* (Belleville, ON: Mika Publishing, 1983), 108, 110.

64   District General Order, Kingston, June 7, 1814, in Duncan Clark Papers, LAC MG 19A39, 243-244; Squires, *104th Regiment of Foot*, 196-240.

65   Harvey to Conran, August 2, 1814, LAC RG 8 I 3174, vol. 685, 32.

66   Ibid., 31-32.

67   Graves, *Merry Hearts*, 183.

68   Tucker to Conran, August 4, 1814, LAC RG 8 I 3174, vol. 685, 34.

69   The four men were Donald Campbell, Peter Chamberlain, Peter Myette, and Louis (Lewis) Norman. Hendry, *British Casualties during the Niagara Campaign of 1814*, annex M; Tucker to Conran, August 4, 1814, LAC RG 8 I 3174, vol. 685, 35; War of 1812 Casualty Database, available online at http://www.1812casualties.org/casualties_database/advanced_search, accessed July 16, 2013.

70   James, *Military Dictionary,* entry for "Fortifications"; David A. Owen, *Historic Fort Erie: An Historical Guide* (Niagara Falls, ON: Niagara Parks Commission, 2001),

3, 6, 8, 10, 50; Graves, *Merry Hearts*, 188; Graves, *Where Right and Glory Lead*, 215; Graves, *All Their Glory Past*, 74.

71   Graves, *All Their Glory Past*, 48.

72   Graves, *Merry Hearts*, 184-185; Hendry, *British Casualties Suffered during the Niagara Campaign of 1814*, annex M; War of 1812 Casualty Database, available online at http://www.1812casualties.org/casualties_database/advanced_search, accessed July 16, 2013.

73   Graves, *Merry Hearts*, 186.

74   The dead included Chandler Copp, Daniel Dillon, and Joseph Dupre. The missing man was James Brown. Hendry, *British Casualties Suffered during the Niagara Campaign of 1814*, annex M.

75   Drummond to Prevost, August 13, 1814, LAC RG 8 I 3174, vol. 685, 108; Malcomson, *Lords of the Lake*, 296-297.

76   Drummond to Prevost, August 15, 1815, LAC RG 8 I 3174, vol. 685, 94.

77   Headquarters Camp Before Fort Erie, August 14, 1814, LAC RG 8 I 3174, vol. 685, 83-84, 90-93.

78   Ibid., 83.

79   Young to Scott, December 20, 1814, LAC MG 24, F 15.

80   William Dunlop, *Tiger Dunlop's Upper Canada* (Ottawa: Carleton University, 1967), 52.

81   Ibid., 51.

82   Drummond to Prevost, August 15, 1814, LAC RG 8 I 3174, vol. 685, 94; Drummond to Prevost, August 16, 1814, LAC RG 8 I 3174, vol. 685, 102; Fisher to Harvey, in Cruikshank, *Documentary History*, vol. 1, 144-145.

83   Drummond to Prevost, August 15, 1814. LAC RG 8 I 3174, vol. 685, 95; Klinck and Talman, *Journal of John Norton*, 349; Graves, *All Their Glory Past*, 87-88.

84   Gaines to the Secretary of War, August 23, 1814, in Cruikshank, *Documentary History*, vol. 1, 153; Drummond to Prevost, August 15, 1814, LAC RG 8 I 3174, vol. 685, 97; Graves, *All Their Glory Past*, 89, 94.

85   Drummond to Prevost, August 15, 1814, LAC RG 8 I 3174, vol. 685, 99; Graves, *All Their Glory Past*, 91; Squires, *104th Regiment of Foot*, 233.

86   Graves, *Merry Hearts*, 188.

87   John Le Couteur to H. Couteur, July 29, 1869, in Cruikshank, *Documentary History*, vol. 1, 168-169; Joseph Whitehorne, *While Washington Burned: The Battle*

for Fort Erie, 1814 (Baltimore: Nautical and Aviation Publishing Company of America, 1992), 59, 63.

88 Graves, "William Drummond and the Battle of Fort Erie," 35.

89 Court-Martial of Brigadier-General E.P. Gaines, United States National Archives, Washington, DC, Record Group 153, Records of the Judge Advocate General, 258.

90 Graves, "William Drummond and the Battle of Fort Erie," 35; Drummond to Prevost, August 15, 1814, RMC CO 42/157, 175-176, 179.

91 Graves, *Merry Hearts*, 188.

92 Ibid., 189.

93 Ibid., 190.

94 Return of Killed, Wounded and Missing of the Right Division, in the Assault on Fort Erie, Drummond to Prevost, August 15, 1814, RMC CO 42/157, 178.

95 Many of those taken prisoner at Fort Erie (and indeed those taken prisoner in the Niagara Peninsula during that summer) — including, for example, Private William Gilfoil — were later moved to a large prisoner cantonment at Pittsfield, Massachusetts; Killed Wounded and Missing of the Right Division at Fort Erie on the Morning of August 15, 1814, Prevost to Bathurst, August 27, 1814, RMC CO 42/167, 182; War of 1812 Casualty Database, available online at http://www.1812casualties.org/casualties_database/advanced_search, accessed July 16, 2013; David F. Hemmings and Joshua J. Lichty, *Captured in the War of 1812: Prisoner of War Camps in America* (Niagara-on-the-Lake, ON: Niagara Historical Society, 2012), 27, 126, 135, 137; Graves, *Merry Hearts*, 191.

96 Dunlop, *Tiger Dunlop's Upper Canada*, 40.

97 Graves, *All Their Glory Past*, 226.

98 Graves, *Merry Hearts*, 194.

99 Ibid.

100 Ibid., 199.

101 Drummond to Prevost, September 24, 1814, LAC RG 8 I 3174, vol. 685, 266-269; District General Order, September 23, 1814, in Cruikshank, *Documentary History*, vol. 1, 227; Glenn A. Steppler, "'A Duty Troublesome Beyond Measure': Logistical Considerations in the Canadian War of 1812" (PhD dissertation, McGill University, August 1974), 191-193.

102 Drummond to Prevost, October 10, 1814, in Cruikshank, *Documentary History*, vol. 2, 241; Lewis Einstein, ed., "Recollections of the War of 1812 by George Hay, Eighth Marquis of Tweeddale," *American Historical Review* 32, no. 1 (1926): 74; Barbuto, *Niagara 1814*, 282, 295.

103 Graves, *Merry Hearts*, 203.

104 Myers to Drummond, October 19, 1814, LAC RG 8 I 3174, vol. 686, 70; Johnston, *Glengarry Light Infantry*, 201; Klinck and Talman, *Journal of John Norton*, 353.

105 Myers to Drummond, October 19, 1814, LAC RG 8 I 3174, vol. 686, 70-71; Graves, *Merry Hearts*, 205.

106 Harvey to Myers, October 18, 1814, in Cruikshank, *Documentary History*, vol. 2, 258; Myers to Drummond, October 19, 1814, LAC RG 8 I 3174, vol. 686, 70-71; Einstein, "Recollections of the Marquis of Tweeddale," 75; Barbuto, *Niagara 1814*, 298; Graves, *Merry Hearts*, 205-206; Johnston, *Glengarry Light Infantry*, 201-202.

107 Cruikshank, *Documentary History*, vol. 2, 260-261; War of 1812 Casualty Database, available online at http://www.1812casualties.org/casualties_database/advanced_search, accessed July 16, 2013.

108 Division General Order, October 22, 1814, LAC RG 8 I 3174, vol. 686, 75.

109 Graves, *Merry Hearts*, 207.

110 Drummond to Prevost, October 20, 1814, LAC RG 8 I 3174, vol. 686, 77.

111 Graves, *Merry Hearts*, 207, 210.

112 General Distribution of the Forces in the Canadas, November 8, 1814, TNA CO 42/157, 336; Hunter to Freer, December 9, 1814, LAC RG 8 I 3255, vol. 789, 147.

113 Squires, *104th Regiment of Foot*, 169.

114 A Return of the Age, Size, Length of Service of the Boys and Lads of the 104th Foot Stationed at Three Rivers and Kingston, February 23, 1814, LAC RG 8 I 3362, vol. 102, 74-75.

115 Graves, *Merry Hearts*, 210.

116 Armstrong to Bradley, September 28, 1814, LAC RG 8 I 2647, vol. 89, 139.

117 Hickey, *Don't Give Up the Ship*, 296; Graves, *Merry Hearts*, 217, 221

Chapter 5

1 Proposed Arrangements for 1815, LAC RG 8 I 3538, vol. 1223, 40; General Order, Quebec, April 24, 1812, LAC RG 8 I 3502, vol. 1168, 129-130.

2 Steppler, "Duty Troublesome Beyond Measure," 141.

3 Report of Board of Officers, February 16, 1815, LAC RG 8 I 2682, vol. 119, 85.

4 Paymaster List, 104th Regiment, January 25-February 24, 1817, LAC RG 8 I 2608, vol. 6, 181-182.

5 Freer to Kirkwood, January 29, 1815, LAC RG 8 I 3527, vol. 1224, 255; Moodie to Foster, May 3, 1815, LAC RG 8 I 3362, vol. 1025, 100, 102; Squires, *104th Regiment of Foot,* 174.

6 Bathurst to Drummond, October 18, 1815, TNA CO 43/23; Fortescue, *History of the British Army,* vol. 10, 228; ibid., vol. 11, 52.

7 Drummond to Bathurst, April 25, 1815, RMC CO 42/192, 49; General Monthly Return, Canada, December 25, 1819, TNA WO 17/1523.

8 Bathurst to Sherbrooke, February 5, 1817, TNA CO 43/23.

9 Fortescue, *History of the British Army,* vol. 4, part 2, 931-934; War Office, *Army List, 1796,* 312-328; S.J. Park and G.F. Nafziger, *The British Military: Its System and Organization, 1803-1815* (Cambridge, ON: RAFM, 1983), 111-117; Estimate Charge of His Majesty's Land Forces, December 25, 1815-December 24, 1815, *Journal of the House of Commons, Session 1814-1815,* 70 (London: 1814): 518; Fortescue, *History of the British Army,* vol. 4, part 2, 938; Bartlett, "Development of the British Army," 105; Roger Morriss, *The Foundations of British Maritime Supremacy: Resources, Logistics and the State, 1755-1815* (Cambridge: Cambridge University Press, 2011), table 2.3.

10 Downes to Lisle, February 8, 1815, LAC RG 8 I 3364, vol. 1035, 198, 200-201.

11 Horse Guards to Sherbrooke, January 23, 1817, LAC RG 8 I 3362, vol. 1026, 82.

12 General Order, Quebec, April 19, 1817, LAC RG 8 I 3504, vol. 1177, 11-18.

13 Six of the regiment's officers currently in England would be placed on half-pay, a form of compensation, as their services were no longer required. General Order, Quebec, May 17, 1817, LAC RG 8 I 3504, vol. 1177, 49-50; Sutherland, *His Majesty's Gentlemen,* 9.

14 Proceedings of a Court of Inquiry, May 8, 1817, LAC RG 8 I 3362, vol. 1027, 45-47.

15 McBean to Harvey, May 31, 1817, LAC RG 8 I 3362, vol. 1027, 48.

16 Dallison, *Neighbourly War,* 130-131, 133; General Order, June 21, 1817, LAC RG 8 I 3504, vol. 1177, 94-95; Sutherland, *His Majesty's Gentlemen,* 110-111; Squires, *104th Regiment of Foot,* 180.

17 List of Invalids, August 21, 1817, LAC RG 8 I 2780, vol. 187, 141; *General Regulations and Orders for the Army, 1811,* 219-220.

18 These honours and their dates include: Detroit (August 16, 1812), Queenstown (October 13, 1812), Miami (April 23, 1813), Niagara (July 25, 1814), and Bladensburg (August 24, 1814).

19 This Battle Honour acknowledged two actions, the capture of Fort Niagara in

December 1813 and the Battle of Lundy's Lane. *London Gazette,* May 27, 1815, issue 17016, 993.

20 *London Gazette,* November 4, 1815, issue 17076, 1; Dunbar and Harper, *Old Colours Never Die,* 30; Alexander Roger, *Battle Honours of the British Empire and Commonwealth Land Forces, 1662-1991* (Ramsbury, UK: Crowood Press, 2003), 33; C.B. Norman, *Battle Honours of the British Army* (London: John Murray, 1911), 45.

21 The source for the casualty figures is the War of 1812 Casualty Database, available online at http://www.1812casualties.org/casualties_database/advanced_search?regiment=104th%20%28New%20Brunswick%29%20Regiment%20of%20Foot&sort=asc&order=Date%20Of%20Death, accessed July 4, 2013.

22 "The Soldier Cut Down in His Prime" is but one version of a traditional tune with variants including different words and titles, such as "The Trooper Cut Down in His Prime" and "The Sailor Cut Down in His Prime."

Appendix Two

1 HRH The Duke of York to Prevost, October 12, 1812, LAC RG 8 I 3172, vol. 677, 132.

2 Ibid., 132-133.

3 Ibid., 133.

4 Ibid., 134; MacArthur, "British Army Establishments during the Napoleonic Wars: Part I," 166.

5 Saumarez to Sherbrooke, October 25, 1813, RG 8 I 3241, vol. 719, 45.

6 Sutherland, *His Majesty's Gentlemen,* 107, 219, 393.

7 Saumarez to Sherbrooke, October 25, 1813, RG 8 I 3241, vol. 719, 40-46.

8 Ibid., 41.

9 Dallison, *Neighbourly War,* 75.

10 Inspection Report, New Brunswick Regiment of Fencible Infantry, May 29, 1815, TNA WO 27/133.

11 Dallison, *Neighbourly War,* 109, 127; Inspection Report, New Brunswick Regiment of Fencible Infantry, May 29, 1815, TNA WO 27/133.

Appendix Three

1 Campbell, "March of the 104th Regiment of Foot," 30.

2   George F.G. Stanley, *Toil & Trouble: Military Expeditions to Red River* (Toronto: Dundurn Press, 1989), 245, 255.

3   Ibid., 39-41.

4   Malcomson, *Lords of the Lake*, 232-233, 240-241; "The Extraordinary March of Lieutenant Henry Kent, from St. John's, New Brunswick to Kingston, Upper Canada," Naval Chronicle 33 (January-July 1815): 123-128.

5   Brereton Greenhous, ed., *Guarding the Goldfields: The Story of the Yukon Field Force* (Toronto: Dundurn Press, 1987), 31-32.

6   Playfair, "Comparison," 2.

7   Ibid., 4.

8   Ibid.

Selected Bibliography

Manuscript Sources

Colonial Office 42, Secretary of State Correspondence, In-Letters, 1807 to 1815.

Colonial Office 43, vol. 22, Letters from Secretary of State, Lower Canada, September 3, 1801-September 16, 1811.

Colonial Office 43, vol. 23, Letters from Secretary of State, Lower Canada, October 22, 1811-March 16, 1816.

Library and Archives Canada, Ottawa.

Massey Library, Royal Military College of Canada, Kingston, Ontario.

National Archives, London.

Record Group 8 C Series, British Military Records, 1811-1815.

Record Group 9, Pre-Confederation Militia Records, 1811-1815.

Record Group 45, Captain's Letters to the Secretary of the Navy, 1813.

United States National Archives, Washington, DC.

War Office 6, vol. 2, Out Letters of the Secretary of State for War and Secretary of State for War and the Colonies, 1793-1859.

War Office 17/1516-1519, Office of the Commander in Chief: Monthly Returns to the Adjutant General Canada, January 1812-December 1815.

War Office 17/2259-2263, Office of the Commander in Chief: Monthly Returns to the Adjutant General Nova Scotia, January 1812-December 1815.

Published Manuscript Sources and Period Works

Adjutant General's Office. *General Regulations and Orders for the Army, 1811*. London: Horse Guards, 1811.

American State Papers, Military Affairs, vol. 1. Washington, DC: Gales and Seaton, 1832

Anonymous. *A Treatise on the British Drill and the Exercise of the Company*. London: W. Clowes, 1814.

Boyd, John Parker. *Documents and Facts Relative to Military Events During the Late War*. No publisher, 1816.

Crawford, Michael J., ed. *The Naval War of 1812: A Documentary History*, vol. 3. Washington, DC: Naval Historical Center, 2002.

Cruikshank, E.A., ed. *Documentary History of the Campaigns upon the Niagara Frontier in 1812 to 1814*. 9 v. Welland, ON, 1896-1908.

———. *Documents Relating to the Invasion of the Niagara Peninsula by the United States Army, commanded by General Jacob Brown in July and August 1814*. Niagara-on-the-Lake, ON: Niagara Historical Society, 1920.

Dudley, William S., ed. *The Naval War of 1812: A Documentary History*, vol. 2. Washington, DC: Naval History Center, 1992.

Dupin, Charles. *A Tour Through the Naval and Military Establishments of Great Britain: In the Years 1816-1820*. London: Sir Richard Phillips and Company, 1822.

James, Charles. *Military Dictionary or Alphabetical Explanation of Technical Terms*. London: T. Egerton, 1802.

Preston, Richard A., ed. *Kingston before the War of 1812*. Toronto: Champlain Society, 1959.

United Kingdom. Army. Horse Guards. *General Orders and Regulations for the Army, 1811*. London: W. Clowes, 1811.

———. Parliament. *Journal of the House of Commons, From November 4th, 1813 to November 1st, 1814*. London: House of Commons, 1814.

———. Secretary of War. *Collection of Orders, Regulations and Instructions for the Army; On Matters of Finance and Points of Discipline*. London: T. Egerton, 1807.

———. War Office. *Army List, 1814*. London, 1814.

Wood, William, ed. *Select British Documents of the Canadian War of 1812*. 4 vols. Toronto: Champlain Society, 1920-1928.

Newspapers and Periodicals

British Standard, 1862.

Edinburgh Annual Register, various.

Kingston Gazette, 1813, 1814.

London Gazette, various.

Naval Chronicle, 1815.

Gentleman's Magazine, vol. 27 (new series), January-June 1847.

Published Personal Accounts, Diaries, Journals, and Correspondence

Andrès, Bernard. *La guerre de 1812: Journal de Jacques Viger.* Québec: Presses de l'Université Laval, 2012.

Dunlop, William. *Tiger Dunlop's Upper Canada.* Ottawa: Carleton University, 1967.

Einstein, Lewis, ed. "Recollections of the War of 1812 by George Hay, Eight Marquis of Tweeddale." *American Historical Review* 32, no. 1 (1926): 69-78.

Graves, Donald E., ed. *Merry Hearts Make Light Days: The War of 1812 Journal of Lieutenant General John le Couteur, 104th Foot.* Montreal: Robin Brass Studio, 2012.

Klinck, Carl F., and James J. Talman, eds. *The Journal of Major John Norton, 1816.* Toronto: Champlain Society, 2011.

Sutherland, Stuart, ed. *"A Desire of Serving and Defending My Country": The War of 1812 Journals of William Hamilton Merritt.* Toronto: ISER Publications, 2001.

Temperley, Howard, ed. *Gubbins' New Brunswick Journals, 1811 & 1813.* Fredericton, NB: King's Landing Corporation, 1980.

Tupper, Ferdinand Brock, ed. *The Life and Correspondence of Major General Sir Isaac Brock.* London: Simpkin, Marshall, 1845.

Viger, Jacques. "Reminiscences of the War of 1812-1814." Kingston, ON: News Printing Company, 1895.

Unpublished Works

Campbell, W.E. "The March of the 104th (New Brunswick) Regiment of Foot." St. John River Society, June 21, 2011.

Graves, Donald E. "The Attack on Sackets Harbor, 29 May 1813: The British/Canadian Side." Ottawa, Directorate of History, c. 1991.

Grodzinski, John R. "The Vigilant Superintendence of the Whole District: The War of 1812 on the Upper St. Lawrence." Master's thesis, Royal Military College of Canada, 2002.

Linch, Kevin. "The Recruitment of the British Army, 1807-1815." PhD diss., University of Leeds, 2001.

McCredy, Stephen D. "Some Military Aspects of Kingston's Development during the War of 1812." Master's thesis, Queen's University, 1982.

Steppler, Glenn A. "A Duty Troublesome Beyond Measure: Logistical Considerations in the Canadian War of 1812." Master's thesis, McGill University, 1974.

Wilder, Patrick. "We Will Not Conquer Canada This Year: The Battle of Sackets Harbor, 1813." [n.d.].

Articles and Biographical Entries

Chartrand, René. "The British Army's Unknown, Regular, African-West Indian Engineer and Service Corps, 1783 to the 1840s." *Journal for the Society for Army Historical Research* 89, no. 358 (2011): 117-138.

Cruickshank, E.A. "Record of Services of Canadian Regiments in the War of 1812: III: The 104th Regiment," *Canadian Military Institute, Selected Papers* 7 (1895-96): 9-20.

Graham, Gerald S. "Views of General Murray on the Defence of Upper Canada, 1815." *Canadian Historical Review* 34, no. 2 (1953): 158-165.

Graves, Donald E. "The Redcoats Are Coming! British Troop Movements to North America in 1814." *Journal of the War of 1812* 6, no. 3 (2001): 12-18.

———. "William Drummond and the Battle of Fort Erie." *Canadian Military History* 1, no. 1 (1992): 25-43.

Hughes, Alun. "Following in Laura's Footsteps." *Newsletter of the Historical Society of St. Catherines* (December 2012): 1-10.

MacArthur, Roderick. "The British Army Establishments during the Napoleonic Wars: Part 1, Background and Infantry." *Journal of the Society for Army Historical Research* 87, no. 351 (2009): 150-172.

Playfair, A.W. "Comparison between the March of the 43rd Light Infantry in 1837 and that of the Late 104th Regiment in 1813, from New Brunswick to Quebec." *British Standard*, January 20, 1862.

Books

Bailey, De Wit. *Small Arms of the British Forces in America, 1664-1815*. Woonsocket, RI: Mowbray, 2009.

Bamford, Andrew. *Sickness, Suffering, and the Sword: The British Regiment on Campaign, 1808-1815*. Norman: University of Oklahoma Press, 2013.

Barbuto, Richard V. *Niagara 1814: America invades Canada*. Lawrence: University of Kansas Press, 2000.

Benn, Carl. *Historic Fort York, 1793-1993*. Toronto: Natural Heritage, 1993.

———. *The Iroquois in the War of 1812*. Toronto: University of Toronto Press, 1998.

Blackmore, Howard. *British Military Firearms, 1650-1850*. London: Greenhill Books, 1994.

Bowering, M. Ian. *A Study of the Utilization of Artillery on the Niagara Frontier*. 2 vols. Manuscript Report 446. Ottawa: Parks Canada, 1979.

Burgoyne, Roderick Hamilton. *Historical Records of the 93rd Sutherland Regiment*. London: Richard Bentley and Son, 1883.

Burnham, Robert, and Ron McGuigan. *The British Army against Napoleon: Facts, Lists and Trivia, 1805-1815*. Barnsley: Frontline Books, 2010.

Burns, Robert J. *Fort Wellington: A Narrative and Structural History, 1812-1838*. Ottawa: Parks Canada, 1979.

Carter-Edwards, Dennis. *At Work and Play: The British Junior Officer in Upper Canada, 1796-1812*. Ottawa: Parks Canada, 1985.

Chartrand, René. *British Forces in North America, 1793-1815*. London: Osprey Publishing, 1993.

———. *A Most Warlike Appearance: Uniforms. Flags and Equipment of the United States Forces in the War of 1812*. Ottawa: Service Publications, 2011.

———. *A Scarlet Coat: Uniforms, Flags and Equipment of the British in the War of 1812*. Ottawa: Service Publications, 2011.

Cruikshank, E.A. *Blockade of Fort George, 1813*. Welland, ON: Niagara Historical Society, 1898.

———. *Fight in the Beechwoods: A Study in Canadian History*. Welland, ON: W.T. Swayle, 1895.

Dallison, Robert L. *A Neighbourly War: New Brunswick and the War of 1812*. Fredericton, NB: Goose Lane Editions and the New Brunswick Military Heritage Project, 2012.

Dunbar, Francis J., and Joseph H. Harper. *Old Colours Never Die: A Record of Colours and Military Flags in Canada*. Oakville, ON: F.J. Dunbar & Associates, 1992.

Dunnigan, Brian Leigh. *Forts within a Fort: Niagara's Redoubts*. Youngstown, NY: Old Fort Niagara Association, 1989.

Facey-Crowther, David. *The New Brunswick Militia, 1787-1867*. Fredericton, NB: New Brunswick Historical Society, 1990.

Fortescue, John. *A History of the British Army*. 19 v. London: Macmillan, 1899-1930.

Fredricksen, John C. *Green Coats and Glory: The United States Regiment of Riflemen, 1808-1821*. Youngstown, NY: Old Fort Niagara Association, 2000.

Graves, Donald E. *All Their Glory Past: Fort Erie, Plattsburgh and the Final Battles in the North*. Montreal: Robin Brass Studio, 2013.

————. *Where Right and Glory Lead: The Battle of Lundy's Lane, 25 July 1814*. Toronto: Robin Brass Studio, 1997.

Greenhous, Brereton, ed. *Guarding the Goldfields: The Story of the Yukon Field Force*. Toronto: Dundurn Press, 1987.

Grodzinski, John R. *Defender of Canada: Sir George Prevost and the War of 1812*. Norman: University of Oklahoma Press, 2013.

Guy, Alan J. *Oeconomy and Discipline: Officership and Administration in the British Army, 1714-1763*. Manchester, UK: Manchester University Press, 1985.

Hall, Christopher D. *British Strategy in the Napoleonic Wars, 1803-1815*. Manchester, UK: Manchester University Press, 1999.

Hannay, James. *A History of New Brunswick*, vol. I. Saint John, NB: John A. Bowes, 1909.

Hemmings, David F., and Joshua J. Lichty. *Captured in the War of 1812: Prisoner of War Camps in America*. Niagara-on-the-Lake, ON: Niagara Historical Society, 2012.

Hendry, Douglas L. *British Casualties during the Niagara Campaign of 1814*. Ottawa: Directorate of History, Dept. of National Defence, 1992.

————. *British Casualties Suffered at Several Actions during the War of 1812: Queenston Heights, Sacket's Harbor, Stoney Creek, Oswego, Bladensburg, Baltimore*. Ottawa: Directorate of History, Dept. of National Defence, 1994.

Hickey, Donald R. *Don't Give Up the Ship! Myths of the War of 1812*. Toronto: Robin Brass Studio, 2006.

Hitsman, J. Mackay. *The Incredible War of 1812: A Military History*. Updated by Donald E. Graves. Toronto: Robin Brass Studio, 1999.

————. *Safeguarding Canada: 1763-1871*. Toronto: University of Toronto Press, 1968.

Horn, Bern, ed. *The Canadian Way of War: Serving the National Interest*. Toronto: Dundurn Press, 2006.

Howard, Martin. *Wellington's Doctors: The British Army Medical Services in the Napoleonic Wars*. Staplehurst, UK: Spellmount, 2002.

Johnston, Winston. *The Glengarry Light Infantry, 1812-1816*. Charlottetown, PEI, 2011.

Malcomson, Robert. *Capital in Flames: The American Attack on York, 1813*. Montreal: Robin Brass Studio, 2008.

———. *Lords of the Lake: The Naval War on Lake Ontario, 1812-1814*. Toronto: Robin Brass Studio, 1998.

———. *A Very Brilliant Affair: The Battle of Queenston Heights, 1812*. Toronto: Robin Brass Studio, 2006.

———. *Warships on the Great Lakes, 1754-1834*. Annapolis, MD: Naval Institute Press, 2001.

Malcomson, Thomas, and Robert Malcomson. *The Battle for Lake Erie*. St. Catharines, ON: Vanwell Publishing, 1990.

Morriss, Roger. *The Foundations of British Maritime Ascendency: Resources, Logistics and the State, 1755-1815*. Cambridge: Cambridge University Press, 2011.

Muir, Rory. *Britain and the Defeat of Napoleon, 1807-1815*. New Haven, CT: Yale University Press, 2006.

Owen, David A. *Historic Fort Erie: An Historical Guide*. Niagara Fall, ON: Niagara Parks Commission, 2001.

Park, S.J., and G.F. Nafziger. *The British Military: Its System and Organization, 1803-1815*. Cambridge, ON: RAFM, 1983.

Roger, Alexander. *Battle Honours of the British Empire and Commonwealth Land Forces, 1662-1991*. Ramsbury, UK: Crowood Press, 2003.

Senior, Elinor Kyte. *From Royal Township to Industrial City: Cornwall 1784–1984*. Belleville, ON: Mika Publishing, 1983.

Smythies, R.H. Raymond. *Historical Records of the 40th (2nd Somersetshire) Regiment*. Devonport, UK: A.H. Swiss, 1894.

Squires, W. Austin. *The 104th Regiment of Foot (New Brunswick Regiment), 1803-1817*. Fredericton, NB: Brunswick Press, 1962.

Stagg, J.C.A. *Mr. Madison's War*. Princeton, NJ: Princeton University Press, 1983.

Stanley, George F.G. *Toil & Trouble: Military Expeditions to Red River*. Toronto: Dundurn Press, 1989.

Sutherland, Stuart. *His Majesty's Gentlemen: A Directory of British Regular Army Officers in the War of 1812*. Toronto: ISER Publications, 2001.

Swindon, Arthur, ed. *A Register of the Corps and Regiments of the British Army*. London: Archives Press, 1972.

Whitehorne, Joseph. *While Washington Burned: The Battle for Fort Erie, 1814*. Baltimore, MD: Nautical and Aviation Publishing Company of America, 1992.

Wilder, Patrick A. *The Battle of Sackett's Harbour, 1813*. Baltimore, MD: Nautical and Aviation Publishing Company of America, 1994.

Winfield, Rif. *British Warships in the Age of Sale: Design, Construction, Careers and Fates*. London: Chatham Publishing, 2005.

Photo Credits

The painting on the front cover, *The Battle of Lundy's Lane*, appears courtesy of *Harper's Weekly*. The painting on page 10 appears courtesy of Don Troiani. The painting on page 23 appears courtesy of Martin Bates and the New Brunswick Museum (X15 765 (2)). The photos on pages 27 (1969.2547.1) and 49 appear courtesy of the Fredericton Region Museum. The photos on pages 33 (R2009.1), 142 (33 485-2), and 143 (1944-335 (1)), and the painting on page 50 (W6798) appear courtesy of the New Brunswick Museum. The maps on pages 43, 46, 58, 69, 82, 85, 94, 108, 119, 121, and 131 appear courtesy of Mike Bechthold. The paintings on pages 45 (C-122463), 63 (C6147), 91 and the back cover (C-000026), and 111 (C000407) appear courtesy of Library and Archives Canada (LAC). The drawing on page 48 and the illustration on page 52 appear courtesy of the St. John River Society. The map on page 59 appears courtesy of Musée de la civilisation, Quebec City. The photos on pages 60, 72, 76, 125, 126, 129 and 162 appear courtesy of the author. The photo on page 133 appears courtesy of Donald E. Graves. The photo on page 146 appears courtesy of Brent Wilson. All illustrative material is reproduced by permission

Index

A

American Revolutionary War 13, 18,
  20, 21, 23, 40, 57, 91, 155
Amherstburg 92
Australia 92
Avery, Colour Sergeant Benoni 180

B

Balls Falls 82
Baltimore 134
Barclay, Commander Robert 92, 160
Barney, Captain William 122, 124
bateaux 63, 68, 69, 71, 75, 78-81, 96, 97,
  103, 115, 116, 137, 138, 143
Battersby, Lieutenant-Colonel Francis
  88, 93
Battle Honours 11, 15, 144, 189
battles
  Beaver Dams 85, 87, 161
  Black Rock 117
  Châteauguay 76, 176
  Chippawa 104, 133
  Cook's Mills 11, 131, 132, 133, 145,
    161
  Crysler's Farm 76, 98, 176
  Fort Erie 118-129, 145, 161
  Lundy's Lane 11, 67, 91, 107-112,
    144, 145, 161, 190
  New Orleans 136
  Ogdensburg 169
  Queenston Heights 24, 67, 76, 84,
    88, 176
  Sackets Harbor 69-75, 145, 161, 162
  Stoney Creek 76, 83, 176
  York 76

Bay Bulls 19
Bay of Fundy 19, 42, 161
Bay of Quinte 63, 79
Baynes, Colonel Edward 37, 38, 64, 66,
  69, 72-74, 138
Beach, Elijah 175
Beaver Dams 83, 85, 87, 88, 100, 107
Beresford 73, 75
Bermuda 17, 149
Besserer, Lieutenant René-Léonard 26,
  129
Bissell, Brigadier-General Daniel 130,
  132
Bisshopp, Lieutenant-Colonel Cecil
  82, 83, 86
Black Rock 89, 116-118
Black Snake 78, 115
Blanchard, Private Joseph 113
Boerstler, Lieutenant-Colonel Charles
  84-86
Bombard, Private James 92
Bonaparte, Napoleon 21, 30, 102, 159
Bourgignon, Private Jean Baptiste 113
Boyd, Brigadier-General John Parker
  84, 89, 90
Bradley, Captain William 44, 45, 67,
  115, 136
Britain. *See* United Kingdom
British Army 9, 13-15, 27, 36, 37, 90,
  139, 149
  Royal Engineers 120
British Army, Artillery
  Royal Artillery 41, 53, 79, 122, 126,
    181

British Army, Cavalry
  1st Dragoon Guards 22
  19th Light Dragoons 83, 130, 139,
    181
British Army, Fencible Regiments
  Canadian Fencibles 22, 78, 83, 139,
    181
  Glengarry Light Infantry Fencibles
    24, 35, 38, 72, 78, 79, 88, 90, 104,
    109, 111, 116, 130, 131, 132, 139
  Island of St. John's Volunteers 20
  King's New Brunswick Regiment
    14, 17, 20, 21, 23, 27
  New Brunswick Fencible Infantry
    13, 14, 22-29, 31-34, 36, 39, 40, 46,
    49, 55, 95, 99, 124, 142, 143, 166,
    168, 173, 181. *See* British Army,
    Infantry, 104th Regiment of Foot
  Grenadier Company 22
  Light Company 22
  No. 1 Company 28
  No. 4 Company 28
  New Brunswick Regiment of
    Fencible Infantry 14, 24, 40, 99,
    138, 155, 157, 166
  Nova Scotia Fencibles 22, 38, 138
  Prince Edward Island Fencibles 20
  Queen's Rangers 20
  Royal Canadian Volunteers 20
  Royal Newfoundland Fencibles 22,
    72
  Sutherland Fencibles 34
British Army, Infantry
  1st Regiment of Foot 53, 71, 72, 79,
    88, 92, 93, 105-107, 109, 113, 122,
    127
  2nd Bengal Fusiliers. *See* British
    Army, Infantry, 104th Bengal
    Fusiliers
  6th Regiment of Foot 20, 104, 160
  6th West India Regiment 40

7th Regiment of Foot 30, 143
8th Regiment of Foot 40, 45, 71-75,
  78, 81, 83, 85, 86, 88, 90, 93, 106,
  112, 123, 134, 155, 160
  1st Battalion 134
  2nd Battalion 45
9th Garrison Battalion 32
10th Royal Veteran Battalion 56,
  116, 135
11th West India Regiment 28
23rd Regiment of Foot 30, 34
24th Regiment of Foot 33
29th Regiment of Foot 27
37th Regiment of Foot 25
38th Regiment of Foot 40
40th Regiment of Foot 28
41st Regiment of Foot 67, 80, 105,
  114, 117, 122, 126, 181
  2nd Battalion 181
43rd Light Infantry 161
43rd Regiment of Foot 28
46th Regiment of Foot 28
49th Regiment of Foot 36, 38, 61, 78,
  83, 85, 90, 93, 96, 97, 181
60th Regiment of Foot 25, 26, 34
67th Regiment of Foot 184
82nd Regiment of Foot 131, 132, 172
89th Regiment of Foot 103-105, 110,
  114, 117, 122, 123, 130, 181
  2nd Battalion 181
93rd Regiment of Foot 34
99th Regiment of Foot 141
100th Regiment of Foot 71-73, 78,
  88, 114, 117, 130, 131, 132
101st Regiment of Foot 30, 39, 155
101st Regiment of Foot (Royal
  Bengal Fusiliers) 13
102nd Regiment of Foot 32
103rd Regiment of Foot 32, 107, 109,
  111, 121, 122, 127

104th (King's Volunteers) Regiment
13
104th (New Brunswick) Regiment of
Foot 9-11, 13-17, 23-25, 29, 31-49,
51-56, 58, 59, 62-67, 71-73, 75-93,
95-99, 101-106, 109-118, 120, 122,
124, 125, 128, 129-146, 149, 150,
152, 155, 159, 160, 161, 172, 175,
180, 181
No. 1 Company 44, 55
No. 2 (Light) Company 10, 15, 44,
46, 67, 84, 112, 117, 128, 129,
132, 133, 145
No. 3 Company 44, 45, 66, 115
No. 4 Company 44, 55
No. 5 Company 44, 46, 115
No. 6 Company 44, 45, 67, 115
No. 7 Company 44, 55, 115
No. 8 Company 44, 45, 68, 115
No. 9 (Grenadier) Company 15,
44, 45, 63, 67, 112, 117, 120,
128, 129, 133, 145
No. 10 Company 44, 55, 115
104th Regiment of Foot (Bengal
Fusiliers) 13
104th (Royal Manchester Volunteers)
Regiment 13
Army of Upper Canada
Right Division 15, 92, 101, 104,
106, 111-114, 116, 118, 120,
128-130, 133
Cape Regiment 28
King's German Legion 37
New South Wales Corps 32
Nova Scotia Regiment 18
Regiment de Watteville 104, 123, 181
Royal African Corps 34
Royal African Rifles 168
Royal Munster Fusiliers 13
British Army, Lower Canadian
Provincial Units

Voltigeurs Canadiens 34, 38, 59, 63,
72, 73, 78, 93, 96, 97, 115, 181
British Army, Loyalist Units, American
Revolutionary War
Loyal American Regiment 21
Royal Fencible Americans 23
British Army, Militias
2nd Militia Brigade 107
4th Battalion Select Embodied
Militia 138
British Army, Provincial Forces
Commissariat Voyageurs 138
Incorporated Militia of Upper
Canada 104
Provincial Light Dragoons 83, 96,
106
Royal Newfoundland Regiment 20
Royal Nova Scotia Regiment 20
British North America 9, 14, 15, 17-22,
25, 26, 29, 30, 37, 38, 43, 62, 68,
90, 91, 138-140, 145, 149, 155,
160, 161
Brock, Major-General Isaac 67
Brown, Major-General Jacob 103, 104,
105, 110, 112, 114
Brown, James 186
Buffalo 88, 89, 103, 105, 116, 118, 120,
134
Burlington Bay 75, 78, 79, 96, 104
Burlington Heights 65, 77, 78, 80-82,
87, 89, 95-97

C

Campbell, Lieutenant Alexander 116
Campbell, Donald 185
Campbell, Captain Dugald 26
Canada Command 149
Canadian Army 11, 15
Canadian Army, Infantry
Royal New Brunswick Regiment 11
Canadian Pacific Railway 160

Cape Vincent 115
Carleton, Governor Thomas 19, 20, 21
Carleton Heights 41
Carter, Lieutenant Thomas 132
Cascades 138
Cataraqui 135. *See* Kingston
Cataraqui River 63
Chamberlain, Peter 185
Chambers, Captain Peter 80
Charlottetown 28, 44
Chase, Sergeant Thomas 90
Châteauguay River 97
Chauncey, Commodore Isaac 61, 66, 74, 75, 77, 80, 89, 95, 105, 113, 128
Chauncey, Lieutenant Wolcott 74
Chesapeake, USS 29
Chippawa 77, 89, 104-106, 109, 114, 130, 133
Chippawa River 107, 130, 131
Christian, Captain Thomas 26
Church, Private Isaac 132
Coffin, Lieutenant-General John 155
Coldstream, Scotland 143
Collingwood 160
Colony of Newfoundland 15, 17, 19, 25, 36, 138, 149
Conjocta Creek 117, 145
Cook's Mills 130, 131, 132, 133
Cooper, Captain Henry 155
Copp, Chandler 186
Cornwall 98, 102, 114-116, 161
Coteau-du-Lac 54, 64, 138
Craig, Lieutenant-General Sir James 26, 29-31, 62
Croad, Lieutenant George 143

D

Darroch, Brigadier-General Duncan 98
De Haren, Major Peter V. 83, 85, 86

de Hautefeuile, *see* von Gerau de Hautefeuile
de Rottenburg, Major-General Sir Francis 64, 65, 87-90, 92, 93, 96, 97
de Salaberry, Lieutenant-Colonel Charles 97
Dearborn, Major-General Henry 62, 80, 81, 84, 88, 89
DeLancey, Lieutenant James 71, 75
Detroit 61, 78, 92, 101
Dillon, Daniel 186
Dobbs, Commander Alexander 120, 122
Drayton, Private William 80
Drummond, Lieutenant-General Sir Gordon 62, 68, 97, 101-107, 109, 111-113, 116, 118, 122, 123, 127, 128, 130, 134, 139, 181
Drummond, Lieutenant-Colonel William 34, 35, 41, 54, 63, 65, 66, 69, 71, 72, 74, 75, 79, 88, 97-99, 101-106, 108, 110-112, 114, 115, 117, 118, 120-126, 128, 131, 134, 146, 168, 181, 183
Drummond Island 138
Ducharme, Captain François 84, 85
Dundas, Henry 20
Dunlop, Surgeon William 101, 123, 128
Dupre, Joseph 186
Durham boats 137
Dysart, Premier Allison 144

E

Earle, Charles 24
Eight Mile Creek 96
Emerson, Thomas 23
England. *See* United Kingdom
English, Private John 80
Evans, Major Thomas 74, 107

Evans, Lieutenant-Colonel William 117

F

Fair American 74
Fayette, Private John B. 113
First Nations 17, 18, 45, 61, 63, 66, 73, 81, 83-85, 87, 90, 93, 95, 105, 106, 111, 116, 120, 124, 160, 176, 183
Caughnawaga 83
Kahnawake 83
Oneida 90
Seven Nations 83, 84, 86
Fischer, Lieutenant-Colonel Victor 122-124
Fitzgibbon, Lieutenant James 83-86
Fort Covington. *See* French Mills
forts
Alexander 160
Cumberland 42
Drummond 41
Erie 11, 77, 103, 104, 114, 116, 118, 119-122, 129, 130, 134, 145, 146, 187
George 11, 60-62, 65-67, 77-79, 81-84, 86-89, 91-96, 100, 101, 104-106, 113, 133, 134, 143-145, 161
Mackinac 134
Niagara 78, 89, 95, 104-106, 189
Schlosser 78, 89, 107
Tompkins 70, 71, 73, 74
Volunteer 70, 74
Wellington 102, 103, 115, 116
York 61, 62, 160
Forty, The 81-83
Forty Mile Creek 81
Four Mile Creek 88, 90, 93, 96
France 13, 18, 19, 30, 31, 144
Fredericton 9, 20, 21, 26, 28, 40, 43-45, 47, 48, 51, 52, 54, 55, 99, 143, 146, 157, 159, 161, 169

Freer, Noah 99
French Mills 98
Frenchman's Creek 130
Fulton, Major James 92

G

Gananoque 80, 81, 89, 98, 114, 115, 161
Garths, Private William 95
General Pike 66
George III, King 102
George IV, King 61, 136, 140, 144, 155, 174
Georgian Bay 160
Gerau, *see* von Gerau de Hautefeuile
Ghent 134, 137
Gilfoil, Private William 187
Gilpin, William 35, 36, 38
Glew, Captain Joseph 126
Gordon, Lieutenant-Colonel 122
Gower, Governor Vice-Admiral Sir Erasmus 25
Grand Communications Route 41
Grand Falls 51
Grand Portage Route 54
Grant, Henry 24
Grant, Private Henry 46
Gray, Captain Andrew 68, 74
Great Lakes 14, 57, 65, 103
Greenwood, Cox and Company 36
Grimsby. *See* Forty, The

H

Halifax 28-30, 41, 45, 55, 56, 160
Halkett, Major-Colonel Alexander 34, 44, 45, 47, 54, 57, 63-67, 174
Hamilton, Lieutenant-Colonel Christopher 107
Hampton, Major-General Wade 97
Harmony 143
Harvey, Lieutenant-Colonel John 81

Haynes, Sergeant Major Joseph 143
Head of the Lake 78
Heriot, Major Frederick 73, 93
Hinckes, Sergeant James 28
Holland, Captain Edward 28, 35, 44, 46, 47, 54, 67, 68, 115
Holmes, Private Moses 113
Horse Guards 27, 31, 36-38, 53, 140, 149
Horse Island 70-72
Hudson's Bay Company 17
Hull, Captain Abraham 113
Hunter, Major-General Martin 22, 23, 26, 28, 29, 31, 35, 37, 38, 40, 42, 44, 45, 67, 68, 115, 134, 143, 185
Hunter, Lieutenant-General Peter 26
Hunter, Captain Thomas 42

I

Île-aux-Noix 138
Indian Department 83, 84
Ireland 15, 20, 25, 32, 34, 36, 37, 41, 138, 145
Irvine, Callender 42
Izard, Major-General George 130

J

Jackson, Private William 92
Jamaica 30
Jay, John 18
Jay's Treaty 18
Jenkins, Lieutenant John 35, 169
Jobling, Lieutenant George 35, 73, 115, 129, 185
Johnston, Lieutenant-Colonel George 27, 31

K

Kane, Private Henry 80
Kelly, Lieutenant Waldron 129
Kingsclear 169

King's Colour 28, 29
Kingston 9, 11, 14, 15, 26, 47-49, 54-69, 73, 74, 76-82, 86, 87, 89, 96-98, 100-105, 114-116, 134-137, 142, 144, 146, 159-161, 180
Kingston Gazette 87
Kirkwood, Major Tobias 155

L

Lachine 138
Lacolle 138
Lady Murray 80
Lady of the Lake 80
Lahore, Corporal Charles 132
Lake Erie 61, 77, 78, 92, 118, 120
Lake Huron 61
Lake Ontario 57, 60, 61, 66, 75, 77, 78, 82-84, 87, 89, 95, 103-105, 113, 137, 144
Lake Washademoak 42
Lake Winnipeg 160
Lammy, Private William 54
Larencell, Private Joseph 80
Le Couteur, Lieutenant John 33, 57, 60, 64, 67, 73, 75, 85, 86, 90, 93, 102, 110, 113, 117, 118, 120, 124, 127, 128, 131, 135, 180
Lee, Private Daniel 92
Lemery, Sergeant Alexis 142
Leonard, Major Richard 44, 45, 65, 67, 71, 75, 81, 104, 106, 109, 110, 113, 120, 127, 128
Leonard, Lieutenant Thomas 129
Leopard, HMS 29
Lindsay, Private William 132
Lock, Private Ednor 113
Lock, Private Lewis 99
London 26, 27, 31, 36, 42, 138, 139
London Gazette 144
Longwoods 101
Lorimer, Captain Robert Roberts 61, 62

Loring, Captain Robert 113
Loyalists 18
Lyon's Creek 130, 131

M

Macaulay, Dr. 81
Macintosh, David 135
Mackinac 61
Mackonochie, Captain James 107
MacLaren, Lieutenant Governor
  Murray 144
Maclauchlan, Major 127
Macomb, Colonel Alexander 70
Macon's Bill No. 2 30
Madawaska River 47
Madison 42
Madison, President James 30, 41, 136
Majoribanks, Lieutenant John 115
Malden 61
Marlborough, John Churchill, 1st Duke
  of 159
Martinette, Private B. John 112
Martinique 29, 31
McBean, Lieutenant-Colonel Donald
  141
McCarthy, Major Charles 31, 34, 35,
  168
McDonald, Ensign William 35
McEachern, Sergeant John 128
McGrierson, Private Thomas 80
McKinsey, Private Malkam 80
McLauchlan, Alexander 135
McLauchlan, Sergeant Hugh 135
McLauchlan, John 135
McLaughlin, Lieutenant James 128
Merritt, Captain William H. 106
Military General Service Medal 143
Militia Act of 1787 19
Miller, Lieutenant David 26
Mills, Private Cornelius 73
Minerva, HMS 56

Mitchell, Private Edward 95
Montreal 15, 26, 47, 51, 54, 64, 83, 97,
  98, 102, 114, 116, 137, 138, 140,
  141, 143, 144, 146
Moodie, Robert 35, 54, 65, 67, 68, 72-
  74, 79, 88, 93, 99, 138, 142, 155
Moore, Lieutenant Fowke (Frederic)
  35, 76
Moorsom, Ensign Henry 33, 111, 113,
  184
Moorsom, Lieutenant Henry Nathanial
  184
Moorsom, Lieutenant-Colonel
  Nathaniel 184
Moorsom, Ensign William 184
Moorsom, Second Lieutenant William
  Richard 184
Morrison, Lieutenant-Colonel Joseph
  98, 104-107, 109
Moses, Major Thomas 143
Mulcaster, Captain William 98
Myers, Lieutenant-Colonel Christopher
  101, 130, 131, 132
Myette, Peter 185

N

Napoleonic Wars 14, 15, 23, 36, 37, 91,
  143, 144
Navy Harbour 68
Navy Point 70
New Brunswick Museum 29, 143
New France 160
New York City 18
Newark 77, 78, 83, 88, 92-95
Niagara 134
Niagara. *See* Newark
Niagara Falls 77
Niagara Frontier 78, 99, 144
Niagara-on-the-Lake 11

Niagara Peninsula 11, 15, 16, 57, 65-67,
    77-82, 85, 87, 96, 100, 101, 103,
    104, 114-116, 134, 142, 144, 145,
    161, 187
Niagara River 61, 77, 78, 83, 87-89, 95,
    103, 105, 107, 113, 117, 118, 129,
    130, 134
Nicholson, Private James 95
Nickerson, Private Nathaniel 110
Non-Intercourse Act of 1809 30
Nootka 18
Norman, Louis (Lewis) 185
Norton, Captain John 106, 108, 183
Nova Scotia Command 149, 150

O

Ogdensburg 114
Ogilvie, Lieutenant-Colonel James 93
Oromocto River 42
Oswego 103

P

Pearson, Lieutenant-Colonel Thomas
    57, 106, 107, 108, 109
Petitcodiac River 42
Philpotts, Lieutenant George 129
Pike 75
Pike, Brigadier-General Zebulon 62
Pittsfield 187
Plattsburgh 130, 134
Playfair, Lieutenant Andrew 47, 51,
    96, 161
Plenderleath, Lieutenant-Colonel
    Charles 93
Point Frederick 57, 58, 59, 65, 67, 68,
    135
Point Henry 58, 59, 65, 68, 135
Point-Lévis 52
Port Weller. *See* Twelve Mile Creek
Portugal 30
Prairie du Chien 134

Prescott 15, 54, 78, 80, 98, 102, 114,
    115, 116, 161
Presqu'Ile 51, 143
Prevost, Lieutenant-General Sir George
    29, 30, 36-38, 41-43, 53, 55, 64-66,
    68-70, 73-75, 77, 87, 92, 93, 95, 98,
    99, 102-104, 138, 139, 161, 180
Prince Regent. *See* George IV, King
Princess Charlotte 134
privateers 42
Procter, Major-General Henry 92, 135
Proctor, Captain William 44

Q

Quebec City 26, 42, 44, 47, 51, 52, 54,
    56, 62, 64, 65, 79, 135, 138, 140,
    146, 161
Queen Charlotte 92
Queenston 24, 67, 76, 77, 83, 84, 88, 93,
    105-107, 113, 130, 177

R

Rainsford, Captain Andrew 40, 71, 75,
    81, 102
Rainsford, James 40
Rankin, Lieutenant Charles 33
Rankin, Lieutenant Coun Douly 33, 40
Reed, Private John 95
Regimental Colours 28, 29, 46, 142, 143
Retaliation 81
Riall, Major-General Phineas 101, 104-
    108, 110
Ripley, Brigadier-General Eleazar 114
Rivière-des-Caps 52
Rivière-du-Loup 41, 51, 161
Robinson, Lieutenant-Colonel Beverly
    21
Robinson, Commissary-General
    William Henry 137
Robison, Elizabeth 60
Rogers, Private Reuben 54

Royal Marines 24, 103, 122, 184
    Corps of Colonial Marines 24
Royal Military College of Canada 159
Royal Navy 14, 24, 42, 50, 87, 96, 99,
    115, 122, 137, 160
    Provincial Marine 57, 61, 177
    Royal Marine Artillery 184
Roy, Sergeant Peter (Pierre) 117, 118
Ruby, Private Sawyer 92

S

Sackets Harbor 10, 14, 57, 60, 62, 66-
    70, 72, 75-77, 80, 82, 96, 100, 102,
    135, 144, 145, 162
Saint John 20, 21, 28, 29, 40-42, 44-46,
    55, 143, 157, 160
Saint-Pierre and Miquelon 18
Sampson, Surgeon James 138
Saumarez, Major-General Sir Thomas
    156
Scotland 15, 20, 25, 27, 37, 40, 65, 143,
    145
Scott, Lieutenant-Colonel Hercules
    106, 107, 109, 122
Scott, Lieutenant John 160
Scott, Brigadier-General Winfield 106,
    107, 109, 122-124, 127
Secord, James 84
Secord, Laura 84
Servos's Mills 88
Seven Years' War 13, 19, 78, 91
Shaffalisky, Lieutenant Frederick 116
Sheaffe, Major-General Robert 61-64,
    67
Sherbrooke, Lieutenant-General Sir
    John 30, 41, 56, 140, 156
Shore, Captain George 28, 44, 46, 60,
    67, 75, 104, 106, 109, 110, 113,
    117, 127, 129, 132
Sir Isaac Brock 61
Six Mile Creek 96

Smelt, Major William 107
Smith, Dennis 135
Smith, Jacob 181
Smith, John 181
Smith, Colour Sergeant Peter 99
Smith, Colour Sergeant Richard 124,
    128
Smith, William 135
Smyth, Major-General George 40, 41,
    156
Snake Hill 118, 122, 123
Spain 17, 18
St. Andrews 20, 21, 28, 44, 143, 161
St. Anne's Chapel of Ease 146
St. David's 84, 86, 88, 92, 93, 96, 106
St. John River 21, 42, 47, 50, 52, 143,
    157
St. Lawrence, HMS 103
St. Lawrence River 11, 41, 52, 55, 56,
    78, 97, 98, 101, 103, 114, 115, 144,
    160, 161
Stewart, Colonel Archibald 79
Stewart, Private William G. 80
Stoney Creek 76, 79, 81, 83, 88, 176
Stoney Point 69
Stovin, Major-General Richard 102
Straton, Lieutenant John 41
Street's Creek 133
Sutherland, Captain A. 26, 181
Sydney 28, 44, 135

T

Ten Mile Creek 96
Thom, Private John 95
Thomas, Surgeon William 53, 138
Thomas, William Dyer 22, 23
Thunder 78
Tinling, Lieutenant-Colonel Isaac 28
Toronto. *See* York
Torrens, Colonel Henry 37, 38, 127
Treaty of Amiens 21

Treaty of Amity, Commerce and
  Navigation. *See* Jay's Treaty
Treaty of Ghent 136
Trimble, Major William 126
Trois-Rivières 56, 135, 137
Tucker, Lieutenant-Colonel John 105,
  106, 117, 118
Tweeddale, Lieutenant-Colonel George
  Hay, 8th Marquess of 130-132
Twelve Mile Creek 83, 92, 96, 106, 107
Twenty Mile Creek 82
Two Mile Creek 88, 89, 93

U

United Kingdom 15, 17-21, 26, 29-32,
  34, 36, 37, 41, 61, 62, 78, 135, 138,
  143, 145, 149, 156, 175, 189
United States 17, 18, 29-31, 34, 39, 41-
  43, 62, 78, 114, 138, 161
  Congress 30, 31, 41
United States Army 14, 42, 85
  1st Brigade 106, 107
  Left Division 97, 104, 106, 114, 116,
    181
  Regiment of Riflemen 42
United States Army, Infantry
  9th US Infantry 113
  19th US Infantry 124
United States Army, Militias
  New York State Militia 71
United States Navy 42, 78, 80
Upper Fort Garry 160

V

Vidal, E.E. 50
Viger, Captain Jacques 34, 59, 64
Vincent, Major-General John 65, 75,
  77-79, 81-84, 93, 96
Virgil 90
von Gerau de Hautefeuile, Captain
  George 39, 44

W

Wadine, Private Stephen 54
Wall, Private Joseph 80
War of 1812 9, 11, 13-15, 24, 39, 41, 57,
  58, 67, 90, 95, 111, 112, 137, 143-
  146, 155, 159, 160
Warren, Vice-Admiral Sir John 160
Washington DC 134
weaponry
  1796 pattern straight-bladed infantry
    sword 50
  1803 curved-bladed sword 50
  British Short Land Musket, India
    Pattern 48, 49, 172
  light muskets 49, 172
  sergeants' fusils 49
  spontoon 50
Wellington, Arthur Wellesley, 1st Duke
  of 115, 161
Welsh, Corporal Thomas 55, 173
Wentworth, Sir John 29
West Indies 18, 19, 20, 24, 29, 34
White, Major John 26
Wilkinson, Major-General James 97,
  98, 114
Wilson, Private John 92
Winslow, Lieutenant John 67, 68, 99
Wolfe 68
Wolseley, Colonel Garnet 160
Woodford, William 24
Woodstock 54

X

Xavier, Private Francis 80

Y

Yeo, Commodore Sir James Lucas 65,
  68-70, 75, 77, 81, 84, 87, 95, 96, 98,
  102, 105, 130, 134, 160
York 26, 60-64, 77-80, 89, 96, 103-106,
  177

York, Prince Frederick, Duke of 31, 37
Young, Colonel Robert 72, 73, 88, 93
Youngstown 105, 106

The New Brunswick Military History Museum

The mission of the New Brunswick Military History Museum is to collect, preserve, research, and exhibit artifacts which illustrate the history and heritage of the military forces in New Brunswick and New Brunswickers at war, during peacetime, and on United Nations or North Atlantic Treaty Organization duty.

The New Brunswick Military History Museum is proud to partner with the Gregg Centre.

Highlighting 400 years of New Brunswick's history.

www.nbmilitaryhistorymuseum.ca
info@nbmilitaryhistorymuseum.ca

The New Brunswick Military Heritage Project

The New Brunswick Military Heritage Project, a non-profit organization devoted to public awareness of the remarkable military heritage of the province, is an initiative of the Brigadier Milton F. Gregg, VC, Centre for the Study of War and Society of the University of New Brunswick. The organization consists of museum professionals, teachers, university professors, graduate students, active and retired members of the Canadian Forces, and other historians. We welcome public involvement. People who have ideas for books or information for our database can contact us through our website: www.unb.ca/nbmhp.

One of the main activities of the New Brunswick Military Heritage Project is the publication of the New Brunswick Military Heritage Series with Goose Lane Editions. This series of books is under the direction of J. Brent Wilson, Director of the New Brunswick Military Heritage Project at the University of New Brunswick. Publication of the series is supported by a grant from the Canadian War Museum.

CANADIAN
WAR MUSEUM

MUSÉE CANADIEN
DE LA GUERRE

The New Brunswick Military History Series

Volume 1
Saint John Fortifications, 1630-1956,
Roger Sarty and Doug Knight

Volume 2
Hope Restored: The American Revolution and the Founding of New Brunswick, Robert L. Dallison

Volume 3
The Siege of Fort Beauséjour, 1755, Chris M. Hand

Volume 4
Riding into War: The Memoir of a Horse Transport Driver, 1916-1919, James Robert Johnston

Volume 5
The Road to Canada: The Grand Communications Route from Saint John to Quebec, W.E. (Gary) Campbell

Volume 6
Trimming Yankee Sails: Pirates and Privateers of New Brunswick, Faye Kert

Volume 7
War on the Home Front: The Farm Diaries of Daniel MacMillan, 1914-1927,
edited by Bill Parenteau and Stephen Dutcher

Volume 8

Turning Back the Fenians: New Brunswick's Last Colonial Campaign,
Robert L. Dallison

Volume 9

*D-Day to Carpiquet: The North Shore Regiment and the Liberation of
Europe*, Marc Milner

Volume 10

*Hurricane Pilot: The Wartime Letters
of Harry L. Gill, DFM, 1940-1943*,
edited by Brent Wilson with Barbara J. Gill

Volume 11

*The Bitter Harvest of War: New Brunswick and the Conscription Crisis of
1917*, Andrew Theobald

Volume 12

Captured Hearts: New Brunswick's War Brides,
Melynda Jarratt

Volume 13

*Bamboo Cage: The P.O.W. Diary of Flight Lieutenant Robert Wyse, 1942-
1943*, edited by Jonathan F. Vance

Volume 14

*Uncle Cy's War: The First World War Letters
of Major Cyrus F. Inches*, edited by Valerie Teed

Volume 15

Agnes Warner and the Nursing Sisters of the Great War,
Shawna M. Quinn

Volume 16

New Brunswick and the Navy: Four Hundred Years,
Marc Milner and Glenn Leonard

Volume 17

Battle for the Bay: The Naval War of 1812, Joshua M. Smith

Volume 18

Steel Cavalry: The 8th (New Brunswick) Hussars and the Italian Campaign, Lee Windsor

Volume 19

A Neighbourly War: New Brunswick and the War of 1812, Robert L. Dallison

Volume 20

The Aroostook War of 1839, W.E. (Gary) Campbell

About the Author

John R. Grodzinski is an assistant professor of history at the Royal Military College of Canada. He is author of *Defender of Canada: Sir George Prevost and the War of 1812* (University of Oklahoma Press, 2013) and editor of *The War of 1812: An Annotated Bibliography* (Routledge, 2007). He has contributed articles to a number of journals and has also authored chapters for several books. Grodzinski appeared in the PBS documentary on the *War of 1812* (2011), an episode of "Battlefield Detectives," and has been a commentator on the War of 1812 for the Discovery Channel and CBC Radio. He is a popular speaker and has addressed historical groups throughout Canada and in the United States. Grodzinski is also editor of the online "War of 1812 Magazine" and over the past decade has organized and led over eighty battlefield studies to sites from the Seven Years' War, the American Revolutionary War, and the War of 1812. He resides in Kingston with his wife Helga.